You're Not Crazy,

You're Responding:

Reclaiming Wholeness In a Pathologized World

By Auroara Leigh

Foreword written by Len Pierre

You're Not Crazy, You're Responding

This book is intended for reflection, understanding, and healing. It is not a substitute for professional medical or psychological care. If you are working with a doctor, therapist, healer, Indigenous elder, or counsellor, please continue that relationship.

Some names and identifying details have been changed to protect the privacy of those involved.

ISBN: 978-1-7781082-2-8 (paperback)

First Edition, 2026

Published by Simply Sacred Solutions

For Dr. Hugo De Burgos,

My Medical Anthropology
Professor from UBC-Okanagan
who first showed me that
the culture was sick,
before I had words for it.

May You Rest in Peace,

You impacted so many.

For the children who were told their pain was their fault.

For the teenagers who sat silent while adults wrote a story that was never true.

For the victims of abuse who were labeled and shamed.

For the adults they became, still carrying that story in their body.

For the powerful matriarchs who were told your worth was tied to your age as you went through menstrual transitioning.

For the men who are told you are only of value if you produce, provide and protect and that your feelings are secondary.

You were never wrong.

You were responding.

Contents

Foreword

There is a question many people have been taught to ask themselves when they are struggling:

What is wrong with me?

It is a question that can follow us into doctors' offices, classrooms, workplaces, relationships, and even into our own quiet moments. It is a question shaped by systems that have too often been quicker to diagnose a person than to understand their story; quicker to manage a response than to ask what created the conditions for that response in the first place.

This book invites us to ask a different question:

What happened to me?

That shift may seem simple, but it is profound.

For far too long, many people have been made to feel as though their anxiety, grief, anger, withdrawal, hypervigilance, numbness, or fear are evidence that they are broken. Yet, when we understand trauma through a more compassionate and relational lens, we begin to see something different. We begin to see that the mind, body, and spirit are often doing what they have needed to do to survive.

You are not broken. You are responding.

As someone who works in the areas of Indigenous cultural safety, trauma-informed practice, and decolonizing systems, I have seen how often institutions can unintentionally repeat harm when they focus only on a person's behaviour, diagnosis, or perceived "deficit." Too often, systems ask, "How do we fix this person?"

rather than, "What has this person endured?" "What conditions have shaped their experience?" and "What might safety, dignity, belonging, and healing look like now?"

This is why Auroara Leigh's work matters.

She offers readers language for experiences that are often misunderstood, minimized, or pathologized. She reminds us that our bodies carry memory. That survival strategies are not character flaws. That healing is not about becoming someone new, but about returning to the parts of ourselves that were always worthy of love, care, protection, and belonging.

This book is also an important reminder that healing is not onesize-fits-all. For some, healing may include counselling, medication, ceremony, culture, community, movement, spirituality, boundaries, rest, or the courage to finally tell the truth about what happened. For many, it will be a braided path, one that honours both professional support and the wisdom already held within the body, family, community, and spirit.

Auroara writes with honesty, vulnerability, and conviction. She does not offer easy answers, nor does she suggest that healing happens overnight. Instead, she offers something more meaningful: permission. Permission to question the stories that have been placed upon us. Permission to see ourselves with greater compassion. Permission to recognize that our responses make sense in the context of what we have lived through.

For readers who have carried shame, labels, silence, or the belief that they are "too much," I hope these pages offer a different possibility.

May this book remind you that your story matters.
May it help you meet yourself with curiosity instead of judgment.
And may it support you in reclaiming the wholeness that was never lost, only covered by the things you had to do to survive.

With respect, **Len Pierre** *Owner & CEO, Len Pierre Consulting*

A Note to the Reader

If you are holding this book while also holding a prescription for anxiety or depression, this page is for you.

You were born whole. You were wired for love, for safety, for real connection. Then life happened. People happened. Systems happened.

The pain you carry is real. The anxiety in your chest. The depression that flattens your days. The shutting down. The hypervigilance. The way you cannot quite show up as the full version of yourself. Much of what we are taught to experience as evidence of malfunction may also be the nervous system doing what it learned to do in the conditions it was given. Anxiety, shutdown, hypervigilance, and depression deserve care. They also deserve context.

You were taught to believe something was wrong with you. That teaching did not happen by accident.

When people come to understand themselves only as broken, something happens. They can become easier to manage. They may stop asking hard questions. They may defer their own knowing entirely to authority. They may take on the shame instead of seeing the harm. They may take the pill, accept the label, and go back to living inside systems that were never built with their wellbeing in mind. Whatever the intention, pathologizing human pain can function as a form of control. It happens in families. In institutions. In whole cultures. It tells people their responses to real harm are the problem, instead of naming the harm itself.

This book names that. Clearly. Without apology.

This is not an anti-medicine book. Medication can save lives. Many people need it as part of their healing. What this book challenges is the story wrapped around the way western medicine has treated human pain. The story that says your nervous system is broken. That you are too much. Too sensitive. Too damaged to function without correction.

You are not too much. You are a person who lived through something. Many somethings, maybe. Your body held the echoes. It adapted. It survived. It is still here.

This book is an invitation. To understand what actually happened in your body, your family, your culture. And to begin, at whatever pace feels safe, to come home to yourself.

You are sacred.

You always were.

A note on professional support. This book is for reflection, understanding, and healing. It is not a substitute for medical or psychological care. If you are working with a doctor, therapist, healer, Indigenous elder, or counsellor, please continue that relationship. This book is meant to walk alongside that work.

A Letter from the Author

I did not write this book from a place of having arrived.

I wrote it from the middle of a journey that began long before I had words for it. From a childhood where I learned my feelings were inconvenient. My pain was a problem. Something fundamental about me was wrong. I wrote it through the years of carrying that story as if it were true. Through the nights of crying alone in a room where no one came. Through the offices where labels were handed to me like verdicts. Through the violations that confirmed what I had already been told. That I was not safe. Not protected. Not worth protecting.

I wrote it after being raped at fifteen, and again at eighteen. I wrote it after the relationship that used my wounds against me and called my collapse a disorder. I wrote it after years of mental abuse, and a decade of dissociating from my own body because living fully inside it was too much to bear.

And I wrote it from the other side of all of that. The side where you understand what happened. Why your body responded the way it did. Why none of it was ever your fault. The side where you can stand upright, heart open, and refuse to apologize for taking up space.

I have spent years studying the meeting points of culture, trauma, neuroscience, and healing. I have worked with health authorities, with communities, with leaders and practitioners trying to build something more humane than what we inherited.

None of that education saved me. What saved me was understanding that I was never broken. That the things I had been taught to call my symptoms were actually my responses. That a nervous system shaped by threat is an intelligent nervous system.

The understanding did not come in a single moment. It came in waves. In a computer room at university at twenty-three, writing a medical anthropology paper, suddenly seeing for the first time that the culture was sick. In a yoga studio, standing in mountain pose with my heart open, feeling the full weight of everything I had been taught to hide. Being open meant being vulnerable. There was a story hardwired in my traum-our about that. In the moment I moved to a new city with my daughter and stepped into a room of people who treated their own feelings as information instead of evidence of disorder. I understood, with a shock of recognition, that this was what safe was supposed to feel like.

The healing did not happen all at once. It happened in the slow gathering of those cracks of light, each one widening what the one before had opened, until there was more light in me than dark.

I wrote this book for the teenager I was. Sitting silent in that office while a story was written about her that was never true. They could not see the nights of torment she had been through. Of course she was withdrawn.

I wrote it for the woman I became, who spent years not knowing she was allowed to question that story.

I wrote it for those who have been abused and then told by the medical system that they are sick or disordered because they are struggling to function. Pain and suffering do not have an end timeline. The body heals at its own pace, when it finally feels safe enough to connect again.

I wrote it for my daughter. The world she grows up in should not require her to shrink herself to survive in it. She does not have to stay the nice girl out of fear of being pathologized for naming what is wrong.

And I wrote it for you.

Whoever you are. Whatever brought you here. Whatever labels you have been handed. Whatever you have been told about yourself. Whatever story you have been carrying so long it began to feel like the truth.

You are not crazy.

You are responding.

Your nervous system has been doing exactly what it learned to do in the conditions it was given. That is biology. That is survival. That is, in the deepest sense, intelligence.

This book will ask you to look at some hard things. The systems that profit from your pain. The families that passed their wounds forward without meaning to. The culture that taught whole generations to pathologize the most human of responses. It will also ask you to look at yourself with a kind of compassion that the dominant culture does not consider normal. And to decide that you are worth that care anyway.

I am not a perfect person. I am not a finished healer. I am someone who has done the work, is still doing the work, and has found, in that work, something worth passing forward.

Here is what I have found. The wholeness you are looking for was always there. It is waiting to be remembered, and reclaimed. It was simply covered over by everything that was done to you, and everything you learned to do to survive it.

This book is an invitation to begin uncovering it.

With love and with truth,

Auroara Leigh

Chapter One
The Myth of Brokenness

When I was young, I was told something was wrong with me.

I was called too sensitive. If I asked for my needs to be met, it was called performing. If I retreated into myself, I was told I lived in my head. If I expressed myself freely, I was told no one would ever want to marry me.

Those words landed like knives. The shame was unbearable. My body carried it as fire. A hot burning in my stomach. A tightening in my throat. The sting of tears behind my eyes as I cried myself to sleep, night after night. My brain would clench tight, as if I could hold back the pain. The words still etched themselves into me. They sank like ink into parchment, settling into my self-worth, staining everything they touched.

I was too young to know why people said such things. Too young to know how false they were. I only knew the weight they left. I began to believe everyone could see my flaws. That I was somehow inherently wrong. The shame felt like hot tar. Sticky. Heavy. Impossible to escape. It seeped into how I saw myself. How I approached relationships. How I made choices for decades to come. I tilted myself away from the world. I never stood fully upright. I was always afraid someone would discover how "bad" I really was.

The damage did not stop at the walls of my home. The shame my family carried became a cover for the abuse. Their shame of their shame was folded into a story that blamed me. If I pushed back, the consequences at home got worse. So I retreated. I obeyed their story. I learned to silence myself.

Schools and systems picked up the script. Teenagers who come from violence, neglect, or hiding get labelled. The misdiagnosis takes root. I was whispered about as crazy. Those words cut almost as deep as the violence itself. When communities and institutions turn their faces away, it changes everything. If the one who causes the harm gets away with it, and the world outside is not a blanket of safety, where in the world is safe? The isolation becomes total.

~

I had three fathers. None of them saw me. None of them protected me. Each one carried his own wound. His own rage. His own shame. His own hunger. Each one, in his own way, left no room for the children around him to be fully safe.

One of my fathers wore a uniform. He was an alcoholic who believed power over others was the same as strength. He ground my fingers together under the dinner table when there was company and he couldn't do it outright. A small, secret cruelty. A sneer on his face that said: I can do this and you cannot stop me and no one will believe you. He threw balls at my head. He threw me down stairs. He took me on high speed chases unbuckled and concussed. He locked me in jail cells when I talked back. He hurt my mother. My brother. Me. The people around him who knew looked away. He wore a uniform. That uniform protected him the way it protected all of them at that time, before there was accountability like today.

I was six when my mother finally left him.

I had a savant's mind. A huge hunger to understand everything. Three grades ahead of myself. That quality should have been nurtured. In a home built on shame and secrecy, it was dangerous. Children who see clearly and ask too many questions are the most threatening children in a broken household. They are the ones gaslit the hardest. Because their clarity, if validated, would unravel everything.

There is a particular kind of harm that happens when a system looks directly at what is real and chooses a different story instead.

I want to tell you about the office. I was sitting in a chair that felt too big for me. I was quiet. My mother did all the talking. She had been told by my stepfather what to say. She said it. I sat with my shoulders collapsed forward. My stomach hot. My body already knew that something in this room was wrong. It was a performance of a particular story, dressed up as a search for truth. The story that needed me to be the problem.

Someone had already seen what was actually happening. A counsellor had named it. Had told us, plainly, that I was being abused. That witness had been the first true thing anyone in authority had ever offered me.

And then I was carted away from that witness and placed in a hollow doctor's office instead.

Because I was too big a mirror. I reflected back everything my family had never faced in themselves. Every wound they had buried. Every pain they had inherited and never processed and passed forward. A child who is being abused and begins to show it, begins to collapse inward and withdraw and shut down, is not convenient. They are evidence. Evidence has to be explained away.

So the story was rewritten in that office. The psychiatrist saw a teenage girl. Collapsed forward. Withdrawn. Uncommunicative. Hot shame coursing through her body. Unable to speak for herself, because speaking had never once been safe.

He saw depression. A chemical imbalance. Something that could be named and medicated and managed. (Later, learning that the simple chemical imbalance story, particularly the claim that depression was caused by a deficiency of serotonin, had never been established in the way it was so often presented to patients. The certainty of the story had outrun the science.)

He did not see a girl who had been taught that her body was wrong. He did not see a girl carrying shame that did not belong to her. He did not ask what was happening at home. Or if he did, he listened to my mother's version and wrote that down instead. He did not see that my collapsed posture was not a symptom of a malfunctioning brain. It was the posture of a person who had learned that making herself smaller was the only way to survive.

What came out of that appointment was a label. The label became the story. The abuse. The home. The years of being told I was too much and too sensitive and fundamentally wrong. All of it disappeared behind a diagnosis. A pill. A story that protected the adults in the room and left a fourteen-year-old girl alone with the understanding that the problem, officially, was her.

I felt the jolts of it through my chest, down the front of me. The specific electricity of betrayal. The world had looked directly at what was happening and chosen a different explanation. One that was tidier. One that came with a prescription pad. One that kept the true source of the pain invisible and profitable. One that protects the abuser and names the victim as the source of the problem.

This is what it costs when a system mistakes the wound for the wounded.

This is what it costs when a corporation profits from that mistake.

And so the lie was officially recorded.

All of it was rooted in the wider system. A medical system built on pathologizing pain, profiting from it, and silencing people became the way it enabled abuse in our entire population.

This is medical gaslighting.

This is the systemic control of women's bodies.

This is the pressure to perform a normal that does not exist.

This was the authorities using their power to dictate countless lives dignity, livelihood, but also missed opportunities to truly heal.

A horticulturist had been brought in to examine the garden. He stood in front of a wilting plant and said the trouble was in her cells. He did not look at the gardener spraying poison on her leaves. He did not see that her sun had been blocked for years. He did not notice that she was thirsty. Leaning toward any direction that might hold water. He wrote his report about her cells. The gardener kept gardening.

I was the plant.
I was thirsty for love.

~

The horticulturist did not work alone.

He carried a manual. The manual told him what a healthy plant looked like. What symptoms meant what diagnosis. What prescription to write for what presentation. He had memorized it the way a Christian child memorizes scripture. What the manual did not contain was a single page on the soil. On the gardener. On the chemicals being sprayed. On whether the sun was reaching the plant at all.

This is an atrocity of priorities. The professionals had their manuals. They did not have curiosity. They followed a DSM checklist. They never asked: what happened to this child? Who hurt her? What is her world like? When there is no inquiry, authority becomes an enabler. If the places we are told to go for help uphold the abuse story, the system itself becomes part of the harm.

If any one of us saw a plant wilting in someone's home, we would think it needs to be moved to a different location, needs water, or needs to be re-planted to give it's roots more room to expand. Yet, we do not do that with humans...and why is that?

The cultural messages that fed into all of it are the chemicals on the leaves. Children are seen, not heard. The adult is always right. Don't be weak. Don't cry. Don't talk about family matters. Only Western medicine is real. Tell on someone and you will be taken away. These are not small things. They create an ecology that trains bodies to hide, to obey, to shut down. They teach girls to police their own bodies so they will not be blamed. They teach boys to be louder and unchecked. They teach adults to fear speaking. They teach institutions to prefer tidy labels to messy human stories.

I did not have the frameworks then to name what was happening. Now I do. Psychology. Health studies. Medical and cultural anthropology. Indigenous knowledge. Trauma expertise. Yogic philosophy. All of them confirm what I already felt in my bones. Children who come from violence, abuse, or neglect have understandable responses to violence, abuse, or neglect. They are not their symptoms. They are responding to the soil they were forced to grow in.

If you were also that child, hear this. The things you were called were never the truth of you. The labels were a horticulturist's report. They described a plant struggling and forgot to describe the garden. They named your cells and forgot the toxins. They wrote you down as the problem and never once examined the gardener. Or the wider social ecosystem. You were not the problem. You were the only one in the room small enough to be blamed for what the adults could not face.

If I could have met the fourteen-year-old who sat silent in that office, I would have loved her differently. I would have watered her first. I would have asked what was in the soil before I asked what was in her cells. That is the work I now intend to do for the young people I meet. And for you, if you are still that child somewhere inside. To witness rather than label. To tend rather than diagnose. To sow rather than cut.

The Biology of Survival

What was happening inside that plant has a name in science.

When a child lives in threat, whether the threat is direct violence or the constant chance of it, the autonomic nervous system learns to protect. It is the system that learns to protect through responses that can include fight, flight, and freezing, alongside the appeasement strategy that trauma practitioners often call fawning. It is the root system of the plant, working beneath the soil to keep the visible parts alive.

In conditions of safety, those roots grow wide and deep. They reach for water. They draw in nutrients. They build a foundation that lets the plant rise tall and steady into the light. In conditions of threat, those roots do something different. They contract. They cluster. They put their energy into the immediate work of not dying, instead of the long work of flourishing.

Repeated threat can make danger easier to notice and safety harder to trust. Stress-related systems develop inside that weather. Researchers have documented differences in threat processing and autonomic regulation after early adversity, but no single brain region or chemical tells the whole story. The root system learns the weather it keeps meeting. It gets quicker at finding danger because danger has been useful information.

Over time, the plant puts survival first because survival is what the environment is demanding. What gets labeled symptoms in adulthood, the withdrawal, the anger, the hypervigilance, the dissociation, is biology doing exactly what biology is supposed to do in an unsafe world.

This is intelligence. This is the nervous system doing what it was built to do. Bruce Perry describes it as a system that remembers patterns of danger and keeps protecting long after the danger has passed. Some experiences clinicians name as symptoms may also contain protective adaptations. The thick bark a tree grows after a fire is a memory of fire. It is the tree's intelligence made visible.

I call this armour traum-our. The words trauma and armour woven together.

Traum-our (n.): the protective armour a nervous system builds after repeated threat. A set of survival strategies shaped by fear and experience, keeping a person alive in dangerous contexts. It shows up as rigidity, hypervigilance, fawning, or emotional shutdown. It is wisdom in the body. With witness and attunement, it can be slowly unwound and reorganized into safety. Somatic practices, relational repair, and trauma-informed approaches let the nervous system experience what it once missed. Attunement. Protection. Love.

The newer science is even more precise. Stress does not land in every body in the same way. The kind of stress matters. How long it lasts matters. When it happens matters. And one of the most powerful buffers we know is the presence of attuned, responsive care.

When a young plant is met with that care, something measurable happens at the cellular level. In landmark animal studies at McGill University, neuroscientist Michael Meaney and his colleagues found that differences in maternal care were associated with epigenetic changes around a gene involved in regulating the stress response, called the glucocorticoid receptor. Rat pups that received higher levels of maternal licking and grooming developed different patterns of gene expression than pups that received lower levels of maternal care. The gene involved stayed more open and expressive with attentive care, and was partly quieted by a chemical process called methylation when care was low. Human research has since found associations between childhood adversity and epigenetic differences in stress-related systems. The science is still unfolding, but the message is profound: early conditions can become biologically embedded. Strip away the laboratory language and the finding is something the old cultures never needed a microscope to know.

Love is a chemical event. It changes which seeds in the soil are allowed to grow.

A child who is repeatedly met with I see you. I believe you. I am with you is receiving conditions that can support regulation and trust. Without reliable support, hypervigilance, self-blame, or shutdown may become more likely. With responsive relationships, flexibility, safety, and trust have more room to grow.

If you did not receive that, hear this too. If you did not receive that, hear this too. Some of the ways your body responds today may carry the shape of what was missing then. Not every response has one origin. Not every pattern belongs to childhood. But unmet needs can become part of the story a nervous system learns. You were growing in a garden that did not always give you what you needed. The fact that you are still standing is evidence of an intelligence the manual cannot measure.

And if you are reading this as someone who serves, hear this too. The people who come to you carrying diagnoses are responding to gardens you cannot fully see. Your work is to wonder about the soil. To ask what was in the air around them. To listen for what their nervous system is still trying to say. You are allowed to be, in your own attention, the kind of weather they have been waiting for. The research is clear that responsive relationships matter. They become part of a new set of conditions. The story is not hopeless. A nervous system keeps learning its whole life long, and researchers are still tracing how far that learning reaches into the body. This much we can say without flinching: safe, responsive relationships are powerful conditions for human healing and wellbeing, at any age.

Safety is the sunlight of human flourishing. Attunement is the soil. Connection is the water.

When the gardener finally tends instead of poisons, when the sun is allowed to reach the leaves again, the plant does not need to be replaced. The nervous system reorganizes. The same roots that learned to brace can learn to drink again. Even biology is more forgiving than the old story of permanent damage let us believe. The early conditions matter enormously. They are not the end of the story. The nervous system keeps learning. Relationships keep shaping us. The soil can still change.

The metaphor is not perfect. No metaphor is. But the principle underneath it is real: living systems develop inside conditions, and human nervous systems keep learning from the conditions that follow.

My first cracks of light came in Kelowna.

I had moved there to study at UBC's Okanagan campus. The geography was beautiful. The lake. The mountains. The light. My body responded to the new ground before I knew what was happening. The yelling was gone. The footsteps overhead were gone. There was room to breathe.

In Kelowna I also found kind people. Not the toxic, mean patterns I had grown used to in the community I came from. People who were soft with each other. Who asked questions and waited for answers. That change of company mattered more than I could have predicted.

I had been a plant in poisoned soil my entire life. Kelowna was different ground. I could feel the difference in my roots before I had words for it.

I began to believe that if I surrounded myself with people who were gentle and curious, I could heal. The simple truth was radical. I did better when I was safe, seen, and protected. The science had said this. My body was finally getting to feel it.

There was one moment, specifically, that I have never forgotten.

~

I was working one-on-one with my yoga instructor. Going deeper into my practice as part of becoming a teacher myself. We started with the most basic pose there is. Mountain pose. Feet planted. Knees gently bent. Spine tall. Shoulders back. Chest open. Crown of the head reaching upward. An intentional alignment, from the ground all the way to the top of me.

A plant standing in its own light.

The moment my shoulders went back and my heart opened and my chest lifted, something happened I was not prepared for.

My whole body flooded with vulnerability. The kind that overtakes you before you can brace.

Standing in proper alignment, with my chest open, was something my body had been taught was dangerous. From the time I was nine years old, I had been learning, in the quiet and relentless way that girls learn things, that my body drew attention I had not asked for. That my developing breasts were something that belonged, in some unnamed way, to other people's eyes. That a girl who stood open and upright and present was asking for something. That my natural posture, the posture a human body is designed to hold, was somehow an invitation. A provocation. A disgrace.

So I had learned to fold. To curve my spine inward. To make myself smaller at the front. To lead with my shoulders hunched and my heart hidden. I had done this so automatically, for so long, that I did not even know I was doing it. My body had learned to hide because of what the world did with female bodies that dared to simply exist. The wrongness was never in my spine. It lived in the eyes that watched it.

Standing in mountain pose, shoulders back, heart lifted, I felt the full weight of that learning all at once.

And then my instructor told me I was not present. That something had taken me out of the moment. That I needed to return.

He was not wrong that something had happened. He could not see what it was. The wellness world, even at its most well-intentioned, is not always trauma-informed. A person who has not lived inside a female body being sexualized from childhood cannot always tell the difference between distraction and devastation. Between a student drifting and a student being flooded by years of accumulated harm.

I did not have language for it then. I was learning, in real time, that I had been swimming through waters of pain I had assumed were just the water. What I was carrying was the weight of every message I had ever received that told me my body was a problem I needed to manage for everyone else's comfort.

Ask many women, many people who grew up in a female body, when they first understood they were being sexualized by adults, and the answers will devastate you. Many can name it. Many were children. From that moment forward, a tax is levied on us that we never agreed to pay. The constant management of how our existence lands in other people's bodies.

The woman who wears a turtleneck and still draws attention. The girl who stands in correct posture and is told she is asking for it. The person who simply breathes and moves and exists in a body and is somehow held responsible for what that body provokes in others.

This is not a small thing. It lives in the spine. It lives in the shoulders. It lives in the way we take up, or refuse to take up, space. It lives in the way a plant that learned to grow crooked around obstacles is still curving even after the obstacles are gone.

Mountain pose cracked me open that day because I had never been allowed to simply stand upright before. Not without cost.

That is what unprocessed pain feels like when it finally surfaces. Quiet. Ordinary. Just a yoga pose that undoes you. Just a body that finally tells the truth.

That day in the studio cracked something open. Once something is open, you cannot un-open it. The seeking that had always been in me found a direction.

The Braided Path

At university, I found medical anthropology and shamanism. The classes I took taught about healing practices around the world and the paradigms they live within. They cracked the broken story even further. In some cultures and healing traditions, adolescence and periods of intense struggle have been understood through initiatory, spiritual, or relational frames rather than only through pathology. In some traditions, people who have wrestled deeply with suffering later become healers, medicine carriers, or witnesses precisely because they know the terrain of pain. Those teachings reframed my own adolescence. The years I had been told were evidence of damage were actually the years I was forming. Against all odds, into something a healing culture would need.

Still, I had to go deeper. Some parts of Western medicine were useful. EMDR helped me reprocess shards of early childhood trauma that talk therapy could not fully reach. Somatic experiencing taught me to listen to the body as a primary source of information. My path became a braided one. Alternative healing. Holistic practices. Cultural approaches to health and wellness. All of it threaded together with evidence-based trauma work.

Over seven years I built a framework that made sense of my body and my mind together. The somatic self is central to mental health. Western medicine's habit of separating mind from body leaves people misunderstood. That separation opens the door to a dangerous story. When we cannot point to a visible wound, the easiest explanation becomes chemical imbalance. A tidy theory that benefits a pharmaceutical marketplace. A business model as old as it is cold. Identify a problem. Sell the quick fix. In some settings, short appointments, prescribing norms, and systems built around billable interventions can narrow the encounter before the person's story has been heard. A prescription may help. It can also become the end of the inquiry too quickly. Whose story is behind the symptoms? What conditions are around them? Those questions should not disappear because a medication is available. That has become the norm of how our medical system treats the inner world.

I am grateful for the teachers from many disciplines who have walked alongside me. From every direction. A plant heals by drawing nourishment from many sources at once. The sun of one tradition. The water of another. The soil of a third. The mycelial network of all the wisdom keepers who came before.

When I finally met myself with all of that knowledge gathered, the science, the somatic practices, the ancestral and cross-cultural wisdom, the tightness in my body began to unbind. The 'broken' story did not disappear overnight. It began to lose its power. I stopped reading my nervous system as a defect and started reading it as a map. Every behaviour that had been pathologized now looked like a meaningful attempt to keep me alive.

When I stopped reading my responses as evidence of brokenness and started reading them as evidence of survival, something in me began to breathe differently. And in that new breath, I began to see something else. The very qualities I had been shamed for were my deepest gifts.

Reclaiming the Gifts

The qualities I had been shamed for, the sensitivity, the metacognition, the seeing-through-to-what-is-real, were not flaws to manage. They were the deepest gifts I would ever carry. The conditions that wounded me were also the conditions that grew me. Both are true. Both must be held.

I have always had the ability to see through to what is real. I never let myself settle for the surface or for the performance. As a child, this was survival. I needed to know people's true intentions because reading them accurately kept me alive. As an adult, the same skill has become a blessing. I can sense genuineness behind someone's eyes. I recognize when authenticity is present. I am drawn toward it. I match with the others who are also authentic. Together we weave a soul tribe of people who are real, grounded, and true.

I have always been metacognitive. Constantly aware of what I was thinking. Reflecting on it. Processing it. For years that felt like a burden. Like my mind never stopped. Now I see it as a profound strength. My metacognition lets me support others as they build their own self-awareness. When we cultivate self-awareness, we open a doorway into empowerment. We begin to understand our own patterns. Our own gifts. Our own choices.

I am also deeply kind. I came to know kindness because I had to learn its opposite first. Experiencing that contrast made me a knower of love in its truest form. My sensitivity means I can no longer tolerate spaces that are unkind, harsh, or dismissive. I ask, instead, for what is softer. Gentler. Kinder. By doing so, I create and hold the kind of space where others can also feel safe and seen and respected.

I am proud of the work I do in naming abuses of power. They are everywhere. In families. In communities. In workplaces. In systems. I had to become strong in my truth, strong in my own empowerment, so I could say a single sentence out loud. I am allowed to want kindness. That declaration changes the room. It gives other people permission to expect the same.

I remind myself, and the people in front of me, that we are sacred. I am sacred. You are sacred. We are whole, even when the world tells us otherwise. Honoring that truth opens the door to the beauty of boundaries. Boundaries are sacred agreements that protect our energy, our worth, and our belonging. When we live inside them, the benefit extends past us to everyone we are connected to.

What this looks like in practice is quieter than it sounds.

I walk into rooms and I see people. The actual person, not the performance. The wound they are working from. The fear that is driving the behaviour everyone else is accepting as normal. I can see the man at the dinner table who cuts people off mid-sentence and understand, without making it a moment, that he is running a seven-year-old's panic about not being enough. I do not need to name it out loud. I do not need him to know I see it. I see it. The seeing changes how I move in the room.

The gift of high pattern recognition, of metacognition, of being able to read what is actually happening underneath what is being performed, is enormously wanted in some rooms and enormously threatening in others. There are rooms that light up when I walk in. People feel seen in a way they have rarely felt before. There are rooms that go quiet. A certain kind of person decides quickly that I am not someone to celebrate. Both are information. Neither is my problem to solve.

This took me a long time to understand. For most of my life I tried to make myself more palatable to the rooms that did not want what I carried. I dimmed the clarity. I softened the truth. I apologized for seeing what I saw. That shrinking was its own kind of wound. The wound of a plant trained to grow crooked even after it had been moved to better light.

What I understand now is that the gift is mine to be. Managing it was never the assignment. When I validate myself, when I model for the people around me that a woman is allowed to see clearly and say so, when I hold my ground without apology or aggression simply because it is true, I am giving something to every person in the room who has been told they cannot do the same. Especially the women. Especially the daughters who were taught that having a clear voice is itself the problem.

I am here to be exactly the human I am. Loved and messy and courageous and willing to say what is real. The universe, or God, or whatever name you give to the intelligence behind all of this, can take care of the rest.

The gifts were always there. Underneath the armour. Waiting for the conditions to be safe enough to come out.

The same can be true for pain. Sometimes it stays quiet until the conditions shift. Sometimes it arrives before we feel ready. Mine had waited a long time. What I am about to tell you is what happened in me when the conditions finally changed enough for something buried to move.

What I am about to tell you is what happened in mine when the conditions were finally ready. Before I take you there, I want to tell you why I walked it.

I was working as a Stopping the Violence counsellor in a small town. I needed to walk the walk. I needed to see what happens when you do, so I could better guide the women coming through my door.

What I found was the crippling reality. My nervous system was in a shaking response just getting close to the same place I was abused thirty years prior. The nervous system remembered even when I didn't. That is the reality. We all have that. Stories in our nervous system every day.

We are so wise. And we are just sometimes afraid to sit with what truly is. Because of the damage it will cause around us. Because of the way others will be upset with us if we do. Because of the fact that people do not want to throw their loved ones under the bus to tell the truth. They think it is selfish, because their whole life they were told it was selfish to say yes to themselves. They were told to be quiet. To numb the pain. To move forward. To do better. To not be the one who asks too many questions.

So I know how hard it is to bring it all up.

I did it so I could survive it and tell about it. That is what I am doing on every page you are reading.

I want you to be safer from prescriptions handed to you without enough curiosity about the conditions around your pain. Medication can help. A prescription should not become the end of the investigation. I want you to ask what else the rates of violence, mental health crisis, addiction, disconnection, and despair may be telling us about the society around the person. I want us to stay brave enough to look at the fire and not only quiet the smoke.

That is why I walked through what I am about to describe.

You do not have to do what I did. You do not have to take anyone to court. You do not have to revisit every place that hurt you. You only have to know that going through is possible. In your own time. In your own way. When your own conditions are ready. A witness who can stay. A nervous system steady enough to hold its own ground. A practitioner who has done their own work. A community that does not flinch. Tools that the body trusts.

If you are not there yet, you are not behind. You are exactly where the conditions have allowed you to be. The fire is patient. The garden is patient. The plant does not bloom on a schedule the gardener can impose.

This is one woman's account of what going through looked like for her.

~

That story is the next chapter.

Before you turn the page, hear this.

This is all to tell you that you are not crazy.

You are responding.

And you can return to wholeness when you sit with what truly is and has been.

Chapter Two
The Soul Echoes
Understanding Neurodevelopmental Trauma

Before I take you into the courtroom, I need to take you back further.

The going through was not just him. It was not just one day in front of a judge. It was all of it. The whole undercurrent of what I had been carrying since before I had language for any of it.

I am going to be honest with you about what happened to me. Not because my story is unique. Because it isn't. Different houses. Different specific harms. Same wiring underneath. I am telling you what happened to me because the only way I know to teach you how neurodevelopmental trauma actually works is to show you how it actually happened. In a real childhood. In a real body. With real consequences that did not stop when childhood did.

This is how I was programmed to believe in the world.

The Soil

I learned something in Peru that has stayed with me for the rest of my life.

I was there in my early twenties, studying for my anthropology degree at the University of British Columbia. The trip was credited coursework. I had gone south to learn from a culture whose wisdom about the body, the mind, and the natural world had developed in directions Western academic frameworks had no way of accessing.

A Quechua teacher took us out to where they plant. He told us about the practice. When the Quechua people plant a tree, they do not put the seed directly in the ground. They first prepare a special mud, packed with the nutrients that particular kind of tree will need to thrive. They wrap the seed in that mud before it ever touches the soil it will grow in.

A seed given that nourishing start, he said, would grow into the strongest tree. Its roots would reach deeper. Its trunk would hold steadier in wind. The first conditions of a seed are the foundation conditions. They are what the rest of the tree will be built on for the rest of its life.

I remember standing there listening to him. I remember a quiet recognition arriving in some part of myself that already knew without having words for it. I did not get that.

I had not been packed in special mud. I had been dropped into ground that had been poisoned by the people responsible for tending it. And in my mother's defense she was given the same alcoholic, unstable, neglectful upbringing that did not have nutritious mud.

That is what this chapter is going to teach you about. The mud the seed was given, or the mud it was not given. The first conditions. The foundation conditions. The ones that shape everything that gets built on top.

A plant has needs. It needs water. It needs sun. It needs soil that has not been contaminated by what was poured into it before. It needs a gardener whose attention is on the plant and not on themselves. It needs the consistent return of conditions that allow it to settle its roots and reach toward what feeds it.

I did not have those things.

The lack of love. The lack of affection. The lack of validation. The neglect so woven into the household that nobody noticed it was neglect. The cry-it-out method, which I have come to believe may have contributed to an early lesson in my own body that distress would not always be met. The adults who liked alcohol more than they liked listening. The rule that children were to be seen and not heard. The understanding that when you said something, you did not get to matter. You were just along for the ride of what the adults were doing. There was no room for a self to grow. No room for a self to blossom.

That was the soil before any of the other things were added on top.

The very first programming taught me that my needs would not be met. Not by anyone. The baby version of me learned, before she had words for anything, that the world she had been born into would not come when she cried. I cannot prove which infant experience wrote which line in me. I can see the larger ecology. Distress existed inside a home where responsive care was inconsistent. My grounded belief is that those early repetitions became one thread in what my body learned about whether comfort would arrive. It happened before autobiographical memory. The lesson, whatever its exact beginning, felt deep.

Then the other things were added on top.

I had three fathers. Each one carried his own wound. Each one, in his own way, left no room for the children around him to be safe. One of them is the one I eventually took to court. None of them brought safety. Each of them added to a soil that was already poisoned.

The man in the uniform is the one I am telling you about now. He is the one who laid the deepest foundation. He is the one I had to face thirty years later to stand up to what no one in his life had ever stood up to. The earliest years are particularly sensitive years for building the foundations of attachment, stress regulation, and development. Those first conditions matter enormously. They shape the mud around the seed. But they are not the end of the story. Development continues, and the nervous system remains capable of learning and change. That is our chance for mud to develop us deeper if we get consistency, love, encouragement, connection, touch, kindness, patience, presence, and slow stable guidance. That was not my experience.

The Authority

He wore a uniform. He was an alcoholic. He believed power over others was the same as strength.

The way he taught me anything was by hurting me until I learned it. When I was three years old, he threw me into the pool and would not let me hold the side. That was how he taught me to swim. The lesson was: figure it out. The lesson was: no one is coming. The lesson was: if you do it wrong, you will pay for it.

That programmed me to believe that asking for help would bring more harm. That my body's only function was to perform what was being demanded of it.

I was hit if I did not learn something fast enough. Spanked. Yelled at. Criticized. A wooden spoon brought down on the palms of my hands. The meatballs at dinner had to be cut a certain number of times before I was allowed to eat. If I missed a cut, I had to wait. If I waited too long, I was spanked.

That programmed me to believe that I had to read other people's minds to survive. Survival was conditional on getting it right by unspoken rules I was never given.

After enough nights of that, my body did what bodies do when there is no way out. I curled up. I went small. I went tired. I went scared. I went defeated. I numbed out. I learned to avoid human interaction. I learned to dissociate from the room I was sitting in even while my body stayed in the chair.

That programmed me to believe that my body was a place to escape rather than a place to live in.

When yelling started in another part of the house, I learned to disappear into the corner of whatever room I was in. The sound did not have to be aimed at me to mark me. The body recorded the air. The walls recorded the air. I recorded everything.

That programmed me to believe that even being adjacent to anger meant I was about to be hit. The air itself became dangerous.

I watched him hurt my mother. There was nothing I could do. The body of a child knows when the person who should be the strongest in the room is being broken. That kind of seeing changes a child. It teaches her two things at the same time. The first is that the people who are supposed to protect you cannot protect themselves. The second is that no one is coming for any of you. Especially when the one hurting you is the authority that people turn to for safety.

That programmed me to believe that strength was a lie. That no one in the world was actually safe.

How does a girl survive that?

Who are the safe men in the world?

There was also sexual abuse. It came from men who were meant to serve the justice in the world. Ruptures like that are more common than anyone talks about, and we will get into silence being a huge part of our culture's unwellness. It took me forever to come out of deep silence programming.

The way he taught me to ride in a car was unbuckled in the back of a metal vehicle at high speed while he was drunk. The effects of those brain injuries live in me still. Some have never fully resolved for me. I have learned how to work around them. They have become conditions I live within. They have become conditions I work within. When my head went blurry and rang and could not focus as a child, there was no care to take me to. What were they going to do? Drive me to a hospital and have someone ask how it had happened. The very thing that hurt me was the thing that prevented the help from coming. The person who would show up for safety wasn't.

That programmed me to believe that when I was injured, no one would come. The source of the injury would be the same person responsible for whether or not I ever got help. And when I did not get medical care and nurturance, it deeply programmed me that I did not matter.

He was allowed to be critical. We were not. He was allowed to be wrong about everything. We were not allowed to be wrong about anything. The asymmetry was total. The world inside that house had only one permitted voice. It was his.

That programmed me to believe that my own voice was dangerous. The only safe thing to do was track his approval and avoid stepping outside of it.

Outside the house, the adults who came around acted like everything was normal. Because of the uniform he wore and the rank he held. The uniform protected the house the way the uniform protected the man wearing it. The neighbours did not look. The relatives did not look. The community did not look.

That programmed me to believe that the world looks away.

I found out years later, through the investigations that came when I finally took him to court, that they had all known. The others he worked with knew. The relatives knew. The neighbours knew. The professionals knew. They knew we were having a terrible time. They were scared of him. All of them. The same fear that kept me silent as a child was the fear that kept the adults around us silent for thirty years. He was not just my problem. He was a community's problem. The whole community was carrying him. The institution itself was covering for him. When my mother finally found the strength to leave, the same community turned on her instead of on him.

That programmed me to believe that the institutions designed to help would protect the wrong person. That help itself could be the harm. That the world I lived in was not the world the world said it was.

There was no calling for help because the help was the one in your house.

When I was small, he would take me into the jail cells where he worked and lock the door. He would tell me, behind that closed steel, what it looked like to be a good little kid. The lesson was the cage itself. The lesson was that if I did not behave, this was where I would end up. The lesson was that he had the keys to my freedom. I learned to associate authority with confinement before I had words for either.

That programmed me to believe that authority was a cage. My freedom was something another person owned.

There was no learning that was not braided with threat. There was no skill that was not also a survival drill.

I have wondered for years what taught him to become that way. Harm can be learned and passed forward, but I cannot know every source of another person's cruelty. I believe he carried wounds of his own. I also know a wound does not force a person to harm a child. Whatever he had lived through, he made choices with power. Other people paid for them. He made other people pay it.

I was the first person ever to stand up to him.

That decision did not come for thirty years.

How the Patterns Compounded

I want to teach you something that is rarely taught and is critical to understand.

The programming does not just persist. It compounds.

I think of trauma as a pattern-recognition system. A child who has already learned one shape of danger may become quicker to recognize pieces of that shape later. A new threat can activate old learning. The second harm is still its own harm, but the body may meet it with a nervous system already trained by the first. This is one way trauma can compound. New experiences can reactivate older expectations of danger.

This is how I know.

After my mother left the man in the uniform, she eventually partnered again. The next man's harm was more verbal than physical. Critical. Undermining. Cutting. In the absence of the first man, his abuse would have been bad on its own.

But the first man was not absent from my body. My body was still using his template.

So when the second man's verbal abuse came, it was filtered through the size of the first man's threat. My nervous system did what nervous systems do. It reached for the most familiar pattern and applied it. The verbal abuse was made bigger by the fear that had already been stored. My body responded as if the first man were back in the room.

This is how trauma compounds. Each new experience activates the original template. The original template keeps growing.

And there was the father whose harm was absence itself. He moved in and out of my life like weather. Never fully showing up. Making promises that evaporated on arrival. Expecting me to perform for whatever approval was on offer, and my fawn response was practically built for him: be pleasing enough, be good enough, be impressive enough, and maybe this time there would be no abandonment. The deepest wound with him was never a single thing he did. It was what he never did. He did not protect me. He made the ending of the marriage about himself rather than about the child who needed protecting, and years later, when he came back around, he handed me his resentment as though it were mine to carry, blaming the child for what the adults had built. He had not integrated his own wound, so he tried to pass it to me. I learned to emotionally safeguard myself around him the way you learn to carry an umbrella in a country of sudden rain. Between the three of them I received the whole curriculum: harm done to the body, harm done in words, and harm done by absence. Three men. Three weathers. One lesson repeating: the people who were supposed to guard the garden were the weather the garden needed guarding from.

The template does not stop growing once childhood is over. It keeps being reached for. Every angry boss. Every critical partner. Every disagreement in a meeting. Every time someone in the world becomes upset with you in any way, the template can be activated. The body does not know that this person is not him. The body knows there is anger in the room. Anger in the room means something really bad is about to happen.

For me, that has meant nothing ever felt safe when there were people in any state of argumentativeness. Not heated discussion. Not productive conflict. Not minor disagreement. The template did not care about the gradations my mind could make. The template knew only one thing. Angry voices mean danger.

That is neurodevelopmental trauma. The original wiring being reached for, over and over, in rooms where the original threat is long gone.

The Lifelong Cost of the Programming

These things are lifelong. They live in the body long after the moments that made them.

The brain injuries live in me still. The fear lives in me still. The body that learned to track every footstep on the floor above it does not forget how to do that, even after the footsteps have stopped. What was done to me in those years is inside me. Time moved on. The programming came with me. I have made a life that holds it. I have made a life that does not let it run me. That is a different kind of healing than people imagine when they imagine healing. It is the reorganization of what was done into something I can live with.

That became the shape of my life.

I grew up as a plant that kept one eye on the gardener at all times. Calibrating. Watching. Pulling back from anything that might bring his attention down on me wrong. Every direction except the one he had approved of came with consequence. The fear of being wrong was the trellis I trained myself around. I grew along that trellis for decades. I did not even know I was on it.

It was about the fear of stepping outside of what was wanted of me. What I actually wanted never entered the room.

That fear followed me out of his house. It followed me into every classroom. Every friendship. Every workplace. Every relationship I would ever try to have. The body that had learned to track the gardener kept tracking. Different gardeners now. Different rooms. Same vigilance.

School was safer than home. The yelling did not follow me to school. But the shape my body had learned was the shape I brought with me. I could not connect the way a child allowed to grow normally connects. I was three grades ahead of myself academically. I could read and reason and analyze at a level that startled my teachers. What I could not do was play. What I could not do was let anyone close. What I could not do was let my body be at rest in any room that contained other human beings. I was five years old. How was I supposed to know how to cope? I did not even know there was anything to cope with. The conditions of my house were the only conditions I had been given. I assumed they were the conditions of being alive.

I put on a traum-our no one could ever get through again. The armour that grew around me was so dense and so practiced that even people who loved me later could not reach through it. The armour kept me alive. The armour also kept me from being known.

This is what the long aftermath of early threat looked like in my adult life. The careful relationships. The withheld voice. The body that cannot rest. The vigilance that never turns off. The marriages declined. The bridges not crossed. The rooms not entered. The truths not spoken. Every one of those is the original wiring still being reached for, decades after the original threat has died.

The Questioner Survived

There was one thing that did survive all of it.

I was a sassy little thing. I was the one who asked the questions. I was the one who did not stop asking. I did not stop in his house. I did not stop in his office. I did not stop in the schools or the relationships or the workplaces that came later. I have been told my whole life that I am too much. That I ask too many questions. That I should know when to leave well enough alone. I have never learned how to do that. I do not intend to learn now. My curiosity has what has kept me alive and seeking, uncovering and finding.

That refusal to stop questioning was the part of me he never managed to break. He bent every other thing. He bent my posture. He bent my sense of safety. He bent my ability to be in my own body. He bent how I would learn to relate to men, to authority, to my own desires. The questioner, the one who knew that what was happening was wrong even when no one would name it, survived him.

That is also part of neurodevelopmental trauma. The part that survives. I believe there is often some part that survives. It might be a single quality. It might be small. It might even be the part you were told was the problem with you. Sometimes that part becomes a gift. The questioner is mine. That questioner is the one who took him to court thirty years later.

That questioner is the one writing this book.

The Parking Lot. The Courtroom. The Lake.

Thirty years after all of that, I sat in a parking lot outside the same building where some of my earliest abuse had happened. I was shaking. Not from cold. From what I had always called cellular memory. Science might speak more carefully of implicit threat learning, conditioned physiological response, or a nervous system recognizing cues before conscious thought catches up. My conscious mind knew where I was. My body had already begun reacting. In the somatic framework I had learned, I understood the shaking as my body moving through a defensive response rather than as evidence that I was falling apart. I thought of the way an animal tremors after a chase. My body was shaking. I let it. I knew what was happening. I had the knowledge by then to name it. Naming it was the thing that kept me from being swallowed by it.

I understood that shaking through the trauma frameworks I had learned: my body recognizing cues connected with the place and reacting before my conscious mind could settle it. The mind knew. The body reacted anyway. That gap, between what the mind knows and what the body has learned to expect, is the gap this chapter has been about. It was the autonomic nervous system in charge.

I was about to give a personal statement. I had taken the man in the uniform to court. I did not know what winning would look like. The lawyer asked me what I was trying to achieve. I told her the truth. I did not know. I only knew I had to do it. The process itself was the point. Truth-telling was the only thing that had ever allowed me to metabolize what happened in my nervous system. Dissociation is a beautiful and powerful protector. It had carried me through things no child should have to survive. The way back from it has always been the same. Naming what was real.

I had not been able to sleep with the light off for thirty years.

Six hours of cross-examination. The defence lawyer's only tool was to pathologize me. To gaslight me. To use the same mechanism that had been used on me since childhood. Make her sound unstable. Make her sound unreliable. Make her sound like the problem. Every response I gave was another step of me anchoring into my own core. Every answer I found was my nervous system remembering who it actually was underneath all of it. It was not a courtroom. It was a ceremony. The plant standing in its own light. Refusing, finally, to fold.

He had no choice but to sit there and hear me. Thirty years later. At the end of it, through everything his lawyers tried, he admitted it. He admitted I had reason to fear him.

It was not full justice. What should have been a full trial became a peace bond, and there was nothing of peace in it. It was another veil placed over violence against women and children, and I name it plainly here because so many women will recognize the shape of it. Still, I had my time. I made him hear me. Some months later, an official letter of apology arrived, acknowledging how the system had failed to protect my family. I asked for it to be addressed to my mother and my brother too. What I had endured to get there needed to give something back to all of us. The letter did not undo a single day of it. And yet it helped something in us heal.

The court was the act of refusing the programming. It was the moment my body, in the room with the original source of the wiring, chose to do something different than what the wiring would have had me do. The wiring would have had me go small. Dissociate. Comply. Perform. The questioner refused.

That refusal is what new growth looks like at the developmental level. It is the choice to act in a direction the wiring would never have permitted, while the wiring is screaming. The wiring stays. The choice is what changes. The old alarm still screams in certain rooms. I go anyway. Or I become discerning about which rooms are worth my time.

I have walked many paths of healing. EMDR helped me reprocess what words alone could not reach. Somatic experiencing taught me how to listen to my body as the truest source of information. Writing music and singing it gave the pain a way out of me. Sharing my story in rooms where people were finally ready to hear it taught me what witness actually feels like. The church, and the moment holy spirit moved through my limbic system and released a fear that had been living there at the most primal level. Reiki, Sundance and sweat lodge. Acupuncture, chiropractic, and cranial sacral therapy.

And Peru. Sitting in ceremony on a mountain, inside an Incan temple most tourists never found, I let myself be fragile in front of men for the first time. The mountain held me. The altitude thinned my breath. Something I had been guarding since I was a child slowly began to lower its arms. I was terrified. I let it happen anyway. That was a first crack of light. The plant medicine that followed cracked everything else open.

Each path was a different way back to the same place.

Then one day I was back at the lake I grew up on. The same water. I was looking out at it and a feeling came over me that I had never felt before, or had forgotten so completely it felt new. Peace. A real, full, embodied peace. The presence of something underneath everything I had ever carried.

In my observing self, I recognized what it was. It was a state of consciousness that people have always been pointing toward when they talk about the garden of Eden or the kingdom of heaven, the Tao or the Buddha. Or Yogic philosophy. Always available. Always present. The thing we never actually lose, only temporarily obscure.

I understood, in that moment, that every yes and every no we give to experiences, thoughts, and people either clouds that peaceful self or returns us to it. The clouds are real. They can be thick. They can last thirty years. The sun is always there. The garden is always there. We do not have to earn our way back to it. We simply have to keep clearing the clouds, one breath, one truth, one ceremony, one conversation at a time, until we can feel what was always underneath.

I was not broken. I was shattered, and then blamed for it.

And even shattered, the light was always inside.

If you are reading this and you are recognizing your own wiring in any of mine, hear this last. The programming you are carrying is not who you are. It is what was done to you, encoded. You can become aware of it. You can refuse it, one room at a time. Your body can learn new templates. The plant can put out new growth that responds to current conditions instead of original ones. That work is real. It is slow. It is yours to do at the pace your body can hold.

If you are reading this as one who serves, who tends, who shows up to rooms where people come carrying programming they did not choose, hear this too. The person in front of you is not their template. They are the plant beneath it. Your attention can be the kind of weather that lets new growth happen. The research is clear that humans remain capable of learning and adaptation across the lifespan. Attuned care, even in adulthood and even decades after early wiring was laid, can become part of the conditions that support that change. You can be part of a new set of conditions.

Whatever brought you to this chapter, you are sacred. You are responding. The wiring was not your fault. The new growth is yours to claim.

Now that you can see the programming, we can look at the specific adaptations it produced. The shutting down. The over-giving. The hypervigilance. The traum-our. The next chapter is an invitation to recognize them as the survival tools they always were.

Chapter Three
Survival Responses
How the Body Adapts

For most of us, the first time we ever felt our hearts race or our hands shake or our minds go blank in the middle of a moment we did not understand, someone told us something was wrong with us. Maybe a parent. Maybe a teacher. Maybe a doctor. The labels followed. Anxious. Avoidant. Defiant. Too much. Too sensitive. Too quiet. Too dramatic. Something to be fixed.

We deserved more curiosity than we were given.

Many of those reactions can make sense as protective responses when conditions exceed what a person can hold. That does not explain every symptom in every body. It does change the first question.

This chapter is going to walk you through three deeply studied threat responses and a fourth relational survival strategy often named in trauma practice. Fight. Flight. Freeze. Fawn. These are protective responses, strategies a body reaches for when survival, safety, or connection feels threatened.

A plant that grows in the shadow of a wall will lean toward the only light it can reach. We do not say the plant is disordered. We say the plant is doing what plants do. A turtle that pulls inside its shell when something looms is not malfunctioning. The turtle is being a turtle. Our nervous systems work the same way. They were built for survival. They are still doing that work even when the threat is no longer present, because they do not know how to stop until they are taught.

These protective patterns are shaped through biology, learning, relationship, and experience. Most of us have one dominant pattern that became most familiar because it worked best in the conditions we grew up under. Recognizing that pattern is not the end of healing. It is the beginning of being able to thank our body for what it has been doing on our behalf.

Fight

Fight is the surge of energy a body releases when its boundaries are crossed. The tightening in the chest. The hardening of the jaw. The hands that want to push back. The voice that wants to rise. Fight is the body's way of saying: something matters here. I will not be small inside this.

In the brain, fight is the sympathetic nervous system firing forward. The amygdala signals threat. Adrenaline and cortisol flood the body. Heart rate climbs. Blood moves to the large muscle groups. Pupils widen. The slow-thinking part of the brain, the prefrontal cortex, goes quiet so fast survival action can take over. The jaw tightens. The hands prepare. The voice gathers force. The whole organism gathers to push back at whatever is in the room.

A plant grows thorns when something keeps grazing on it. A rose puts spikes between itself and what would tear at it. A cactus learns to protect its flesh with armour that says do not touch. The thorns are not decorative. They are the plant's intelligence about what has been done to it.

In our culture, fight is one of the most pathologized survival responses. A child who yells is called defiant. A teenager who pushes back is called difficult. A woman who asserts herself is called aggressive. A man who refuses to comply is called unstable. The body's intelligent refusal to be hurt again gets renamed as a character defect.

There is also another way fight can show up that is often misread. For someone whose dominant pattern has been freeze or fawn, the return of fight energy in adulthood is often a sign of the nervous system thawing. The energy that has been bound up for years in shutdown or appeasement begins to move. The body that has been quiet for too long begins to push back. To outside observers, and sometimes to ourselves, this can look like backsliding. Like getting worse. Like being more reactive than we used to be. It is the opposite. It is the body finding its way back to the response it could not access at the time of the original wound. The thawing is healthy. The fight energy is the body remembering it has a voice.

If fight became your dominant pattern, it programmed you to believe that softness was a luxury you could not afford. That the world was something to be braced against rather than received. That your safety lived in your willingness to push first.

Flight

Flight is the body's urge to get out. It can show up as actually running. It can show up as busyness. Distraction. Overworking. Restlessness. The inability to be still. It can show up as the constant low hum of needing to be somewhere other than where you are.

In the brain, flight is the same sympathetic nervous system, firing in the other direction. The chemistry is the same as fight. The same adrenaline. The same cortisol. The same accelerated heart rate. The energy goes toward escape rather than confrontation. Blood moves to the legs. The body wants to be elsewhere. The prefrontal cortex narrows to one thing only. Get out. This is the body's strategy when staying and engaging would cost more than leaving.

Flight can also show up as dissociation. When the body cannot physically leave the room it is in, the consciousness can leave the body. Dissociation is flight in its most internal form. It is the self stepping out of the self so that whatever is happening does not have to be fully felt. It is one of the most sophisticated survival adaptations a body has. It is often labeled by clinicians as a symptom of something wrong rather than understood as the brilliant strategy it is.

A vine creeps over walls to find better light. A strawberry plant sends out runners to find new ground when the old ground is exhausted. Roots grow outward instead of down when the soil is poor. The plant does not stay where it is being hurt. It moves to where survival is possible.

Flight is often mislabeled as avoidance. As attention deficit. As not being able to commit. Flight is wisdom. If you cannot fight your way out, you find the door. If there is no door, you make movement itself a kind of door.

If flight became your dominant pattern, it programmed you to believe that no room was safe enough to stay in. That stillness was when bad things happened. That movement, work, distance, and busyness, anything that kept you away from being pinned, was where survival lived.

Freeze

Freeze is the body's emergency brake. It stops us when overwhelming danger is too close to escape. It conserves energy. It plays dead. It hides us inside our own bodies until the danger has passed.

In the brain, freeze is the firing of the dorsal vagal complex, the most ancient branch of the parasympathetic nervous system. The body slows everything down. Heart rate drops. Breath becomes shallow. Blood moves away from the limbs and toward the core. Digestion slows or stops. The body goes still. This is the same response that allows a mouse caught by a cat to go limp. The same response a deer uses when the predator is closer than its legs can carry it. It is older than fight. Older than flight. It is the body's most ancient way of saying: if I cannot get away, I will become unreachable.

A tree drops all its leaves and goes dormant when winter comes. A bulb retreats underground and can wait there for years if it has to. A plant that looks dead is not always dead. Sometimes it is doing the most sophisticated thing a plant can do, which is wait.

Of all four responses, freeze is probably the most widespread and the least recognized. Most people who are living in freeze do not know that is what is happening. They simply know they are tired. They know they cannot quite get themselves to start the thing they want to start. They know their feelings feel muted. They know there is a flat quality to their days that should not be there.

This is what is called functional freeze. The body has chosen the freeze response, and the person is still moving through life. They get up. They go to work. They care for their children. They show up. From the outside, nothing is wrong. From the inside, almost nothing is reaching them.

The signs of functional freeze are more common than the world tends to admit. A low fatigue that does not lift with rest. Trouble starting things, even things that matter. Brain fog. Lost time. Trouble remembering. A flat or muted emotional range. Watching your life from outside the body instead of living it from inside. Procrastination that feels heavier than choice. The feeling that nothing really lands. No joy. No real grief. Just a low hum. Disconnection from desires, dreams, hunger, body sensations. A constant low-grade overwhelm that does not match anything in your day. Sleep that is not rest.

If any of that felt familiar, you are not alone. Researchers in the trauma field have observed for decades that a huge portion of the adult population, especially those who lived through chronic childhood stress or long-term relational harm, are running on dorsal vagal shutdown underneath their daily lives. The reason it goes unnamed is that it does not present as crisis. It presents as fine. The world has stopped looking for fine to be a symptom.

Freeze can look like laziness. Like depression. Like procrastination. Like checking out. Sometimes those words are describing something else entirely. Sometimes a person is also clinically depressed. The point is that outward stillness does not tell us its cause. We have to ask what is happening underneath it.

If freeze became your dominant pattern, it programmed you to believe that disappearing was the only way through. That being seen meant being hurt. That if you could just not be there, in your own body, the danger would pass over you.

Fawn

Fawn is the survival response of appeasement. It is the body's strategy when neither fighting nor fleeing nor freezing is going to keep you safe. The only thing that might keep you safe is making the dangerous person happy.

A vine wraps itself around whatever stronger structure is available. It grows to fit the shape of its container, reshaping itself to whatever room it has been given. The shape is not the plant's true shape. It is the shape survival required.

Fawn shows up as the over-giver. The peacemaker. The one who reads the room before she enters it. The one who knows what everyone in the meeting needs before anyone has spoken. The one who says yes when her body is saying no. The one whose generosity is so reliable that no one notices it is costing her something.

Fawn looks like sensitivity. It looks like kindness. It looks like the very qualities our culture rewards in women. That is part of why fawn is the hardest of the four responses to recognize. It does not look like a wound. It looks like virtue. It is praised in the very directions that quietly drain the person doing it.

Fawn is also the response most reinforced by the wider world, especially in women. The woman who appeases is called gracious. The woman who self-erases is called selfless. The woman who carries everyone else's emotional weight is called a good friend, a good partner, a good daughter, a good mother. The same world that rewards fawn punishes the moments she stops doing it. The first time a fawning woman says no, the people who depended on her saying yes will often call her selfish. The fawn knew this. The fawn was protecting her from that exact moment.

Fawn is not only a woman's response. Many men and boys carry it too. Boys who were abused. Boys who learned that pleasing the dangerous adult was the way to survive. Boys who grew up into men still running on that wiring, in rooms where it is no longer needed. The cultural conditioning that hides fawn in men is different but just as real. Men have been taught to be strong instead of being held. They have not been given the vocabulary to name the fawn that lives in their bodies. Their abuse is often less believed, less named, less witnessed. Many men carry fawn quietly, alone, never recognizing it as a wound.

The cost of fawn is hidden because the appearance of it is so socially acceptable. The cost lives in the body. The chronic exhaustion. The illness that comes from never resting. The relationships that drain her because she has trained the people around her to take what she offers. The slow disappearance of the inner self underneath the relentless attention to other people's selves. Fawn does not look like an emergency from the outside. It looks like a very pleasant person who happens to be tired all the time.

Trauma practice often groups four protective patterns under the language fight, flight, freeze, and fawn. Fight, flight, and freezing are deeply studied threat responses. Fawn is a newer clinical and trauma-practice term for appeasement: becoming agreeable, pleasing, useful, or easy to reduce relational threat.

I use the four together because the map is useful. I do not mean they are four anatomically equal branches of one biological hierarchy.

Protective responses also do not always arrive in a neat order. A body may fight in one context, freeze in another, flee when escape becomes possible, and appease when connection itself feels necessary for safety. Biology, learning, relationship, and the situation all shape the pattern.

Fawn, in this book, is the relational armour. The body learns: keep the connection. Read the room. Become what is needed. Reduce the chance of conflict. That pattern can be extraordinarily intelligent in a dangerous relationship. It can also follow a person into rooms where pleasing is no longer required.

The vagus nerve, the long nerve that runs from the brainstem through the heart, lungs, and gut, is the central organ of this. The same vagal pathways that allow us to read another person's face for warmth, to soften our voice, to attune to someone we love, can be drafted by the body into reading another person's face for danger and mirroring it back in whatever shape will keep us safe. The body uses the same machinery it would use for love. It uses it to survive instead.

This is why fawn looks like kindness. The biology of fawn is the biology of connection, running on a different operating system. The fawning body is producing oxytocin. It is reading micro-expressions. It is mirroring the tone of the dangerous person. It is using the social engagement system to stay alive. Polyvagal theory describes this as the survival mode of the same wiring that ordinarily creates safe relationship. The fawn is not faking connection. The fawn is using real connection wiring as armour.

If fawn became your dominant pattern, it programmed you to believe that your worth lived in what you could give. That love was something you earned through usefulness. That to ask for anything was to risk losing the connection. That your own needs were the most dangerous thing in the room.

My Experience with the F's

I want to tell you about this from inside it. Somewhere a woman is going to read these sentences and find her own body inside them. Something that has been frozen in her for a long time will begin to unlock. That is the only reason I am telling it.

Before I tell you what happened, I want you to see who I was.

He was the first lover I had let into the parts of me I had been tending alone. I was young. I was tender. I was a young woman growing into what it meant to be a sexual being. I was taking care of myself. I cared very much for every sacred part of me. The sensual. The sweet. The kind. The caring. The gentle. The soft. Those parts were what drew people to me. They were also mine. I was being a good gardener to them.

The world around me was not.

I was living in a place where the air was misogynistic. The jokes about women were crude and constant. The eyes did not look away. The gazes on my hips, my breasts, my body, were the weather of every room I walked into. The female form was something to be objectified before it was something to be treated like a person. You could not just be a human in that place. You were a body first.

At that time I had a dream. I wanted to get into deep police work. I wanted to help protect people. I wanted to be someone who showed up for the people who could not show up for themselves. I had begun by going on ride-alongs with police officers to learn the work from inside it. I was a young person taking my dream seriously and putting myself in the rooms where I could learn.

The women in the community complained.

Not because of anything I had done. Because of how I looked. Because I had a body that became the thing they could see instead of the dream I was pursuing. They complained to the department that police men should not be riding with girls. The department listened. The program was stopped.

I could not just be a young person with a dream and the work ethic to pursue it. A sexualizing lens was projected onto a youth by people carrying their own internalized misogyny. The institution gave in to the projection. The narratives they wrote about me were a soup. They cooked it all around me. I was supposed to live inside it.

Before I tell you why I had wanted to be police, I need to tell you something that had happened to me when I was still just a girl.

The man I had thought was my first relationship had been selling me into sex trafficking. I had been a child meeting what looked like attention from someone older. The attention had turned out to be something else entirely. I did not fully understand at the time what was happening. It was police who got me out. The system worked that time. Officers I had not known until they showed up for me became the reason I lived another day.

That is why I wanted to be in police work. I wanted to be that person for someone else.

Now back to the night.

He came home from the bar with dark eyes. I had never seen those eyes on him before. He had been drinking. He had been seething. The misogyny in the air around us had been working on him all night. The friends he drank with had been working on him. The whole town had been working on him. He came home with whatever had been poured into him pouring out toward me.

My freeze came first. I did not know to call it freeze then. I only knew that my body went somewhere I could not follow. I felt the cold sleep of dissociation pull me down through the floor. The cable cord he was about to whip me with in his hand. I went still. I went small. I went where the body of a child goes when the body of an adult is too dangerous to confront.

I want to tell you about the lubricant before I tell you what he did with it. The lubricant lived on the bedside table because I had only ever allowed any kind of penetration with lubricant first. That was a tender way I treated myself to care for myself. I deeply cherished my heart, my body, my mind in those years. The lubricant was a way of cherishing my own anatomy. It was a small ritual of self-tending. It was the practice of a young woman who had decided her own body deserved softness on its way in.

He grabbed the bottle. He poured it over my head.

The degradation I felt in that moment is something I never forgot, and it collapsed me inside. The act inverted everything the lubricant had ever meant to me. The thing I had been using to cherish myself was being used to make me into the disgusting thing he wanted me to see in myself.

In that moment, words I had carried inside me for years came flooding back. They were the words my stepfather had spoken to me when I was younger. No one will ever want you. You are wrong. You are terrible. I had carried them inside me as an inheritance without ever believing them in my body. They had been a seed. The night the lubricant came down over my head, the seed found its soil. I thought, somewhere underneath the freeze, he must have been right. I do not deserve love.

The shame had been a seed. That night it had soil. It bloomed.

What followed that night was not one night. It was many. Countless nights of him taking my body without the lubricant, dry, while I was shut down and dissociated and not in my body at all.

The dissociation was flight. My body could not leave the room, so my consciousness left the body. The flight was internal because no external flight was possible. The sex became something I performed. It was no longer something I felt. It was no longer about me. I lay there while it happened. I waited for it to be over. I did what I needed to do to keep the next night from being worse.

The freeze that had been there the first night could not stay forever. The body cannot hold a freeze across hundreds of nights. The freeze became something else.

The freeze turned into fawn.

That was the moment fawn became my dominant pattern. I had not been a fawning person before. My childhood had laid the seed. The events of eighteen were the soil. After the night at the party and the rape, my body chose a new strategy. The strategy was: appease whatever might hurt me. Make myself smaller. Pull my femininity inward so it would not provoke. Pine and please in case I might be hurt again. The fawn was automatic. It was my body's intelligent answer to having learned, twice in one year, that being a tender young woman in that world was unsafe.

When the rape that first night ended, I just turned over. I did not speak. I did not cry where he could hear me. I had no one to go to. My family was not a place I could call from. The ownership happened. Whatever the intention of those dark eyes was, it happened. My sweetness was a flower that collapsed and turned grey into the residue of what once was.

I was not allowed to breathe the same after that.

I turned more deeply into the arms of the person who had done it. Not because I did not understand what had happened. Because I did not see how to survive otherwise. My psyche, my heart, my mind were shattered. My nervous system was on a vigilance it had never come down from for decades after. The only conclusion my body could reach was: let me become whatever you want me to be so I can live another day.

I gave him everything. My dreams. The self I had been before he came home from the bar that night. I became completely his.

I told only one person. My best friend. But he promised not to tell. I carried shame for it even though it was not my shame to carry. The story stayed buried inside my body the whole time. I went back to school. I was still finishing school. I carried on with the daily tasks I had to do. From the outside there was nothing to see. Inside, the freeze had become fawn. The fawn had become the wiring my body now ran on every day. My healing would come in layers. Slowly. Over years. It would not happen fast.

What I knew, in some part of me that did not yet have language for it, was that I did not want another boyfriend. I did not want another man near me. Years later, in another season of life entirely, when my daughter came, I wanted to be alone with her. I wanted her safe from anyone who was unpredictable. That instinct was older than any conscious choice I made. Before I knew how to bring my own nervous system back to safety, before I knew how to relearn how to connect and trust, I knew I had to protect her.

The reconnecting has been slow. It is still slow. The body does not rush back into trust after it has been taught that trust was the door. Trust is a slow return. Future boyfriends I had, I never fully felt safe with to fall asleep at night until I learned how to somatically move the trauma out of my body. Until I let myself be deeply held, and let my psyche release the fear of sleeping next to a man.

There were moments, in those slow years of return, when fight came back to me. It would arrive when I was overwhelmed. It would arrive when something reactivated the old wiring without warning. To anyone watching, including sometimes me, it looked like reaction. It looked like I was getting worse. In the somatic frameworks I was learning, I began to interpret some of that fight energy differently. Not automatically as getting worse. Sometimes as access to anger, protest, or boundary that I had not been able to feel before. I cannot tell you every surge of anger is healing. I can tell you mine sometimes carried a voice I had been trained not to use.

The fight was the body remembering it had a voice.

In one body, in one story, all four responses moved through me. The freeze came first, in the cable cord and the cold sleep. The flight came as dissociation, the consciousness stepping out of the body it could not protect. The fawn came in the countless nights and the years that followed, as appeasement became the only strategy the body had left. As healing began, the fight returned. Not as backsliding. As thawing. As the body finally letting itself respond the way it could not respond on the night this all began. All four responses were the body's intelligence. None of them were broken. All of them kept me alivc.

I have come to understand something about him over the years that I could not understand then. He had been raped as a boy. The violence I received from him was the violcnce thal had been done to him as a child, passed forward, into the body of the woman he claimed to love. The wiring of his nervous system had been teaching him, since he was small, that love and harm lived in the same room. He had learned that lesson before he ever met me. He was running it on autopilot the night he came home from the bar with dark eyes. None of that excuses what he did. All of it explains it. The cycle of trauma is one of the most heartbreaking patterns our species carries. Hurt can travel through bodies. It does not have to. Love can travel too. The work of healing is part of choosing what we will pass on. So many of those who turn violent are carrying the generational pain of their lineages lifestories, passed on like cancer cells...mutating and forgetting what healthy cells are structured like. Healing the hurt inside the lines is the only way through for next generations to heal. The silencing of our culture, to turn away from domestic violence, female harassment and sexualization, enabling violence to be condoned, has led to the statistics that we have today. Within silence is complacency, and within complacency is an eruption of the things we cannot control. Like deep fear and pain programming from sexual violence and physical violence that so many children endure, become adults and then inflict on one another. Healing as a culture is possible.

I am not the only one returning. Nearly one in three women globally has experienced intimate partner or sexual violence in her lifetime. The numbers do not feel like numbers when you are inside them. They feel like a private secret you alone are carrying. The numbers tell us something different. The numbers tell us we are not alone. The story I have just told you is a one-in-three story. Mine is only one telling of it. I am writing it because witness is what heals first. Tender witness of how safety lands in the body. Slowly. Tenderly. Returning to the soft feminine beauty we all deserve to have, to live in, to be inside, while remaining safe and loved and protected. The witness work is what allows the body to trust again. The witness work is what the next nervous system, and the next, and the next, will need from those of us who have walked far enough to be able to offer it.

For many years after that, this is what fawning sounded like inside me.

You are too much. You are too sensitive. You are annoying when you try to make everyone happy. You are exhausted because you are weak. You always attract users because you are naive. You cannot say no because you are not strong enough. Something is wrong with you.

That was the story I lived inside for decades. The wiring from my childhood had been the seed. The events of that year had been the soil. What grew was a way of being in the world that I would not recognize as fawn for many more years. It looked like generosity. It looked like sensitivity. It looked like caretaking. Underneath, my nervous system was constantly scanning. Constantly attuning. Constantly working overtime. I learned to smile when I was hurting. I learned to give when I had nothing left. I learned to read every room for danger and try to soothe it away.

That programmed me to believe that connection required disappearing myself, and that my survival depended on knowing what someone else needed before they did.

I did not know what boundaries were. I thought love meant carrying everyone else's weight. I thought safety meant erasing myself. Because I was constantly fawning, I became a magnet for people who took and took, leaving me burned out and hollow.

For years, I thought this meant I was broken.

Here is the truth I came to learn. My nervous system was not broken. It was brilliant.

Fawning was the only strategy my body had after what had been done to it. My body knew that connection, even one-sided, meant survival. The constant impulse to please others was not weakness. It was wisdom. The brilliance was that it kept me alive. The cost was that it kept me from fully arriving in my own life for many years after.

The Harm of Pathologizing

A clinical label can sometimes describe a pattern that overlaps with protective responses without telling us the whole story of how that pattern formed. Defiance may contain fight. Anxiety may contain mobilization or flight. Depression may include states of low energy or withdrawal. Appeasement may appear inside dependent relational patterns.

Diagnoses can offer access to care. They can offer the relief of a name for what has been nameless. They can open doors that would otherwise stay closed. They have a real role. I am not against diagnosis when it serves the person.

What I am against is the framing those diagnoses too often carry. The framing that says: this is who you are now. This is your defect. This is the thing in you that is broken. That framing is what does the harm. It takes the body's most intelligent adaptations and calls them disease. It takes survival and calls it illness. It blames the plant for the soil it was given.

When we label the body's wisdom as disorder, we disempower the person living inside that body. We also stop asking the deeper question. The question that this entire book is asking. The question that any honest mental health framework would have to ask. What created this stress in the first place? What were the conditions the body was responding to?

A society that cannot ask that question will keep producing the same wounds and treating them as personal failings. We do not have to be that society. The point of naming a survival response is not to mark you with it. The point of naming it is to thank it, and then to slowly teach the body that the conditions have changed.

Intergenerational and Cultural Survival

Survival responses are inherited. They pass through families and cultures the way any other memory does. Science now confirms what many traditional cultures have known for generations. Stress responses can be passed down through the body itself. The field is called epigenetics. It describes how the conditions of an ancestor's life can shape the chemistry of a descendant's nervous system.

Children of parents who survived war carry war in their bodies. Children of residential school survivors carry residential school. Children of displacement, of slavery, of famine, of refugee passage, of generational racism, carry those things in their bodies even when they themselves did not live through any of it.

This is why Indigenous communities, immigrant families, and any people who have been on the receiving end of historical violence often carry a vigilance the dominant culture does not understand. That vigilance is not paranoia. It is biological memory of what was done.

The cruel irony is that the very systems that produce historical trauma often pathologize the people surviving it. A child acting out under the weight of racism in school is diagnosed with a behavioural disorder. A refugee parent in grief is labeled depressed while their resilience goes uncounted. The wound made by the system gets renamed as the wound of the person who carried it.

Anti-pathologizing means seeing the whole soil. It means refusing to call the plant defective when the soil itself is what was devoid of nutrients.

My Story of Restorying

For most of my life, I carried the silent weight of believing that something was fundamentally wrong with me. When I would shut down in the middle of conflict, when my body froze in moments that seemed ordinary to others, I judged myself as weak. I thought I was broken. Defective. Incapable of handling life the way everyone else seemed to. Even professionals reinforced this story. Labels like anxious, depressed, and avoidant were written into my file. Each one layered over the last like heavy blankets that smothered my spirit.

That story of deficiency lived in me for years. It coloured the way I saw myself. The way I entered relationships. The way I tolerated mistreatment. If I was broken, then maybe I did not deserve better. If I was defective, then maybe all I could do was manage my flaws. That story narrowed my life into survival. It left no room for thriving.

Then slowly, through learning about trauma, the nervous system, and the body's wisdom, I began to ask a different question. The old question had been: What is wrong with me? The new question was: What happened to me?

The moment I began asking that question, the story started to shift. I began to see that my freeze response was not weakness. It was my body protecting me in moments when escape or fight was impossible. It was a survival strategy. It was the body's intelligence at work.

My anxiety was not irrational. It was my nervous system, tuned by years of lived experiences, always scanning for danger to keep me safe.

My patterns of fawning, people-pleasing, over-giving, and abandoning my own needs were not proof of my lack of boundaries. They were evidence of how brilliantly my younger self had learned to keep peace in unsafe environments.

When I reframed my story through the lens of adaptation, I found compassion for myself. I began to honour the intelligence of my body rather than fight against it. I could look back at the moments of shutdown and instead of whispering, you failed again, I could now say, of course you froze. You were protecting yourself. Thank you for keeping me safe.

The new story became one of resilience. The new narrative was: I am not defective. I am adaptive. My body has always worked to keep me alive, even if those patterns no longer serve me today.

Once I could see my survival responses as wisdom, I could begin to integrate them rather than shame them. The freeze response softened when I offered myself safety. The fawn response loosened its grip when I learned that my worth was not dependent on others' approval. Even the moments of fight or flight became invitations. They were no longer occasions for condemning myself for overreacting. They were chances to listen to what my body was asking for. Space. Safety. Boundaries. Care.

Restorying my inner narrative changed how I saw myself. It also changed how I live. I moved from believing I was broken to knowing I was whole. From carrying shame about my responses to honouring them as sacred. From living in survival to stepping into the possibility of thriving.

Restorying the Inner Narrative

Once we can see our survival responses as wisdom, the story we have been carrying about ourselves can begin to shift.

This is the work of restorying. We take the same life. The same memories. The same patterns. And we tell the story in a way that honours what our bodies actually did. The labels we picked up along the way get set down. The shame we have been carrying gets returned to whoever handed it to us. The new story is one of intelligence rather than defect.

A simple practice for restorying:

Identify the old story. The label you have been carrying. The thing you have believed about yourself. I am too sensitive. I am lazy. I am too much. I cannot keep a boundary.

Name the survival response underneath the label. That sensitivity was fawn. That laziness was freeze. That too-muchness was fight. That inability to keep a boundary was the wisdom of a body that knew connection was survival.

Ask what happened to me. Not what is wrong with me. What conditions was this body adapting to. What was it trying to keep me safe from.

Offer the body compassion. Thank it. Speak to it the way you would speak to a small child who had been doing the work of an adult.

Rewrite the story. I am not broken. I am adaptive. My body has been working on my behalf for as long as I have been alive.

Integrate. Let the new story be the one you tell yourself when you catch the old one rising again. The new story does not erase the old conditions. It changes your relationship to them.

This is a practice. It asks to be returned to. You will go back to it many times.

If you are reading this and recognizing your own dominant response in one of these four, take a breath. Whatever your body has been doing all this time, it has been doing it for you. The shutting down. The over-giving. The hypervigilance. The lashing out. Every one of those is your body's love language for keeping you alive. That work was not your fault. That work was your wisdom.

If you are reading this as one who serves others, who tends, who shows up in clinical rooms or healing spaces or the offices of organizations carrying these patterns, hear this too. The person sitting in front of you is not their diagnosis. They are the plant that survived. Your attention, your patience, your refusal to pathologize, can be the change in soil conditions that allows them to put out new growth. Research across developmental and relational science has shown that responsive relationships matter. Your attention and attunement can become part of the conditions that support learning, regulation, and adaptation. You are participating in a relational process that can matter psychologically and biologically over time. The service is the smallest part of what you provide.

Whichever side of the room you are reading from, you are sacred. You are responding. The new growth is yours to claim.

The responses do not stay liquid forever. Repeated often enough, over enough years, in enough rooms, they harden. The fight becomes a permanent edge. The flight becomes a permanent restlessness. The freeze becomes a permanent fog. The fawn becomes a permanent smile that does not reach the eyes. The body builds armour around the responses. The armour stops being a strategy and starts being a structure. The next chapter is what that armour is. Traum-our. The turtle shell that was meant to be temporary and became the shape of a life.

Chapter Four
Traum-our and the Turtle Shell
When Survival Becomes Structure

The body does not stay in liquid response forever. The fights become permanent edges. The flights become permanent restlessness. The freezes become permanent fog. The fawns become permanent smiles that do not reach the eyes.

This is where Chapter Three closed. This is where Chapter Four begins.

The four responses you came to know in the last chapter are alive in the moment. They can rise and fall in a single afternoon. A car horn can trigger sympathetic flight. A conflict at work can trigger fawn. A grief that did not get to be felt can trigger freeze. When the conditions of the moment have passed, a regulated nervous system returns to itself.

There is another version of these responses. One that does not rise and fall. One that does not return to itself. One that hardens, over years, into a structure the body forgets it is wearing.

This is what is called traum-our. Trauma armour. The repeated activation of survival responses, in a body that never gets the conditions of safety it needs to soften them, becomes a fixed shape. The body forms a shell. The shell starts being the body. The body forgets it had a different shape before.

This chapter is about that shell.

Defining Traum-our

Traum-our is the layered protective casing the nervous system builds when it has endured repeated overwhelm without enough periods of safety to come back to itself. It is not a disorder. It is the body's response to chronic conditions that should never have required it to be there in the first place.

In the moment, traum-our shields. It keeps the danger at bay. Over time, if the danger does not lift and the body cannot soften, the shielding does not lift either. The armour stops being something the body wears. It becomes something the body is.

This is where the trouble begins. We can lose ourselves inside the armour and forget that anything beneath it ever existed.

A tree that grew through fire develops thicker bark. The bark is intelligence. The bark is the tree's memory of what it lived through. Years later, in a forest that does not burn, the bark is still there. Thick. Heavy. Slow to feel the rain. The tree has not stopped being a tree. It has forgotten how to bend in soft weather.

Traum-our can look like silence, avoidance, hypervigilance, numbness, over-functioning, or people-pleasing. It is the body's way of saying: I cannot let the arrows of life pierce me anymore, so I will carry armour instead. The armour, once forged, runs on autopilot. The body forgets it is wearing it. The world starts to feel like the kind of place that requires this armour at all times, because the body sees the world through the slits in the armour and nothing else.

What Builds the Armour

Traum-our is built by everything the nervous system was wired to expect and did not get. The big events are only part of the record. The body learns the world is dangerous in many more ways than only direct violence.

The body learns to brace from bullying. The chronic small humiliations of a schoolyard, a workplace, or a family. The repeated experience of being singled out, called names, excluded, watched, made small by people who held more power. Each instance leaves a deposit in the body. The deposits accumulate. After enough of them, the body walks into rooms already braced for what it has learned rooms can contain.

The body learns to brace from humiliation tactics. Public shaming. Mockery dressed as humour. The look that says you are not what you should be. The performance of one person's superiority at the expense of another person's dignity. The body remembers humiliation in the chest. In the heat that rises in the face. In the impulse to disappear. After enough of those moments, the body stops waiting for them. It carries the disappearing with it everywhere.

The body learns to brace from projection. When the people around us cannot see their own pain and so they aim it at us. When their stories about who we are come from their wounds rather than from anything we have actually been or done. The body is being asked to carry something that does not belong to it. Projection is one of the most disorienting harms because the body cannot defend against what is not actually about the body. It can only absorb. Over years, the absorption becomes armour.

The body learns to brace from lateral violence. The harm that comes from peers. From community. From the people who should have been on the same side. Often this is the passed-along trauma of systemic harm, expressed sideways because the original direction was not safe. The wound from a friend, a sibling, a colleague, a community member, lands differently than the wound from a stranger. It teaches the body that even allies are not safe. The armour gets thicker for that lesson.

The body learns to brace from neglect. Not the loud absence of an obvious harm. The quiet absence of what should have been there. The cry-out that did not bring comfort. The need that did not get met. The signal that did not reach anyone who could respond. Neglect is the wound of nothing happening when something should have. It teaches the body that distress signals do not work. The body stops sending them.

The body learns to brace from the absence of love. The nervous system was wired for connection. It expected attunement. It expected the comforting voice and the steady gaze and the warmth of being looked at by someone who wanted to know you. When the conditions of love are chronically absent, the body crystallizes into the shape it had to take to survive without them. The armour becomes a substitute for what should have been care. The body stops waiting for what it has learned will not come.

What the nervous system was wired to do was to soften in the presence of love. To trust. To play. To risk being seen. To attach. When those conditions are present, the body opens. When those conditions are chronically denied, the body builds the shell this chapter is about. The shell is not the problem. The conditions that required the shell are the problem. Healing is not the work of fixing the shell. Healing is the slow work of restoring the conditions the body was wired to soften in.

This is the soil we have been talking about throughout the book. The Quechua teacher in Peru taught us that a seed wrapped in nourishing mud grows into the strongest tree. The same principle is true at the level of the nervous system. A body wrapped in love, in attunement, in protection, in real and consistent care, develops the deepest roots and the most flexible bark. A body deprived of these conditions develops something else. Hard bark. Heavy bark. Bark that will not soften for any season. Traum-our is what grows when the mud was missing.

The Warrior in the Marketplace

Imagine a warrior on a battlefield. Their armour is essential. It deflects arrows. It shields their chest. It allows them to survive what is being thrown at them. Without it, they would not make it through the fight.

Now imagine that same warrior years later, walking through a village marketplace. The battle is over. The armour is still on. It is heavy. It rubs against their skin. It restricts their breath. It exhausts them to wear it every single day. The armour that kept them alive when the danger was real now prevents them from hugging their children. It prevents them from dancing in celebration. It prevents them from moving freely through life.

This is what traum-our feels like in a body. The body that adapted to survive cannot easily un-adapt once the conditions have changed. The armour is wisdom. The armour is also a weight. Healing is not the act of ripping the armour off. Healing is the slow, conditional process of learning, in real safety, that the armour can be set down.

Soldiers do not wear armour because they are weak. They wear it because the environment is dangerous. The same is true for us. Our nervous systems forged armour out of necessity. The challenge comes when the danger passes, yet the armour remains, keeping us alive, and keeping us separate.

The Turtle Shell

The turtle gives us another image of traum-our in motion. The turtle is not weak for hiding inside its shell. The shell is its intelligence about a world that contains predators. The turtle pulls in when threat is near. The turtle peeks out when conditions feel safer. The turtle moves between the two states fluidly when the nervous system is healthy.

When the nervous system is in traum-our, the turtle stops moving between. The shell stays closed. Or the rim of the shell stays half-open and the turtle stays scanning. The flexibility goes. The autonomic system that was supposed to be a wave becomes a fixed posture.

In trauma-aware terms, we can name three positions in the turtle. The first is inside the shell. The body in shutdown. Dorsal vagal collapse. Numb, silent, heavy, far away from itself. The second is at the rim. The body in hypervigilance. Sympathetic activation that does not turn off. Heart pounding, eyes scanning, muscles tense. The third is head and feet extended. The body in connection. Ventral vagal engagement. Curious, open, able to feel, able to be felt.

A regulated nervous system moves between these three positions throughout an ordinary day, depending on what the day brings. A nervous system in traum-our gets stuck. The work is not to abandon the shell. The work is to remember that the turtle is allowed to come out.

This is the clinical map polyvagal theory has offered us: ventral social engagement, sympathetic mobilization, and dorsal immobilization. The model has become deeply influential in trauma-informed practice, although parts of its evolutionary and neuroanatomical explanation remain scientifically debated. I use it here as a map, not as the only possible description of the autonomic nervous system. Within this model, the three positions can be understood this way. Polyvagal theory describes the dorsal vagal complex as the evolutionarily older pathway. Within this framework, it is the shell. The sympathetic state is the rim. Ventral vagal engagement is the head and feet extending. In this model, a body shaped by chronic harm may spend less time in states associated with social engagement and safety, moving more readily into mobilization or shutdown. The work of healing becomes the work of slowly, slowly expanding the body's available range of safety and connection.

The Three Nervous System States

Here is what each state feels like, in plain language.

Within this model, ventral describes states associated with social engagement and felt safety. It can feel calm, grounded, open, connected, able to play and create. Experiences of consistent care, comfort, and attunement may help a body build greater access to this kind of state.

Sympathetic describes mobilization. Fight or flight. Alert. Restless. Tense. A faster heart. The urge to move, confront, or escape. Repeated threat and unpredictability can make mobilization easier to trigger.

Dorsal, in the polyvagal map, describes immobilization and shutdown. Heavy. Numb. Disconnected. Frozen. Not quite here. Chronic overwhelming stress, inescapable threat, and prolonged deprivation may be associated with shutdown-like states. This is the body deciding that the safest thing left is to go still.

The map is useful because it gives language to felt experience. It is not a diagnostic test, and these states do not map one-to-one onto specific diseases.

Within this framework, the key word is flexibility. The more access a body has to states of safety and connection, the more room there may be for regulation and relationship. Prolonged activation can place wear on the body over time. Nobody simply chooses these patterns. Our histories. Our conditions. Our biology. What we learned to expect. All of it can shape how readily we move between activation, connection, and shutdown.

When Sympathetic and Dorsal Happen at the Same Time

There is one more experience worth naming because many trauma survivors recognize it: intense activation and immobilization can appear together. The heart may race while the body feels unable to move. The mind may go blank while the chest is pounding.

Researchers describe forms of tonic immobility and fear-related freezing. Polyvagal practitioners may map parts of this experience as simultaneous mobilization and shutdown.

I call it the fire and the brake.

This kind of experience can appear in trauma-related conditions. It should not be used to explain every case of panic disorder, chronic fatigue, or autoimmune illness. Those conditions have multiple possible pathways. The map is here to make the body more understandable, not to turn one theory into a diagnosis. Many times, autoimmune is linked to chronic stress and appeasement.

The work of healing is to slowly, slowly, slowly create new conditions in which the body can find that a way through has become possible.

If traum-our became the shape of your life, it programmed you to believe that the world required armour. That setting the armour down was unsafe. That the version of you who lived before the wound is unrecoverable. That who you have become through survival is who you have to be.

My Years Inside the Shell

You already know the night this began. I told you about it in the last chapter. What I want to tell you about now is what happened after. The decade I spent inside the shell my body built to keep me from feeling that night had ever happened.

After the second time, I split. That is the only word for it. Some part of me went somewhere else and stayed there for over a decade. The pain was too large to live inside consciously. My nervous system did what nervous systems are designed to do. It moved me away from it. In my life, dissociation had functioned as protection. It gave me distance when being fully present felt intolerable. That is not the only way dissociation can arise, and it is not harmless simply because it once protected me. But I can meet the pattern with compassion instead of shame.

Then the person who had violated me turned the story around. He told me I was crazy. He told other people the same. I was distant, yes. I was collapsed inside, afraid, ashamed. He named those things as evidence of my disorder rather than evidence of what he had done.

Here is what that did to me. I had never fully believed my parents when they called me the problem. Some small, stubborn part of me had always known they were wrong. When the person you have given yourself to most completely, the person you have shown the most tender and unguarded version of yourself, looks at all of that and says you are bad and wrong, something breaks differently. Something deeper.

If even this person, who has seen the most beautiful parts of me, says I am broken, then it must be true. It must be something I cannot see in myself. It must be real.

It was never real. I could not hold that truth anymore. The internal validator, the part of me that had always known, had its strength snapped. In that snapping, the gaslighting became easy. Not because I was weak. Because I was exhausted. Because the pattern of being told I was the problem had started so early and been reinforced so many times that the newest voice confirming it simply joined the chorus.

That programmed me to believe that I was unreliable to myself. That my own knowing could not be trusted. That if enough voices said I was broken, I must be the broken one.

What followed was the trauma bond. The mindless allowing. The dissociation during sex, learning to be gone while something was being done to my body. The part of me that broke when violation became ordinary was the part that had held my dignity, my power, my capacity to fight back. It was like a balloon that had been filled with everything brave in me. It popped. I did not know how to fill it again.

I was hopeless. I was alone. I was too weakened to fight the stories being told about me. The same tactic my stepfather had used, telling strangers lies to explain away why I acted the way I did, was now being used again by someone who claimed to love me. Denounce the person before they can speak. Make them unbelievable. Hide behind their wreckage.

She needs pills, he would say. There would never be accountability for the verbal and emotional abuse that left me frowning and collapsed and then outbursting when I could not take it anymore, that left me flat and hollow. It was my stepfather's voice in a new mouth. So I tried the pills, because I felt guilty for being sad, and for a while the pills made the pain quieter. Quieter is not healed. The pain I had suppressed worked harder and harder to surface, slipping out in the memories of lying alone at night as a child, crying for hundreds of nights, waiting for someone to come.

No one came. My nervous system learned a lesson it would carry into adulthood. The cry-out was broken. Distress signals did not bring comfort. They brought nothing, or they brought more harm. So it stopped signaling outwardly. It turned the alarm inward instead.

That programmed me to believe that my pain was not worth bringing into the world. That bringing it in would either be met with silence or punished. That the only safe thing to do was to bury it inside me and let it eat me from within.

The people around me, when I kept returning to the abusive relationship, would laugh and mock. Why don't you just leave. As if leaving were simply a decision the mind makes and the body follows. My nervous system had been programmed from childhood to expect harm from the people closest to me and to stay anyway, because staying had always been the only option. I could not help it. The more they mocked me for it, the more I internalized that I must be the unwell one. That this, too, was evidence of my brokenness.

It was never brokenness. It was the most logical response in the world to an illogical amount of harm.

I want you to read that again if you need to.

Collective Traum-our

What is true for one body is true for many bodies together. Communities, families, and entire peoples can carry traum-our as a shared layer of protection that has been passed down through generations.

Imagine an entire village this time. Not just one warrior. Generations ago, they endured invasion, famine, or forced removal from their land. To survive, they learned to wear armour together. Not physical armour. Silence. Guardedness. Vigilance. Parents taught children to keep their heads down, to never trust authority, to work twice as hard just to be safe.

That armour was wisdom. It protected the community from further harm. Generations later, even when the danger has shifted, the armour remains. Children inherit patterns of hypervigilance, withdrawal, or perfectionism without ever being told where they came from. Entire families and cultures move through the world as if still under attack, because history has taught them they are.

This is what I mean by collective traum-our. Armour can live in individuals. Patterns can also travel through families and communities through story, silence, parenting, discrimination, poverty, displacement, chronic stress, prenatal conditions, and the social worlds descendants are born into.

Epigenetics has added one possible biological dimension to that conversation. Human intergenerational epigenetic research is still difficult to interpret, and it does not show that an ancestor's autobiographical memory is copied directly into a descendant's cells.

Indigenous communities living with the ongoing effects of colonial violence may carry collective traum-our. Black communities living with the ongoing effects of slavery and racial violence may carry it. Jewish families after the Holocaust. Refugee families. Waraffected communities. Women living inside generations of misogyny. The pathways are not identical. The histories are not interchangeable.

What they share is this: history can remain present through more than conscious memory. The body exists inside family, culture, biology, and continuing conditions. The world often diagnoses the person while forgetting the history still moving around them.

The world that built that wisdom rarely admits its role in producing it.

Healing at the collective level asks a different question than healing at the individual level. It asks: how can we honour the armour that kept us alive, while creating spaces safe enough to set it down together? That work is bigger than this chapter. It is bigger than this book. But naming collective traum-our is the first step. A people cannot soften what it cannot see.

How Traum-our Gets Misnamed

Before we move into the arc of healing, I want to give you four short portraits. They are composites, not clinical case reports. I am not claiming the diagnosis in each portrait is false or that one environmental change would cure the person. I am showing the question anti-pathologizing practice adds: what might we miss if we name the pattern before we fully examine the conditions?

Sofia, the Silent Teen

Sofia used to love speaking up in class. She would wave her hand high, eager to answer questions. The bullying started in middle school. Whispers about her clothes. Cruel notes in her locker. Shoves in the hallway. She tried to laugh it off at first. Every attempt to defend herself was met with more ridicule. The teachers saw her growing quieter. They did not stop the bullies. Eventually, Sofia stopped speaking altogether. Her grades slipped. Her voice went away.

The school referred her for assessment. The diagnosis was Major Depressive Disorder. Medication was recommended. No one asked why she had gone silent. No one stepped in to protect her from what had made her go silent.

Sofia's nervous system was not broken. It was in dorsal traum-our. The shell had come up around her in response to a danger no adult had named. Inside the shell she carried the beliefs the danger had given her. No one will protect me. I do not matter. It is safer if I disappear.

When one teacher finally intervened, called out the bullies, created a safer space at lunch, and started checking in with her gently, Sofia's shell began to soften. The voice came back. As the bullying was addressed and a trusted adult began checking in, Sofia's voice started to return. In this composite, safety and protection are part of the intervention. The point is not that depression is never real. The point is that the bullying cannot be left outside the formulation.

David, the Anxious Worker

David had always been the reliable one. First in, last out. Deadlines always met. The company began restructuring. The ground shifted under him. Leadership changed every quarter. Rumours of layoffs spread. Expectations rose without clarity.

He lay awake at night with his heart pounding. He fidgeted at work. He snapped at coworkers. He forgot small details. HR wrote him up as unstable and sent him to a doctor. The diagnosis came back as Generalized Anxiety Disorder.

David felt broken. His body was doing exactly what it was designed to do. It was scanning for danger in an environment that genuinely contained danger. His sympathetic traum-our was hypervigilance. Armour against chaos. Armour that had once kept him alive in a chaotic childhood and was now being asked to keep him alive in a chaotic workplace.

When a new manager came in who offered clear communication, realistic timelines, and permission to rest, David's body began to calm. Grounding practices helped. Walks helped. Longer exhales helped. He came to understand that his anxiety also contained information about instability. Whether or not he met criteria for an anxiety disorder, workplace conditions belonged in the story.

Leanne, the Numb Parent

Leanne had dreamed of being a mother her whole life. After the baby was born, exhaustion and overwhelm set in. Some days she rocked her baby and felt nothing. Blankness where love should have been. Other times, panic surged inside while her body sat completely still.

The doctors wrote down flat affect and noncompliant with treatment. The diagnosis was Postpartum Depression. Leanne left every appointment feeling like a failure, whispering to herself: I am broken. My baby deserves better.

Her nervous system was not defective. It was in dorsal traumour, sometimes overlapping with sympathetic panic. The same immobilization-with-fear we named earlier in this chapter. The shell had come up because the conditions of new motherhood, on top of whatever her body had already been carrying, exceeded what it could metabolize.

When her partner started taking night feedings so she could rest, and told her softly that her body was protecting her, something shifted. With more sleep, less shame, and practical help, she began to reconnect with her baby in small, safe steps. Rest, practical support, and less shame became part of what helped her reconnect.

Maya, the Over-Giving Friend

Maya was the friend everyone could count on. She drove people to appointments. She stayed late to finish other people's projects. She always apologized first in conflicts, even ones that were not her fault. From the outside she looked dependable. Inside she was exhausted, resentful, and afraid.

Friends teased her for being too nice. A counsellor suggested she had Dependent Personality Disorder. To Maya, the label felt like proof of what she had been afraid of all her life. Inside she believed: if I say no, I will be abandoned. My needs do not matter.

Maya's people-pleasing made more sense when the childhood conditions around it were explored. The pattern may still cause impairment. The armour question asks what the pattern once helped her protect. It helped her to survive.

Healing began when a friend told her, one ordinary afternoon, that she did not have to say yes for her to love her. In therapy, Maya practiced small refusals. No to one extra shift. A pause before apologizing. Each time she discovered that she was still loved. Her armour began to loosen. She learned, slowly, that she could be loved for being herself rather than for erasing herself.

Each of these portraits shows the same pattern. The body's intelligent response to its actual conditions gets renamed as a disorder. The actual conditions get ignored. The label gets applied. The medication gets prescribed. The work of changing the conditions that produced the response in the first place never happens. The smoke gets treated. The fire keeps burning. This is what anti-pathologizing is about. To see the smoke as smoke. To trace it back to the fire. To name the fire, and to put it out. The label is rarely the place healing begins. The conditions are.

The Traum-our Arc

Healing is not the act of ripping the armour away. When we force ourselves or others to get over it or snap out of it or be strong, we create more harm. True healing is the work of watching a turtle slowly remember how to come out of its shell.

I think of the softening of traum-our as an arc. This is my map, not a universal sequence every nervous system must follow. People move back and forth. Some phases overlap. Some people use different language entirely. The map helps me notice five kinds of conditions that can support change.

One is shelter. The body stays in armour because it needs to. The armour is not the problem. The conditions that required the armour are the problem. Survival is the first priority. Honour it.

The second is orientation. The body begins to notice. Where am I now? Is this the original room? Are these the original people? What is here that was not there before? The body learns to ask whether the conditions of the moment match the conditions the armour was built for.

Another is co-regulation. Another nervous system, calm and attuned and willing to be present, offers the body something it could not generate on its own. The breath of a person sitting with you. The steady voice. The hand that does not flinch from your difficulty. Co-regulation is the first proof the body has that conditions have changed. Another is self-regulation. Over time, the body learns to do for itself what another nervous system once did for it. Grounding. Breath. Naming what is real. Pausing before reacting. The capacity to anchor in your own body is built slowly, through repetition, in real safety.

Another is play and creation. The body that has learned it is safe begins to do what bodies were made for. Curiosity. Joy. Risk in the soft direction. Beauty. Connection that is not survival. This is the marker that the nervous system is no longer in traum-our. The armour is still there in memory. The body just no longer needs to wear it every day.

Each phase matters. Healing is the body learning, one condition at a time, that it is safe to move between states without shame.

If you are reading this and recognizing yourself in the armour, hear this. The armour is not who you are. It is what you became to keep what you are safe. The work is not to hate it. The work is to thank it. The work is to slowly, in real safety, allow it to soften. The version of you who lived before the wound is not gone. She is underneath. She has been waiting.

If you are reading this as one who works with armoured people, hear this too. The person in front of you is not their armour. They are the body the armour was built to protect. Your patience, your steadiness, your refusal to demand that they hurry, can be the conditions under which their armour softens. You are not just witnessing. Your steadiness can become part of a relational environment that supports learning, regulation, and change. The psychological and the biological are not separate worlds. Whichever side of the room you are reading from, you are sacred. The armour was wisdom. The softening is also wisdom. Both are how a body keeps itself alive. *Traum-our does not form in isolation. The conditions that build it are everywhere. The culture we live in is asking us to perform. Productivity, comparison, distraction, achievement. Softening was never on the list. It is asking us to scroll, consume, hustle, optimize. The conditions of modern life are themselves a force that compounds traum-our, in every body, every day. The next chapter is what those conditions are doing to us. Not just to me. Not just to you. To all of us, together.*

Chapter Five
Social Conditioning
How a Culture Built on Violence Cannot Hold Pain

You are tired.

I want to start there. Because you are.

You are tired in a way that does not lift with a weekend. You are tired in a way that wakes you up at three in the morning with your heart racing or your mind blank or both. You are tired in a way that finds you scrolling at midnight for something you cannot name. You are tired in a way that smiles at the appropriate moments. Answers the email. Meets the deadline. Shows up at the dinner party. Gets home and cannot remember anything from any of it.

You are tired and you have started to wonder if the tiredness is who you are.

Or maybe the tiredness shows up differently for you. As anxiety that arrives unannounced. As irritability you cannot trace to a cause. As a numbness that has been with you for so long you have stopped looking for what used to be underneath it. As an over-giving to the people around you that has hollowed you out. As a need to optimize everything, including your rest. As the suspicion, growing quietly in some part of you, that something is wrong with how things are.

You are not the problem.

The conditions of modern life are doing this to you. They are doing it to almost everyone you know. The exhaustion is not a personal failure. The numbness is not a character flaw. The anxiety is the predictable result of a body trying to function inside a culture that was never designed around what the body actually needs.

This chapter is about what the culture is doing to you, and why. It is going to name some hard things. It is not doing that to add to your weight. It is doing that because naming the conditions is what allows the body to stop blaming itself for responding to them.

You are not broken. You are responding. The thing you are responding to is much larger than you have been told it was.

What This Culture Is Doing to Your Nervous System

The conditions are everywhere.

The workplace you walk into has been engineered, often without anyone meaning it that way, to keep your sympathetic nervous system activated for eight to ten hours a day. Restructuring is constant. Expectations exceed available time. Communication is partial. Rumour fills the gaps. The body, sensing danger in the form of uncertainty about its own survival inside the institution, stays in low-grade fight or flight from the morning meeting to the evening commute. By the time you get home, the system has been firing for so long that returning to baseline is no longer something the body remembers how to do. So it tries to discharge. It finds the easy outlets. The screen. The drink. The food that promises comfort. The scroll.

The screen you reach for has also been engineered. The platforms that hold your attention have spent billions of dollars studying how to keep you on them. Every notification is a small dopamine event. Every comparison with another person's curated life is a small wound to your own sense of enoughness. Every algorithmically chosen piece of content has been selected to provoke a response in your nervous system, because nervous systems that are provoked stay on the platform longer. Your attention is the product. Your dysregulation is the business model.

This is a story about what happens to a body that spends its day in chronic activation at its workplace and its evening in chronic activation on its phone. The screens are the smallest part of it. The body does not know that the danger is not real. The body responds to the cues it is given. The cues it is given say: stay alert. Compare yourself. Watch out. There is something to be afraid of. There is something to optimize. There is something you are missing.

Porn addiction is a survival strategy. Binge watching is a survival strategy. Gambling is a survival strategy. Endless scrolling is a survival strategy. Compulsive shopping is a survival strategy. Substance use is a survival strategy. They are all the body trying to discharge or numb or escape from conditions it was not designed to live inside without rest. Your body is not weak for reaching for those things. Your body is smart. The fact that you cannot stop reaching for them is not a personal moral failing. It is the wisdom of a body that has been given inadequate tools for what it has been asked to endure.

The comparison culture is doing its own work. The endless aestheticization of other lives. The constant reminder that someone, somewhere, is doing it better, looking thinner, making more, parenting smarter, healing faster. The body that grew up needing approval to feel safe now lives in a world where there is never enough approval to fill the well. The condition the body developed in childhood as a survival response to a particular dangerous adult is now being commercially exploited by an entire industry that needs you to feel not-enough so you will buy what is being sold.

The hustle culture is the final layer. Sleep less. Optimize more. Wake up earlier. Push harder. Build the brand. Side hustle on the weekend. Productivity above all. The body that is already being told it is not enough is now being told the answer is to do more. The exhaustion compounds. The disconnection from the self deepens. The performance gets thicker.

This is what is happening to nervous systems, every day, in millions of bodies. The body did not ask for this. The body did not consent to it. The body is just responding to what is in the room.

Why the Culture Cannot Hold Pain

The natural question is: why? Why has the culture allowed itself to become this? Why does it not stop and ask what is happening to the bodies inside it?

The honest answer is one many people do not want to hear. The body knows it anyway.

Pathologization is not an accident. It is the defence mechanism of systems that have produced enormous pain and do not want to be named as the source of it. If you are told that your exhaustion is a personal failure, you look inward for the fix and outward to the market for the solution. If you understood that the conditions of your life were producing your exhaustion, you would look outward at those conditions and inward to your own sovereignty for the solution. One of those directions makes you a customer. The other one makes you a threat.

The systems that hurt us cannot afford for us to know that they are hurting us. So they invest, heavily, in stories that locate the problem inside the individual. You are anxious. You are depressed. You have ADHD. You are codependent. You are noncompliant. You are difficult. You are too much. The labels do work the systems need done. They turn structural harm into individual pathology. They turn cultural design flaws into personal disorders. They turn the witness into the patient.

North America, in particular, was built on violence and has not stopped depending on the original conditions of that violence to function. The violence against Indigenous peoples that established the continent as European-claimed territory. The violence of slavery that built the wealth of the colonial economy. The violence done to women in homes and workplaces and courtrooms. The violence done to children in residential schools, in religious institutions, in factories that exploited child labour, in school systems designed to produce compliant workers rather than free thinkers. The violence done to anyone whose body or mind did not fit the role the system needed performed.

We are standing on a foundation that has not yet been repaired. The ground beneath us was never neutral.

A culture built on violence cannot easily hold pain with compassion because the pain it would have to hold is the pain it has caused. Looking at the pain would require looking at the cause. Looking at the cause would require accountability. Accountability would require redistribution of power, wealth, voice, land, agency, decisionmaking, healing. Those are not things any system surrenders easily. So instead the system produces a story in which the pain is mysterious, individual, biological, perhaps inherited, perhaps a chemical imbalance. The story does not include anything anyone in power did or is still doing.

This is the work pathologization performs. It is the protection racket the system runs to keep itself from being named.

There is another layer to why this persists. It lives in the bodies of the people who hold power inside the systems we are describing.

Those people are also human. Their nervous systems were also shaped. Many of them were shaped specifically by power. By the unique conditions of growing up inside privilege, ambition, expectation, performance, the family lineages that produced leaders for the institutions of their time. The wiring that took them to the top of the institution they now run was often built on the same conditions of overwork, emotional suppression, comparison, and inherited shame that wired the people they manage. The difference is that they got promoted for it instead of pathologized for it.

Power, when it is held by people who have not done their own healing, becomes destructive in fairly predictable ways. It becomes defensive. It becomes accumulating. It becomes terrified of being lost. It becomes unable to hear feedback that threatens it. It becomes invested, often unconsciously, in keeping things exactly as they are. The person inside that kind of power often cannot tell, from the inside, that they are inside it. They feel, from the inside, like they are doing their best. They are not lying when they say that.

This is why structural accountability so rarely comes from the people in the structures. The people in the structures are bodies frozen inside their own armour, doing their best inside the patterns they inherited, terrified of what naming the patterns would cost them. They are also wounded, cast in roles the structure wrote long before they arrived. The wounding has shaped them in ways that prevent them from doing the work that would interrupt the harm they are participating in.

Healthy power is something else entirely. Healthy power knows itself to be borrowed and temporary. Healthy power listens more than it speaks. Healthy power redistributes. Healthy power apologizes. Healthy power knows its limits and stays inside them. Healthy power emerges from a body that has come home to itself. That kind of body cannot be threatened by another person's wholeness. That kind of body wants more wholeness, in everyone.

The work of building a culture that can hold pain is the work of growing different people inside every layer of every institution, including the layers that hold the most. Swapping the people at the top changes the faces. It leaves the layers untouched. Some of those people will rise. Some are rising already. The slower truth, the one harder to feel patient with, is that cultures shift one body at a time.

We are not taught to be sovereign because sovereign people do not need what the system is selling. We are not taught to self-validate because self-validating people do not bend to false authorities. We are not taught to love ourselves because people who love themselves do not consume to fill the emptiness, do not stay in jobs that hollow them out, do not settle for relationships that diminish them, do not buy the products that promise to fix what was never broken to begin with.

The teaching gap is not accidental. The things you were not taught are the things that would have made you ungovernable.

You were not taught how your nervous system worked because a regulated nervous system is harder to manipulate.

You were not taught about co-regulation because co-regulating populations build solidarity, and solidarity is a threat.

You were not taught about ancestral wisdom because cultures with intact wisdom traditions cannot be sold cheap substitutes for what they already have.

You were not taught how to grieve in community because grief held in community heals. Grief held alone festers and creates the customers the market needs.

You were not taught how to discharge stress through movement, sound, ritual, or shaking because a body that knew how to discharge stress would not need the medications, the substances, the screens, the scrolling.

You were not taught any of these things because the system that benefits from your unwellness invested centuries in making sure you would not learn them, would not remember them. If you stumbled upon them, you would be told they were superstitious, primitive, unscientific, woo.

The perpetuation of pain depends on silence. The systems that built themselves on violence depend on the bodies they hurt staying silent about the hurt, or being made to look unreliable when they are not silent. This is why naming what is happening matters so much. Naming the conditions interrupts the silence the system needs to keep functioning. Naming the violence makes the system visible. Once visible, the system can be questioned. Once questioned, the system can be changed.

Collective Gaslighting

The word for what I am about to describe came from a film. In 1944, Ingrid Bergman starred in a movie called Gaslight. She played a young woman whose husband slowly convinced her she was losing her mind so that he could control her, isolate her, and steal what she had inherited. He moved objects in their home. He hid her letters. He turned the gaslights up and down and then told her the lights were not flickering. He kept telling her she was sick, unwell, imagining things, unreliable in her own perception. By the end of the film she could no longer trust her own mind.

The husband in that story was helped by a medical narrative that made his wife seem unstable. He needed her to be defined as unwell so that he could keep what he wanted to keep. The medicalization of her was not a description of her condition. The medicalization of her was an instrument of his control.

That is where the word gaslight comes from. The term has expanded since then. We use it now to describe anyone who manipulates another person into doubting their own reality. The word has stayed useful because the pattern keeps happening, on every scale humans live at.

Collective gaslighting is the same pattern, performed by systems instead of by a single husband.

The voice in your head that says it is your fault may not have started as your voice.

Sometimes blame comes from outside first. Repeated by someone, or something, with power. A child or dependent person may take that blame inward because maintaining a workable relationship with the source of power feels necessary. Over time, the external voice can become difficult to distinguish from the internal one. The blame that came from outside begins speaking in the first person. This is how blame works inside one home. It is also how blame works inside one culture.

There is an analogy here, and I am drawing it on purpose. An abusive partner protects himself from accountability by making the victim doubt her own perception. He tells her she is crazy. He tells her she is too sensitive. He tells her she is imagining it. He tells her she is the problem. He is doing it because he needs to. Belief was never part of it. If she trusts her own perception, she will see what he is doing. If she sees what he is doing, she may leave. If she leaves, the abuse loses its host. So the abuser invests, constantly, in making her doubt herself. The doubt is his protection.

Cultures built on violence run the same play at scale.

The history is in the record, when anyone bothers to read it. Women were committed to asylums by husbands and families under legal and medical systems that gave women limited authority over their own lives. Hysteria became a diagnosis attached disproportionately to women, and some medical interventions were invasive and harmful.

In parts of twentieth-century obstetric practice, women were given drug combinations associated with Twilight Sleep, producing sedation and amnesia. The history of that practice now sits inside a wider critique of how women's pain, consent, and memory were handled in medical institutions.

Indigenous ceremonies were criminalized and suppressed in Canada, and Indigenous people were subjected to institutions that treated cultural and spiritual difference as inferiority or pathology.

These histories are not identical. I place them beside one another because they show what can happen when authority decides it knows the meaning of another person's body before listening to the person living inside it.

Queer people who refused to perform a straightness they did not feel were given electroshock to teach the body to feel what the culture demanded it feel. Enslaved people who tried to flee captivity were diagnosed with a condition called drapetomania. An actual medical diagnosis invented by an American physician in

1851 to explain, in clinical language, why a human being would not want to be owned. Soldiers who came home from war unable to function were called weak before the language of shell shock existed, and treated as defective after that language did.

The pattern did not end with history. The pattern only changed its uniform. Companies have built business empires on the deeming of people unwell based on responses that are entirely normal in the conditions those people are living inside. Anxiety in a society that produces relentless instability may also be correct information. Depression in a life shaped by isolation and overwork may also be telling us something true about the conditions. A diagnosis does not make the information disappear.

Burnout in a workplace that demands continuous output without rest is not simply a personal failure to manage stress. Sometimes the body is reporting honestly on what the conditions are costing.

What is normal in a sick culture is not healthy or well. Adapting successfully to a dysregulated environment can look, from inside that environment, like wellness. It is not wellness. It is the cost of fitting in to conditions that should never have been the conditions. The medicalization of the person who is not fitting in often misses, completely, the question of whether the conditions themselves are the problem.

These are the pattern. They are still running. The pattern is the same as the pattern inside the abusive home. The system that is causing the harm protects itself by pathologizing the bodies that are showing what it has done.

People do try to push back. Many of us do. The problem is that pushing back inside a culture of collective gaslighting is exhausting. The system has more positions of power than any one person has hours in the day. The person who names what is happening gets labeled difficult, unstable, paranoid, sensitive, angry, ungrateful, divisive, problematic, hysterical, unprofessional. Those labels are the modern equivalents of being sent to the asylum. After enough of them have been applied, most people stop pushing back at the source of the harm. The pain does not go away. The pain has to go somewhere.

What often happens is that the pain travels laterally. The employee who could not push back at the boss takes it out on the coworker beside her. The middle manager who could not push back at leadership takes it out on the team she leads. The community member who could not push back at the institution takes it out on the neighbours, the comment section, the people in their own community who are also struggling. The partner who could not push back at the system takes it out on the partner. The parent who could not push back at any of it takes it out on the child.

This is lateral violence. It happens in households. It happens in workplaces, where coworkers tear one another down through gossip, exclusion, and small daily cruelties. It happens in communities, where people harmed by the same structures can turn harm sideways onto one another instead of upward toward its source.

Pain does not automatically make a person harm someone else. People remain responsible for what they do. And still, conditions of chronic powerlessness, humiliation, scarcity, and unprocessed harm can help us understand why lateral harm takes root.

Context is not an excuse. Context is part of the map.

The voice that tells you the work is to fix yourself rather than to gather with others and shift the conditions is the voice the system needs you to keep listening to.

It was never your voice.

How Shame Travels

Once the blame is inside, it becomes something else. It becomes shame.

Shame is what blame becomes when it has been internalized long enough to stop feeling like a foreign object and start feeling like a fact about the self. The voice that began as someone else's accusation now feels like a true description of who you are. You stop hearing the accuser. You only hear the conclusion. The conclusion is that something is fundamentally wrong with you.

Shame is rarely original to the person carrying it. Shame is rarely as individual as it feels. So much shame is inherited, learned, absorbed, and handed forward relationally. It came from the abuser. It came from the household. It came from the institution. It came from the culture. It came from the generation before, who got it from the generation before them, who got it from the generation before that.

Shame travels through bodies the way a cancer cell travels through tissue. It enters one cell. It mutates that cell. The mutated cell touches the cells around it. Those cells begin to change too. They lose the memory of what they were before. They begin to copy the distortion as if the distortion were the natural shape. After enough generations of this, no one in the line remembers what the original cell looked like. They only know what they have become. They assume that is what they always were.

The plant that grows in distorted soil will distort itself to keep growing. It is responding correctly. It is doing what a plant has to do in those conditions. The shape it ends up in is a record of the conditions the plant survived. Anyone who looks at that plant and calls it ugly has misunderstood what they are looking at.

So the question that comes is the only question worth asking. Who, then, is truly to blame?

If the shame you carry came from the parent who raised you, and the shame they carried came from their parent, and that shame came from theirs, and theirs, and theirs, how far back do you have to go to find the first hurt? Sometimes eight generations. Sometimes thirteen. Sometimes twenty-five. Somewhere, far enough back that no living person remembers, there was a first moment. A first wound. A first separation between the person and their own sense of being whole and good and held by what surrounds them. That first hurt set everything in motion. Everything since then has been the body's adaptation, generation after generation, to soil that was poisoned before anyone now alive was born.

This is not an excuse for harm. People who pass on harm are still responsible for what they pass on. The point is bigger than excuse. The point is that blame, when followed back honestly, dissolves into a chain that has no real beginning anyone can point to. There is no first guilty person. There is only a long human story of pain travelling through bodies that did not know how to set it down.

In the middle of that long story, there are people who decide to set it down.

These are the healers. Every generation produces them. They are the people who carry the inherited weight, recognize what it is, and refuse to pass it forward. They do the work no one in their line did before. They unlearn the patterns. They sit with the discomfort. They feel the feelings their grandmothers were not allowed to feel. They speak the truths their grandfathers were silenced into hiding. They break trauma bonds. They learn nervous system regulation. They go to therapy or to ceremony or to both. They build different relationships. They raise different children. They live differently in their own bodies. Their bodies become the place where the line bends.

Generational change is observable. Children can grow up in different conditions than their parents did. A parent who changes patterns of violence, silence, fear, or emotional neglect changes part of the developmental environment around the next generation. That does not guarantee a regulated child or erase every inherited risk. It does change the soil. Patterns that felt permanent in a family can begin losing their grip when someone starts doing something different.

You may be one of those people. You may already be doing it. If you are reading this book, you are probably doing it. You are the person who refused to keep transmitting what was transmitted to you. You are the bend in the line. You are the place where the inheritance stops.

The collective version of this is what is happening now, across the world.

We are living in a moment when collective traum-our is being named at a scale it has never been named at before. Indigenous communities are reclaiming languages and ceremonies and land. Black communities are speaking the truth of generational racial violence. Survivors of religious abuse, institutional abuse, sexual violence, war, displacement, and disability injustice are finding one another and naming what was done. Women are telling stories their mothers kept silent. Men are unlearning the violence that was modelled to them. People who never had names for what they carried are getting language for it from each other. The healing that used to happen quietly inside one family is happening now across continents.

We have global healers because we have global pain. The pain of colonization touched every continent. The pain of patriarchy touched every culture. The pain of industrial capitalism reached every workplace. The pain of ecological destruction is reaching every body, every animal, every river. The corresponding healing has had to become global too. The remembrance is global. The awakening is global.

We are so sacred. All of us. Every one. In my own experience, when I began treating my body as sacred, it responded. It opened. It softened in ways it never had when I treated it as a problem to be fixed. I can only offer you what I found. Your body will tell you what is true for it. The body of the person in line behind you at the grocery store is sacred. The body of the person who hurt you is sacred too, even if that does not mean they are owed your forgiveness, and even if naming their sacredness alongside yours is the hardest work in this chapter. Sacredness is not a reward for behaving. Sacredness is what we are.

I sometimes use the phrase epigenetic warrior, but I want to be precise about what I mean. I do not mean your cells literally store your ancestors' songs, medicines, or autobiographical memories. Human epigenetics does not establish that.

I mean you stand inside a living inheritance. Biology. Pregnancy. Family patterns. Language. Food. Story. Silence. Culture. Land. The ways people loved. The ways people survived. Some of that inheritance can wound. Some of it can resource you.

The lineage reaches us by more than one road.

The true battle of this work has been misnamed.

The battle is not against the pain. The true battle is denouncing the power of the pain and the shame, removing it from the psyche, the heart, the mind, until the cells awaken and aliven and remember the true structure that was there before the cancer spread.

That structure is still in you. It has been in you the whole time, underneath everything.

The healing is not constructing something new. The healing is uncovering what is already there.

The Economy of Pain

There is a clearer way to say what I have been saying.

The economy of pain runs like this. Conditions are created that produce dysregulation in bodies. The dysregulation is labeled as individual disorder. The disorder requires treatment. The treatment is sold. The pharmaceutical industry profits. The wellness industry profits. The self-improvement industry profits. The diet industry profits. The beauty industry profits. The supplement industry profits. The therapy app industry profits. The performance coaching industry profits. The biohacking industry profits. The luxury sleep mattress industry profits. The mindfulness app industry profits. The functional medicine industry profits.

There is an economic tension inside every industry that earns revenue by selling responses to human distress. Many people inside those industries genuinely want to help. Many products and services have real value. And still, a market built around recurring need has different incentives than a community built around reducing need at its source. That tension deserves to be named.

The structural reality is that wellness is not what they sell. They sell products and services that promise wellness. The economic engine depends on you continuing to need them. The more resourced, connected, informed, and supported people become, the less vulnerable they may be to products that depend on shame, fear, or the promise that wholeness can be purchased.

Communities that nourish one another can reduce dependence on markets for some forms of care. Food shared. Children watched. Skills traded. Grief held. Knowledge passed locally. That does not make a community self-sufficient or free of harm. It does show why reciprocity matters.

Colonial and industrial systems have disrupted many local knowledge systems, land bases, kinship structures, and community practices across the world. The histories differ by place. Some disruptions were deliberate. Some followed economic change, urbanization, privatization, law, schooling, missionization, or forced displacement. The result, in many communities, was greater dependence on institutions or markets for things once held more locally. Every village restructured into nuclear families that depend on the market for what the village used to provide.

The cost of all of that, to the human nervous system, is incalculable. The exhaustion you carry is your share of a centuries-long project, the pulling of humans out of the conditions they evolved to live inside.

What the Nervous System Was WiredFor

The body did not change. The conditions changed.

The body that walks into your office carries the same broad human biological inheritance as the bodies of generations before you. We are not genetically or developmentally identical to any one ancestor, and ancestral lives were never one simple world. They held danger, illness, violence, love, kinship, and survival in different combinations.

What we do know is that human beings are deeply social. We develop in relationship. Light and darkness influence circadian biology. Movement matters. Sleep matters. Play matters. Social connection matters. The environments our species has lived in across history have varied enormously, but no human nervous system develops outside a social and physical world.

I think of the old needs this way: connection. Rest. Movement. Rhythm. Belonging. Time to play. Ways to grieve. Ways to celebrate. Food. Shelter. Touch when touch is wanted. Love that is not entirely transactional.

The exact form changes across cultures. The needs do not arrive in one universal village-shaped package. But modern systems should still be asked whether they are making basic human needs easier or harder to meet.

The body was wired for love. Real, embodied love. Steady. Reliable. Not transactional. Not performance-based. The kind of love an infant expects when she is born and would receive in any healthy human community on earth. That love is the original soil. The mud the Quechua teacher told us about. The conditions the nervous system was built to grow in.

Modern life provides very little of this. The body has been asked to function on substitutes for what it was wired to expect. Productivity instead of presence. Optimization instead of attunement. Likes instead of being known. Followers instead of belonging. Self-care instead of community care. Products instead of practices. Experts instead of elders. Diagnosis instead of witness.

The body is not failing in modern conditions. The body is being failed by them.

Collective Homeostasis

Every body has homeostasis. The system that brings the body back to baseline. The breath that slows after the alarm passes. The heart rate that settles after the run. The temperature that adjusts to the room. The blood sugar that regulates with food and rest. Homeostasis is the body's wisdom about what its own baseline is and how to return to it.

I borrow the word homeostasis here as a cultural metaphor. A society is not one nervous system. It does not have a literal autonomic baseline. But groups do develop norms. Paces. Expectations. Rituals. Shared ideas about what is ordinary.

Some social environments make regulation easier. A calm caregiver can help an infant settle. A steady practitioner can change the feel of a therapeutic encounter. A trusted group may make it easier for someone to speak, breathe, or stay present. The reverse can happen too. Chaotic, threatening, or humiliating environments can increase stress.

I think of the petri dish as a metaphor for the field. Human beings are not cells in culture media. We have agency, history, biology, and difference. The image helps me remember that conditions are part of the outcome.

The field shapes the body. Not always. Not completely. But enough that we should stop pretending context is background scenery.

Cultures also change when enough people, institutions, laws, practices, and relationships begin moving differently. There is no single nervous-system tipping point I can calculate. Social movements are more complicated than regulated bodies entering a room.

My thesis is simpler: individual healing matters, and social conditions matter. We need both. A person should not have to regulate alone against a field that keeps producing threat. A culture should not wait for every individual to heal before changing the conditions it can change now.

A Different Culture Is Possible

I want to spend a moment on what it could be.

A culture that understood pain would not rush to medicate it. It would sit with it. It would ask what produced it. It would change the conditions that produced it where it could. It would hold the people inside it with patience.

A culture that understood pain would not pathologize anger that comes from real harm, grief that comes from real loss, exhaustion that comes from real overwork, withdrawal that comes from real betrayal. It would receive those responses as information about conditions that needed attention.

A culture that understood pain would teach children how their nervous systems worked. It would teach them to identify what they were feeling. It would teach them how to ask for what they needed. It would teach them they had a right to need things.

A culture that understood pain would build co-regulation into its institutions. Workplaces with rest. Schools with breath.

Healthcare with time. Public space designed for slow encounters. Community rituals for grief, for celebration, for transition.

A culture that understood pain would centre the wisdom of the people who had been on the receiving end of its violence. Indigenous knowledge would be honoured, not extracted. Women's wisdom would be sought. Disabled bodies would be taught from, not just accommodated. The people the system had hurt would be the people the system listened to as it learned to do better.

A culture that understood pain would teach self-validation as a basic skill. It would name self-love as the foundation of safe community. It would teach sovereignty in the body as the precondition for sovereignty in the world. It would understand that an autonomous person is not a threat to community. An autonomous person is the only kind of person who can fully show up inside one.

That culture is not impossible. It exists already, in pockets, in lineages that survived the dismantling, in communities that resisted the imposition of the dominant model. It is possible to learn from those pockets. It is possible to build outward from them. It is possible for the rest of us to learn from those who never forgot.

That is the work of the next chapter, and of the rest of this book.

If you have read this chapter and recognized your tiredness in it, your numbness, your anxiety, your over-functioning, your scrolling, your numbing, hear this. None of these experiences has to become the whole definition of who you are. Some may be responses to conditions. Some may also involve illness, biology, injury, or causes you never fully identify. The work is not to blame yourself. The work is to become curious about the full ecology. What is happening inside you? What is happening around you? What can be changed? What needs care?

You are responding. Context belongs in the room.

The work is not to fix yourself. The work is to recognize the conditions. The work is to start, one tiny choice at a time, to interrupt the conditions where you can. The work is to find one or two people you can be real with. The work is to stop apologizing to yourself for being affected by what is affecting everyone. You are responding. Your body has been responding correctly to incorrect conditions. That is the only piece of pathology in the whole arrangement. It is not in you.

If you have read this chapter from inside one of the systems we have just been describing, as a teacher, a doctor, a therapist, an HR leader, a manager, a designer, a parent, a journalist, an academic, a policymaker, hear this too. You are not the system. You are a body inside it, doing your best with what you have been given. You also have, by virtue of the position you hold, a particular ability to interrupt some of the harm the system does. Refuse to write noncompliant on a patient's chart. Build rest into the calendar of the team you lead. Resist the metric that measures everything except humanity. Tell the child in front of you that her exhaustion is information, not a problem to fix. Every interruption matters. The system maintains itself through compliance. It can also be unmade through refusal.

Whichever side of the room you are reading from, you are sacred. The pain is real. The cause is structural. The healing is both personal and collective. Both are needed. Both are yours.

The conditions I have described in this chapter are affecting every body that lives inside them. Yours is one of millions. The collective consequences have become visible in numbers that should be taken as an emergency. Burnout. Anxiety. Depression. Suicide rates. Chronic disease. The body of an entire population is showing what an unwell culture produces. The next chapter looks at what those numbers tell us, and at the cultures around the world and across time that have organized themselves around the nervous system's actual needs. The conditions can be different. We are not the first people to try.

Chapter Six
Stress Loops and Collective Emergency
What an Unwell Culture Produces

The previous chapter described what the conditions of modern life are doing to one body. This chapter looks at what happens when those same conditions act on millions of bodies at once. The pattern is observable. It is countable. The numbers have been gathered for decades by health agencies, public health researchers, and statistical bodies in every country that collects this kind of data. The numbers are not normal. They are the body of an entire culture telling us, urgently, that something is wrong with how we have been asked to live.

There is a phrase from medical anthropology that captures what these numbers represent. The late Dr. Hugo De Burgos, a medical anthropologist at the University of British Columbia Okanagan who passed away in 2021, used the term social poisoning to describe what happens when a society systematically disrupts the conditions humans need to enjoy what he called experiential health. He defined experiential health as freedom from illness and alienation. The capacity for human development, self-discovery, self-actualization, and transcendence of alienating circumstances. Social poisoning, in his framework, is what happens when those conditions are taken away by structural design, often invisibly, often slowly, until people start showing up sick and the medical system blames the people instead of the design.

Hugo was a teacher at the university where I studied anthropology. His work on lead contamination in his home country of El Salvador documented in painful detail how the bodies of an entire community were poisoned by a battery factory while the medical authorities, under social pressure, denied that the lead was making people ill. He called the response of those medical authorities medical bad faith. It is when medical authority adopts false values under pressure and refuses to see what the bodies in front of it are clearly showing.

The lead in his research was literal. The soil he was naming was bigger than the literal. The soil of a culture is what every body inside that culture grows in. When the soil is contaminated, the bodies show it. When the contamination is denied, the bodies get blamed for showing it.

He also taught this framework around mental health. His medical anthropology courses on mental health, cross-cultural perspectives, and healing completely changed my life trajectory.

The numbers in this chapter are evidence of social poisoning at scale. They are what an entire population's body shows when the structural conditions it has been asked to live inside have stopped supporting wellbeing. The medical response, much of which I will describe in coming chapters, is too often the same medical bad faith Hugo observed in El Salvador. The bodies showing the symptoms get blamed for the symptoms. The conditions producing the symptoms are protected from accountability.

With that frame in place, let me show you what the numbers are.

The Numbers

I want to begin with mental health, because it is where the population-level signal is loudest.

Anxiety and depression are now among the most common mental health conditions worldwide. The World Health Organization, in its 2025 mental health report, identified more than one billion people worldwide as living with a mental health disorder. That is approximately one in seven human beings alive. Anxiety disorders, the most common category, affect roughly 360 million people globally. Depressive disorders affect roughly 330 million. Only about one in four people who need treatment for anxiety receives any.

In the United States, the percentage of adults reporting symptoms of anxiety rose from 15.6 percent in 2019 to 18.2 percent in 2022. Depression symptoms rose from 18.5 percent to 21.4 percent over the same period. Roughly one in five US adults currently shows symptoms of depression in any given two-week window. Canada and other high-income countries follow a similar pattern.

Suicide is the hardest number to write. Approximately 727,000 people die by suicide every year worldwide, according to WHO data. In Canada, around 3,800 people die that way every year. In the United States, the number for 2024 was 48,824, slightly down from 49,316 in 2023, but still one death every eleven minutes in that country alone. Suicide remains one of the leading causes of death among adolescents and young adults in both Canada and the United States. Men are roughly four times more likely than women to die by suicide, in part because they are less likely to seek help and more likely to use lethal means when they act on their distress.

These are not abstract figures. Each one is a body that could no longer hold what it was being asked to hold.

The cardiovascular system is keeping score on a different scale. The World Health Organization's 2025 Global Hypertension Report identifies 1.4 billion adults aged 30 to 79 as living with hypertension, roughly 33 percent of that age group worldwide. Approximately 600 million of them do not know they have it. Only about 320 million, roughly 23 percent, have the condition under control. Chronically elevated blood pressure is one of the world's largest contributors to cardiovascular disease and premature death, driving millions of deaths through stroke, heart disease, and related conditions each year.

Hypertension is more than diet and exercise. For some bodies, chronic stress is part of the story. A body braced for impact year after year lives under a load a resting body never carries. Blood pressure has many authors. Culture, chronic stress, and the conditions a person lives inside are among them.

Hypertension is culture made visible in the body.

The workplace is its own dataset. Gallup's State of the Global Workplace 2025 report shows that only 21 percent of employees worldwide feel engaged at work, down from 23 percent the previous year, the sharpest drop since the COVID lockdowns. Only 33 percent globally report that their lives are thriving. Manager engagement dropped from 30 percent to 27 percent in a single year, with young and female managers reporting particularly significant declines. The economic cost of this disengagement, by Gallup's own calculations, is approximately 438 billion US dollars in lost productivity. In Europe, only 13 percent of employees report being engaged at work. In the United Kingdom, the figure is 10 percent.

These numbers are people. They are people getting up every morning and going to a place where their nervous system stays in low-grade activation for eight to ten hours and they cannot fully participate in their own life.

Twenty percent of employees globally, in the same Gallup data, reported feeling lonely a lot of the previous day. Among remote workers, that figure rose to twenty-five percent.

These numbers, taken together, represent something more than statistics. They represent the body of an entire culture, on every continent, telling us that something the body needed has been removed and not replaced.

And then there is violence.

Violence in the Numbers

The World Health Organization, in its most recent global report released in November 2025, estimates that approximately 840 million women have experienced intimate partner or sexual violence in their lifetime. That is nearly one in three women globally. The figure has barely moved in twenty years of measurement. The progress has been described by the WHO itself as painfully slow. In the United States, the Centers for Disease Control puts the figure at more than one in three women, approximately 43.5 million people, who experience contact sexual violence, physical violence, or stalking by an intimate partner during their lifetimes. For men, roughly one in five experiences sexual violence in his lifetime when sexual violence is counted to include rape, attempted rape, and contact sexual violence other than rape. Approximately one in six men experiences intimate partner violence specifically.

These numbers are conservative. Violence is one of the most underreported categories of human experience. The actual figures are higher. They have been higher for as long as humans have measured them.

Approximately 137 women and girls worldwide are killed every day by an intimate partner or close family member. In 2024 alone, the United Nations documented roughly 50,000 women murdered by partners or family. One every ten minutes. The Director-General of the World Health Organization said, in releasing a previous version of these figures, that violence against women cannot be stopped with a vaccine. The implication is one we have not wanted to look at. The conditions producing the violence are inside the culture, not outside it.

Two researchers have helped me hold what these numbers mean.

Judith Herman's *Trauma and Recovery* placed domestic violence and political terror in the same trauma conversation. She argued that chronic interpersonal violence can produce trauma responses with important parallels to other forms of prolonged threat. The experiences are not physiologically identical in every body, and a battlefield and a home are not interchangeable settings. Her contribution was to refuse the idea that terror becomes less serious because it happens in private.

Lundy Bancroft, drawing on decades of work with abusive men, has argued that entitlement and beliefs about control are central to many patterns of intimate partner abuse. That is a framework, not a biological law and not the only theory of violence. It shifts attention away from the excuse that abuse is simply uncontrolled anger and toward the beliefs, choices, power, and social conditions surrounding the harm.

Together, these bodies of work ask a cultural question: what beliefs and structures make violence easier to excuse, hide, repeat, or survive without accountability?

These two researchers together hold the truth the numbers point to. Violence is not random. Violence is not what happens between unlucky individuals. Violence is what a particular kind of culture produces when it does not name and dismantle the structures of entitlement that grew certain bodies inside it.

There is also an economic dimension to the violence the culture is producing. The World Bank has estimated that in some countries, violence against women costs up to 3.7 percent of national GDP. That is more than double what most governments spend on education. The economic cost is being paid by the same societies that have, at the level of policy, treated violence as a private matter between individuals rather than a public health crisis with measurable structural causes.

A culture producing these violence statistics has, at its structural level, accepted certain bodies as available for harm and certain other bodies as protected from accountability. The previous chapter named this. The numbers repeat it. The numbers will keep repeating until the culture that produces them is rebuilt.

Stress loops are not broken people. They are broken promises by society.

What a Stress Loop Actually Is

Before we move to alternatives, I want to be precise about the biology, because the precision matters.

The nervous system has a complete cycle. Activation, response, return to baseline. The cycle is the same one your ancestors used to survive lions and famines and storms and rivals. The body fires. The body acts. The body discharges. The body rests. Then the body is ready for the next threat. The cycle is brilliant. It has kept human beings alive for hundreds of thousands of years.

Robert Sapolsky, a Stanford neurobiologist who spent thirty years watching baboons in Kenya, captured this with a phrase that has stayed with me. Zebras do not get ulcers. Zebras get chased by lions, run for their lives, and then go back to grazing. The body does what it was designed to do. The activation fires, the threat is met, the body discharges, and the body returns to baseline. Humans get ulcers, Sapolsky observed, because we run that same emergency physiology for months while worrying about mortgages and meetings and the relentless background hum of a life that never quite arrives at safety. We turn on a system designed for minutes of acute crisis and leave it on for years.

I use the phrase stress loop for what happens when activation keeps being re-triggered and recovery never gets enough room. The threat may be over, but the next demand arrives. Then the next.

Stress hormones and autonomic activation are meant to change over time, not remain identical every minute of the day. Under chronic stress, those systems can become dysregulated. Heart rate, sleep, attention, inflammation, appetite, and mood may all be affected.

Somatic traditions often describe this as a cycle that did not get to complete. Biomedical researchers may speak instead about chronic stress, altered recovery, allostatic load, and repeated activation. I use stress loop because it names the lived experience: the body keeps getting called back to emergency before it has fully come home.

The body does not literally store an event in one muscle or one organ like a file in a drawer. But trauma and chronic stress can shape patterns of tension, breathing, sleep, attention, autonomic responding, and behaviour.

The score is kept in patterns. In systems. In what the organism has learned to expect.

Bruce McEwen, a neuroscientist at Rockefeller University, gave the accumulated wear a name. He called it allostatic load. The body's price for adapting too long. Every system we run too hard for too many years, the cardiovascular, the immune, the metabolic, the hormonal, eventually shows what the running has cost. McEwen mapped the price across blood pressure, cortisol patterns, inflammatory markers, waist-to-hip ratios, and cognitive decline. The load is measurable in the body, year after year, as the receipts of a life lived under conditions the body was never meant to sustain.

Stress research has also examined telomeres, the protective structures at the ends of chromosomes. In a 2004 study led by Elissa Epel, women reporting higher perceived stress had shorter telomeres on average. The researchers estimated that the difference between the highest-and lowest-stress groups was comparable to at least a decade of additional aging.

It was an association in a relatively small study. It did not prove that caregiving stress adds a fixed number of years to every body. Later research has continued exploring links between adversity, stress, and telomere biology, with results shaped by age, health, exposure, and study design.

The careful truth is still important: chronic stress can become biologically embedded. The exact pathway is not one simple cellular clock.

When stress loops become the baseline of an entire culture, the numbers I just walked through are what you get. Burnout. Anxiety. Depression. Hypertension. Suicide. Violence. Loneliness. Premature death itself. The body of the culture showing its activation through the bodies of its people, all the way down to the chromosomes.

The Cost of Collective Emergency

When stress loops become the cultural baseline, the cost is not borne only by the bodies showing the symptoms. The cost is borne by the entire fabric of community life.

Richard Wilkinson and Kate Pickett, two British epidemiologists, published a book called The Spirit Level that tracked eleven different health and social outcomes across wealthy nations. Physical health. Mental health. Drug abuse. Education. Imprisonment. Obesity. Social mobility. Trust. Violence. Teenage pregnancy. Child wellbeing. Across all eleven, the more unequal the society, the worse the outcomes. Not for the poorest only. For everyone inside it. Inequality measurably damages the bodies and minds of even the people at the top of an unequal system, because the entire field of status anxiety and competitive striving wears every body inside it down.

Robert Putnam, a sociologist at Harvard, watched American civic life come apart over four decades. He titled his book Bowling Alone, because Americans were still bowling, more than ever, but no longer in leagues. The fraternal organizations, the parentteacher associations, the neighbourhood clubs, the church groups, the bowling leagues themselves, all collapsed across the same span of years. The structures that used to hold human beings in regular contact with one another were dismantled, often quietly, often without anyone naming what was being lost. The result is a culture full of people who have nowhere to put their loneliness.

Julianne Holt-Lunstad has done some of the most rigorous research on what that loneliness costs the body. Across studies pooling more than three million participants worldwide, the absence of strong social connection produces a mortality risk on the same scale as the worst lifestyle factors we already worry about. The body without other bodies dies sooner. The data is overwhelming and consistent enough that the United States Surgeon General published a public health advisory in 2023 naming loneliness as a national emergency.

Anne Case and Angus Deaton, two Princeton economists, gave us the most disturbing single phrase. Deaths of despair. They tracked the rising mortality among American adults without college degrees, especially in deindustrialized regions, and found that drug overdose, alcohol-related liver disease, and suicide were claiming about 158,000 American lives every year. They called that the equivalent of three full passenger plane crashes a week, every week, for a year. The bodies of the people the economy stopped needing have, for two decades now, been dying in numbers that would shut down any other industry overnight if the deaths were not so spread out and so quiet.

Eric Klinenberg, a sociologist at New York University, has been studying what he calls social infrastructure. Libraries. Parks. Swimming pools. Sidewalks. Community centres. The physical spaces where people encounter one another without an economic transaction. When these spaces are well maintained, even neighbourhoods full of strangers can hold their people. When they decay, even the wealthy fragment. The 1995 heat wave that killed 739 people in Chicago killed them disproportionately in neighbourhoods where the social fabric had been allowed to thin. The bodies that died had no one nearby to check on them.

Philosophers and physicians have begun to name what economists and epidemiologists have been measuring. Byung-Chul Han, a Korean-German philosopher, wrote a small, devastating book called The Burnout Society. He observed that the illnesses of our century are no longer infections coming from outside. They are infarctions, exhaustions of a body that has been told to push itself past its own limits in the name of self-optimization. Mark Fisher, a British cultural theorist, named the phenomenon the privatization of stress. The cost of an unwell system is paid by the individual bodies inside it, who are then asked to treat their suffering as a personal failing rather than the predictable output of the structure they are living within.

Gabor Maté, the Canadian physician whose work has reached so many of us, wrote The Myth of Normal to argue that much of what we now call ordinary life is producing the diseases we then treat. The normal is not the healthy. The normal is the average of a population that is, in measurable ways, growing sicker. Johann Hari, the British journalist, framed depression and anxiety as forms of grief. Grief for connections the culture is no longer providing. Grief for purposes the economy is no longer honouring. Grief for a sense of belonging the design of modern life has been quietly dismantling for decades.

The pattern across all of this work is clear. The disease is downstream. The culture is upstream. The bodies showing the symptoms are not the source of the problem. The bodies are doing what bodies do when they have been asked to live too long inside conditions that wear them out.

This is the lived texture of social poisoning. It does not look like Hugo's lead in the soil. It looks like neighbours who do not know each other's names. Coworkers who stay silent during the meeting and gossip after. Families that share a home and not much else. Friendships that fade because no one has the bandwidth to maintain them. Political polarization that runs deeper every year. The slow shrinking of the spaces where people used to encounter one another and now do not.

A culture that cannot offer safety to the bodies inside it cannot offer connection either. Connection requires nervous systems with bandwidth. Nervous systems in chronic stress loops do not have bandwidth. They have just enough capacity to get through the day. The day after day after day. The body learns to conserve. Connection gets cut first because connection is what the body has been told is optional.

The truth is the opposite. Connection is not optional. Connection is survival. Restoring the conditions that allow nervous systems to come back down is the only way the body of the culture can begin to repair itself.

Parenting in Chronic Emergency

The cost of chronic stress at the cultural level shows up most clearly in how children get raised.

In cultures running constant emergency, parenting bends to accommodate what is required to survive the conditions. Long hours. Economic precarity. The glorification of productivity. The shrinking of extended family. The disappearance of village support. The pressure to look like everything is fine. Parents are asked, increasingly, to do alone what every functional human culture across history has done collectively. Many of them are doing it without sleep, without help, and inside their own unaddressed stress loops.

The shortcuts that result, often without parents intending them, embed stress into the developing nervous systems of the children being raised.

Infant care has shifted, over generations, from constant co-regulation to early sleep training, long hours in swings or cribs, and less physical contact. What was once biologically expected, nearconstant carrying and proximity, becomes framed as indulgent. The cry of an infant whose nervous system is asking to be held gets read as manipulation. The body of the infant learns, in those first months, that distress does not necessarily bring connection. That lesson does not get unlearned later. It becomes the substrate of every relationship the child will have for the rest of their life.

Childcare gets outsourced. Parents love their children deeply. The reason childcare goes to institutions is that economic structures make full-time presence financially impossible for most families. Many children spend most of their waking hours in institutional settings where caregiver-to-child ratios do not allow for consistent attunement. Nervous systems adapt by down-regulating their needs or up-regulating their behaviours to compete for the attention available. Both adaptations leave marks.

Schooling mirrors the workplace. Rigid schedules. Standardized testing. Little room for rest, play, or emotional expression. Children spend their formative years inside the same kind of low-grade chronic activation their parents spend their adult years inside. By the time they reach adulthood, performance under stress feels like the baseline of being human. They have not known anything else.

The cycle continues, generation after generation. A mother who was taught not to cry hushes her own child's tears. A father who learned that worth came from productivity pushes his child to excel even when the child is exhausted. Children learn not only through what is said to them. They learn through nervous system resonance, the body-to-body signals exchanged in every moment of contact between a developing nervous system and the more regulated, or more dysregulated, nervous systems around it.

This is why breaking the cycle of cultural stress is not a matter of self-care tips or small tweaks. It demands a reframe of how families, workplaces, and communities are designed.

It also demands acknowledging something the research has been clear on for decades. The bond between caregiver and child is so foundational that it cannot be separated. Nervous systems shape one another in those years. A regulated parent raising a child creates the conditions for a regulated adult. A dysregulated parent, doing their best inside dysregulated conditions, will pass forward what they themselves never had the chance to set down.

Stress loops are patterns, and patterns can be interrupted. Patterns, once seen, can be interrupted.

Healing Together: Parent and Child

The best evidence we have shows that the most lasting outcomes come when parents and children are supported together, rather than in isolation. Stress is relational. It travels body to body, nervous system to nervous system. A child learns safety by borrowing the calm of a caregiver. A parent regulates more easily when supported in meeting a child's needs without shame, urgency, or judgment from the people around her.

The clearest evidence base we have for this comes from a body of work that began at the Child Trauma Research Project in San Francisco. Alicia Lieberman, a developmental psychologist at the University of California San Francisco, developed an approach called Child-Parent Psychotherapy. The premise is straightforward. When a young child has been through something hard, especially something involving the people who care for her, the healing cannot happen with the child alone. It cannot happen with the parent alone either. The work happens between them, in the same room, with a trained therapist holding the field while the relationship begins to repair.

Five different randomized controlled trials have now shown the same thing. Children and their caregivers who receive Child-Parent Psychotherapy together show greater reductions in trauma symptoms, behaviour problems, and the parent's own distress than children who receive traditional individual therapy. The gains hold at six-month follow-up. The treatment is now listed as evidence-based by SAMHSA, the United States agency that maintains the national registry of mental health treatments. Of all the approaches we have for healing the youngest bodies who have been through something hard, Child-Parent Psychotherapy has the strongest evidence base for keeping the dyad intact while the healing happens.

Attachment and Biobehavioral Catch-up, developed by Mary Dozier and colleagues, is a brief home-based intervention for caregivers of young children who have experienced early adversity. In randomized studies, children receiving ABC showed more typical patterns of cortisol regulation than comparison groups. Later follow-up also found sustained differences in cortisol and parenting sensitivity.

Changing caregiving conditions can be accompanied by measurable changes in stress regulation.

The reason these approaches work was first documented in a small laboratory at the University of Massachusetts in the late 1970s. A developmental psychologist named Ed Tronick designed an experiment that has since become one of the most replicated findings in developmental psychology. He called it the Still Face. A mother engages playfully with her infant for two minutes. She then holds a still, expressionless face for two more minutes. Even babies as young as two months sober, look away, reach back toward the mother, vocalize, try harder to bring her back, and eventually withdraw from the interaction. From a trauma-informed lens, there is something painfully recognizable in that movement away from an exchange that is no longer responding. The infant has registered the disruption in attunement. The whole sequence can unfold in less than two minutes.

Tronick's broader work emphasizes mismatch and repair. Caregivers and infants are not continuously synchronized.

Interaction moves in and out of coordination.

The important observation is that return matters. A caregiver re-engages. The interaction finds its rhythm again. Repeated experiences of repair may help a child develop expectations that disconnection is not always permanent.

Repair is not a guarantee against later difficulty, and one missed cue does not write a lifelong wound. The research gives us a more humane picture than perfection: relationships can miss and return.

This research is part of the foundation under what I want to ask next. When providers can hold both the child and the caregiving relationship in view, the unit of care becomes larger than one isolated individual.

That does not mean every child must be treated with a parent, every parent is safe to include, or dyadic treatment is always superior. Family violence, custody, age, developmental needs, culture, safety, diagnosis, and the person's own wishes all matter.

Sometimes the adult begins first. Sometimes the child needs urgent individual care. Sometimes parallel treatment makes sense. Sometimes dyadic or family work is especially useful.

The honest answer to who heals first is the answer you already reached: it depends. The research supports taking relationships seriously.

A team at Harvard, led by a pediatrician named Jack Shonkoff, has been mapping what happens to a child's developing nervous system under stress. Their framework distinguishes between three kinds of stress that a child can experience.

Positive stress is the brief, mild activation that comes with a new experience. A first day of school. A vaccination. A challenging game. The body fires, the body recovers, the body has learned something about its own capacity.

Tolerable stress is heavier. The death of a grandparent. A frightening injury. A move to a new home. The activation goes deeper. It lasts longer. The hormones run higher.

Toxic stress is what happens when serious adversity, chronic abuse, neglect, household instability, deep poverty, ongoing violence, hits a child's developing body without buffering.

The single most important word in that framework is buffering. What turns tolerable stress into toxic stress is the absence of a regulated, attuned adult. The severity of the event matters less than who is standing beside the child when it lands. A child who loses a grandparent in a household where someone holds the loss with her, names what is happening, lets her cry, sits beside her through the nights when sleep does not come, will metabolize that loss as tolerable. The same loss in a household where she is told to stop crying, where no one acknowledges what has happened, where she is left to make sense of it alone, becomes toxic. Her body absorbs the stress without any vehicle for moving it through.

Urie Bronfenbrenner, one of the architects of American developmental psychology, named this in language that has stayed with everyone who has read him. To develop normally, a child requires progressively more complex joint activity with one or more adults who have an irrational emotional relationship with the child. Somebody, he wrote, has got to be crazy about that kid. That is number one. First, last, and always.

The body of a child whose nervous system has someone who is crazy about her develops differently from the body of a child who does not.

This is where research that began with rats has changed how we understand human children.

Michael Meaney, a neuroscientist at McGill in Montreal, ran a series of experiments through the late 1990s and early 2000s that became foundational. Some mother rats lick and groom their pups frequently. Others do not. The pups raised by high-licking-andgrooming mothers grew up calmer, with measurably different stress hormones, different gene expression in the hippocampus, and different responses to adult stressors. When his team cross-fostered the pups, taking pups from low-licking mothers and putting them with high-licking mothers, several of the stress-related behavioural and biological patterns tracked by the researchers shifted toward those seen in pups raised by high-care mothers. The biology was not destiny. The biology was what the early caregiving had taught the body to expect.

In Meaney's animal studies, the conditions of early maternal care were associated with measurable differences in stress-related gene expression. The findings gave researchers a powerful demonstration that biology is not simply a fixed starting point operating independently of experience. Early conditions can become biologically embedded.

The science has spent the years since being careful about how far to carry that into human lives, and the care is warranted. Researchers including Frances Champagne have continued exploring how early care, stress, and development interact with epigenetic processes. Human beings are far more complex than laboratory animals, and we cannot draw a straight line from a particular act of caregiving to one molecular outcome in a child's brain. What the wider developmental literature does show is that relationships matter. Touch, responsive care, gaze, soothing, and repeated experiences of co-regulation are part of the environment in which a developing nervous system grows.

This is not only poetic language. Development is biological. Experience and biology are in constant conversation.

And the brain remains plastic. Early conditions matter enormously, but they do not finalize a human being at one age. When a parent repairs a rupture, returns with greater attunement, acknowledges what happened, and begins relating differently, the relationship receives new information. The child or adult may begin developing new expectations about what is possible in that relationship.

That does not erase what happened. It does mean the story can continue.

A parent who reads this book when her child is twenty-six and decides to repair something from when the child was six cannot rewrite those twenty years. She can bring something different into the relationship now. A grandparent who recognizes a pattern and chooses not to repeat it with her grandchildren changes the conditions of the present generation.

The window for influence does not suddenly slam shut. Human beings continue learning through relationships across the lifespan.

Development begins before birth. Researchers including Vivette Glover have studied associations between prenatal stress and later child development, including stress regulation and attention. Other researchers have examined telomere length in adults in relation to maternal stress during pregnancy. These studies do not mean a mother's stress writes a fixed destiny into a fetus. Prenatal stress is one possible influence among genetics, physical health, nutrition, exposures, obstetric factors, postnatal care, and the child's later environment. It is especially important not to turn this research into another way to blame mothers. The hopeful part is not that postnatal attunement can simply erase whatever happened in pregnancy. The hopeful part is that development continues. Early conditions matter. Later conditions matter too. It is not too late to begin bringing different information into a relationship. The story keeps being written.

Factors to Consider

Several variables shape which pathway makes sense for a particular family at a particular moment.

Severity and urgency. In moments of crisis, such as suicidality, acute behavioural risk, or immediate safety concerns, the child's needs may take immediate priority. Parallel support for the parent must follow quickly. Crisis is not the end of the conversation about who needs care. Crisis is the beginning of it.

Parental capacity. Parents struggling with addiction, untreated trauma, severe burnout, or their own acute mental health symptoms may need stabilization before they can be fully present for a child. They cannot offer regulation they do not have. This is not a moral failing. It is the same nervous system biology that runs in every body.

Systemic barriers. Poverty, housing instability, food insecurity, immigration precarity, and unsafe neighbourhoods make healing difficult for both adult and child. Providers and policymakers who try to address symptoms without addressing material conditions are working against the actual problem. The body cannot heal inside conditions that keep producing the wound.

Cultural context. Healing pathways differ across cultures. In many Indigenous and collectivist traditions, the family and community are inseparable from the healing process. The question of parent first or child first is less relevant when the worldview holds that everyone heals together, in ceremony, in relationship, in the rhythms of the community that surrounds them.

The truth underneath all of these factors is that the bond between caregiver and child is so foundational it cannot really be separated for the purposes of treatment. Nervous systems shape one another in those years. Caregiver-child relationships are foundational, but they are not the only forces shaping development. Nervous systems influence one another in those years. A more resourced caregiver may be able to offer more consistency and co-regulation. The child still brings temperament, biology, health, other relationships, and a wider world. Supporting parents and children can change the conditions the next generation receives.

The Study That Should Have Changed Everything

I want to tell you about a body of research that should have changed how every health system on this continent operates, and mostly has not.

In the mid-1990s, two physicians began a study at Kaiser Permanente in San Diego. Vincent Felitti was a doctor who ran the hospital's obesity clinic. He had noticed something strange about his patients. The ones who succeeded in losing significant weight were often the same ones who relapsed most dramatically. He started asking why, expecting to hear about willpower or biology. What he kept hearing about instead was childhood. Sexual abuse. Violence in the home. A mother's mental illness. A father's addiction. The weight, his patients began to tell him, had been protection. As they lost it, they felt unsafe again, and the body went looking for the layer that had been holding the old wound.

Felitti partnered with Robert Anda, an epidemiologist at the Centers for Disease Control. Together they designed one of the largest studies of childhood adversity ever conducted in North America. Over seventeen thousand adults, mostly middle-class, mostly white, mostly insured, were asked about ten different categories of adverse childhood experiences. Physical abuse. Emotional abuse. Sexual abuse. Physical neglect. Emotional neglect. A household where someone struggled with addiction. A household where someone had untreated mental illness. A mother who was treated violently. Parental separation. A household member who had been incarcerated.

Each yes counted as one. The total became what is now known as the participant's ACE score.

What they found shifted public health.

The more categories of adversity a person reported, the higher their risk was for a wide range of adult health problems. Heart disease. Cancer. Stroke. Lung disease. Alcohol and drug problems. Depression and suicide attempts. The relationship was graded: as the ACE score rose, many risks rose with it.

The original study found that people with four or more ACE categories had substantially higher odds of several health-risk behaviours and conditions than people with none. Later ACE research found a strong graded association between ACE scores and suicide attempts.

These studies show association and dose-response patterns. They do not mean childhood adversity is the single cause of every later illness, or that a high ACE score is destiny.

That distinction matters. Adversity can shape health through many roads: stress physiology, development, access to resources, relationships, sleep, substance use, health care, racism, poverty, and other exposures across a lifetime. The childhood did not become the disease in a simple one-step conversion. The childhood became part of the body's ecology of risk.

Roughly two-thirds of the original sample reported at least one ACE. More than one in five reported three or more. This was a sample of mostly insured, mostly middle-class adults at a Kaiser Permanente clinic in California. The number was coming from what was assumed to be a stable middle of American society. Childhood adversity is not rare. It has been hiding in plain sight, inside the bodies of the people who were never supposed to be affected by it.

The study was published in 1998 in the American Journal of Preventive Medicine. It has been cited more than twenty-five thousand times. It is considered one of the most important public health studies of the twentieth century. The CDC has continued to track ACEs in population surveys. Subsequent research has expanded the original ten to include community violence, racism, food insecurity, housing instability, and other structural conditions that shape a child's early life. California launched ACEs Aware in December 2019, and MediCal began reimbursing eligible providers for ACE screening on January 1, 2020. This research has existed for more than twenty-five years. A few years ago, I was invited to give a workshop for Public Health Canada. The room held about one hundred health policy makers and decision-makers. I was speaking about trauma-informed approaches in public health, and at one point I asked, casually, expecting many hands to go up, who in the room was familiar with the ACE study.

Not one hand went up.

One hundred health policy decision-makers. The people writing the strategies that shape the conditions of population health in this country. None of them had encountered the foundational research connecting childhood adversity to adult disease, a body of work that has existed for a quarter century, that has been cited by tens of thousands of subsequent studies, that has reshaped how an entire generation of clinicians understand the bodies in front of them.

I have thought about that room many times since. What does it tell us when people shaping public health policy have not encountered a major body of research linking childhood adversity with later health risk? It tells me context is still too easy to leave outside the chart. The ACE literature does not explain how every disease develops. It does make one thing difficult to defend: the idea that childhood conditions are irrelevant to adult population health. I left that room more convinced that we have to keep asking about the fire and how we are applying trauma-informed perspectives into health initiatives, priorities and budget allocations.

Where are our priorities? Is it to medicalize pain and continue building system approaches that are themselves part of what has caused the dysfunction? Or is it to actually help heal people and design ecosystems of social wellness that grow well bodies inside well conditions?

We have had the evidence for a long time. What we have not had is the institutional courage to act on it. The ACE study did not surprise the people who already knew. It surprised the institutions that did not want to know. And the institutions, twenty-five years later, are still finding ways not to know.

An Urgent Call to Become a Healing Culture

I want to name something the previous sections of this chapter have been pointing at without quite saying.

Just living in North America, or in any developed culture organized around the same value system, just being raised inside the conditions this book has been describing, means that children are being raised inside a soil that produces unwellness regardless of how hard their parents try.

This is not a critique of parents. This is a description of the soil.

The soil is not unique to one continent. Any developed culture that has organized itself around the same value system is growing the same kind of body in its children. Wherever a culture has come to value greed as virtue, individualism as identity, self-promotion as the measure of worth, and personal advancement as the highest organizing principle of a life, the children of that culture inherit the same wear. North America is one expression of the pattern. Western Europe is another. Parts of East Asia have absorbed it. Increasingly, every economy that has industrialized along the same lines is producing the same nervous systems.

The values that built this soil are old. They have been pushed forward in the last few centuries with more intensity than at any other time in human history. Greed got rebranded as ambition. Individualism got rebranded as freedom. Self-clout got rebranded as personal brand. Egoic striving got rebranded as success. The content of the value system stayed the same. The packaging changed. The bodies that grew inside the packaging have shown what the package contains.

The alternative values are also old. They have existed in every culture that has ever organized itself around the wellbeing of its many rather than the accumulation of its few. Reciprocity. Kindness. Right relationship with everything alive, including the land, the water, the animals, the air. The understanding that a single human life is one strand in a much larger web. That the strand thrives or fails based on the health of the web it is woven into.

Ego is not the foundation of a self. Belonging is.

These are the values most human cultures have held for most of human history. They have been overwritten, layer by layer, in the dominant cultures of the last few centuries. They can be uncovered again.

The most attuned mother in the world, the most present father, the most well-resourced caregivers doing their absolute best, are still raising their children inside a culture that runs on chronic activation, comparison, productivity, isolation, and the steady erosion of community. The soil is contaminated. The water the children are given to drink, the cultural messages, the institutional structures, the daily pace, the absence of village, is contaminated too. Even the best individual effort cannot fully insulate a developing nervous system from the conditions of the field it is growing inside.

This is the limit of individual healing. It is also why individual healing alone has never been enough.

What this kind of culture is producing in its children, despite the love of millions of devoted parents on every continent it has reached, is a population whose baseline nervous system is set higher than it should be. Whose comparison machinery is more active than it should be. Whose sense of enoughness is more fragile than it should be. Whose capacity for embodied presence is shallower than it should be. None of these are failures of the children. None of them are failures of the parents. All of them are predictable consequences of a soil that has needed overhauling for a long time.

This is the urgent call.

We need to overhaul the cultural norms. Not piecemeal. Not eventually. Not when it becomes convenient for the institutions that benefit from the current arrangement. Now. The conditions of our culture must be redesigned around psychological safety. Around active healing as a community practice. Around the willingness to talk about the work, openly and often, so that the next generation grows up watching the adults around them tend to their own nervous systems and naming what they are doing while they do it.

A healing culture would make it safe to be truthful. It would protect people who come forward with what has happened to them. It would believe survivors. It would hold the people who caused the harm accountable for the harm. It would do this even when the people who caused the harm hold positions of power, social standing, or institutional protection. It would do this consistently enough that survivors stopped having to weigh whether telling the truth would cost them more than the harm itself did.

A healing culture would name harm as harm. Not difficulty. Not personality conflict. Not interpersonal misunderstanding. Harm. The naming would be specific. The accountability would be real. The systems that have protected harmful people would be dismantled and rebuilt around the safety of those they were originally designed to protect.

A healing culture would understand that accountability is not punishment. Accountability is the ecosystem function that allows trust to exist between bodies. Without accountability, bodies cannot trust the field they are inside. Without trust in the field, nervous systems cannot regulate. Without nervous system regulation, communities cannot heal.

Accountability is the keystone. Restore it and the rest of the architecture begins to hold.

A healing culture would talk about the healing. Out loud. In public. The way our current culture talks about productivity and achievement. Therapy would be a normal subject for conversation. Nervous system regulation would be taught in schools. Grief would have community structures. Trauma would be discussed without shame. The process would be visible, so that the children watching would learn early that being human means feeling, tending, repairing, and growing.

This is not a fantasy. Every element of this is being practiced somewhere right now. The body of our culture is showing us that the current arrangement is no longer working. The question is whether we are willing to be the generation that begins the rebuilding.

Cultures That Have Done This Differently

This is the part of the chapter I find most necessary, and I want to spend time on it.

Cultures across history and geography have organized themselves in ways that protect the nervous system instead of overwhelming it. Many of those cultures still exist. Some of them have been actively dismantled by colonization and capitalism and are now reclaiming what they nearly lost. None of them are utopias. All of them have something to teach about what the body actually needs.

This is anthropology's gift to the conversation. The discipline I trained in for years, where Hugo De Burgos taught for decades, has spent more than a century carefully documenting the diversity of ways human beings have organized themselves. The lesson, when you sit with the literature long enough, is that there is no single human nature being expressed by the conditions modern North America is living inside. There are choices being made about how to organize collective life. Other choices have been made elsewhere.

Cyclical time. Many Indigenous communities across the world organize daily and seasonal life around cyclical time rather than linear time. The sun rises and the sun sets. The seasons turn. The body works when work is needed and rests when rest is needed. Ceremonies mark the transitions. Rest is not earned. Rest is woven into the design.

A contemporary echo lives in the Mediterranean siesta tradition. In Spain, Italy, Greece, and parts of Latin America, the middle of the day has historically been a time of slowing down. Lunch is long. Shops close. The body has space to digest, to nap, to be still for a moment before returning to activity. Even as globalization has pushed against this rhythm, research has shown that siesta cultures have lower cardiovascular risk and improved mood compared to cultures that work through the middle of the day without pause.

Care built into structure. In the Scandinavian countries, parental leave policies represent something the rest of the wealthy world has not yet matched. Sweden offers more than a year of parental leave, shared between parents, with financial support that allows both to be present during the early months of a child's life. The infant gets co-regulation. The parents get time to attune. The household nervous system has a chance to settle into rhythm before either parent is asked to return to economic productivity.

Anthropologists who have studied egalitarian hunter-gatherer societies note that infants in those communities were carried almost constantly, surrounded by multiple caregivers, and rarely left to cry alone. This is the original design of human infant care. Attachment science increasingly confirms what those communities understood. Infant nervous systems require steady, embodied presence to wire for safety rather than threat.

Ritual and embodied discharge. Across cultures, communities have developed practices that allow the body to discharge stress through movement, sound, sweat, and shared rhythm. Drumming circles in many African traditions. Sweat lodges among Indigenous peoples of North America. Dance ceremonies across Polynesia, the Caribbean, West Africa, and India. Wailing as a practiced form of communal grief in many Mediterranean and Latin American cultures.

These are nervous system practices, carried in the shape of a song or a dance. They give the body a culturally legitimate channel for the activation that stress loops keep stored.

Western culture has, by and large, pathologized these natural discharges. Crying in public is awkward. Wailing is unprofessional. Dancing without alcohol is strange. Shaking is alarming. The body, denied these channels, holds the activation instead. The pathologization of natural discharge is part of what produces the numbers I named earlier in this chapter.

Many Indigenous communities in Canada and beyond are reclaiming land-based healing practices, including sweats, fasting camps, and ceremonies. The research on these practices is increasingly clear. Trauma symptoms decrease. Cultural pride increases. Nervous systems begin to settle in ways no medication has been able to produce. The medicine was always there. What was missing was permission, access, and safety to practice it.

Community grief and communal witness. The work of Sobonfu Somé and Malidoma Somé, both teachers from the Dagara people of Burkina Faso in West Africa, brought Dagara grief ritual into Western awareness before each of them passed. In the Dagara tradition, grief is not a private matter that a person works through alone with a therapist over many years. Grief is held by the community. There is structure. There is sound. There is movement. There are witnesses. The body of the grieving person is held inside the body of a community that knows what to do.

Western cultures have largely lost this capacity. We send our grieving people home alone. We give them a few days off work. We ask them to be back to functional within weeks. The body that has lost someone is asked to metabolize that loss in private, on a schedule that does not match how grief actually moves. The result is grief that goes underground and shows up later as depression, addiction, illness, rage, and despair.

Community grief rituals are now being adapted in Western contexts, often guided by teachers from cultures that retained the practice. They are reclamations of what was once human and what could be human again.

Reciprocity and the gift economy. Robin Wall Kimmerer, the Potawatomi botanist and writer, has described how Indigenous gift economies frame wellbeing as sustained by reciprocity between people, land, and spirit. Wealth is not accumulation. Wealth is the depth of relationship and the ongoing exchange of care, knowledge, food, and beauty between humans and the more-than-human world around them.

A nervous system inside a gift economy does not have to fight for survival the way a nervous system inside a competitive market economy does. The baseline assumption is that there is enough, that others will share, that one's own contribution will be received and met with care in return. Scarcity is real in some seasons. Scarcity is not the operating principle of the culture. Reciprocity is.

Contemporary cooperative housing models in Canada and parts of Europe gesture toward the same principle on a small scale. Residents share resources like childcare, cooking, gardens, and tools. The structure of daily life builds trust into routine. The nervous system finds the safety of we are in this together, and the wear of constant individual problem-solving begins to lift off the body.

What These Cultures Have in Common

Look across these examples and a pattern emerges.

Cultures that hold the nervous system well share certain design choices. They build rest into structure. They normalize embodied discharge. They centre community over individual achievement. They honour cyclical time. They keep ceremony alive. They distribute care across many bodies instead of placing it all on one or two. They treat the more-than-human world as relative rather than resource.

These are cultural design principles, tested across millennia. They show us what humans across history and geography have done when they have had the chance to organize themselves around what bodies actually need.

The point of naming these cultures is not to romanticize them. Every culture has carried its own wounds. Indigenous peoples have survived genocide. Mediterranean and Latin American cultures have lived under various forms of authoritarianism and economic precarity. African communities have endured slavery, colonization, and ongoing extraction. Scandinavian countries face their own quiet crises of loneliness and ecological grief. No culture is perfect. No body is fully held by any single set of practices.

The point is more modest, and more important. Wellness is not a private achievement available only to those with sufficient income and willpower. Wellness is a cultural design. It has been designed before, in many places, in many ways, by many peoples. The soil has been good before. The soil can be good again.

Reclaiming What the Culture Has Hid—en

There is one more pattern worth naming in the difference between cultures that hold the nervous system well and cultures that do not.

A culture that runs on chronic stress tends to hide certain human qualities. It hides them because those qualities slow down the productivity machinery the culture has organized itself around. It hides them by ridiculing them, by reframing them as defects, by punishing the bodies that carry them too visibly. The qualities go underground. The bodies that carry them learn to mask. The culture loses access to what those qualities would have offered, and the masking itself becomes another layer of stress.

Sensitivity is one of the qualities that gets hidden. The body that is highly sensitive is reading the room with extraordinary precision. It is noticing what other bodies are missing. It is sensing what is unsaid. In an unwell culture, this body gets called too much. Too sensitive. Too dramatic. Too emotional. The body learns to mute itself. The signal it was sending, which was useful, gets turned down to a level the culture can tolerate.

Sensitivity is not fragility. Sensitivity is attunement. It is the capacity to know what is happening in a room before the room has the words for it. A culture that listened to its sensitive bodies would be a culture with much earlier warning systems for harm.

Metacognition gets hidden. The body that thinks about its own thinking, that reflects on its own patterns, that learns from its own behaviour, has been called overthinking, anxious, neurotic. The body learns to stop reflecting. To act faster. To not look too closely at the consequences of its own action.

Metacognition is not overthinking. Metacognition is wisdom forming in real time. It is how growth happens. A culture that valued its metacognitive bodies would be a culture that learned from its own mistakes faster than ours does.

Kindness gets hidden. The body that keeps its heart open in a hardened world has been called weak, naive, soft, a doormat. The body learns to harden. To match the temperature of the room. To stop offering what it would have offered if the room had been able to receive it.

Kindness is not weakness. Kindness is courage. It is the radical refusal to let the conditions of the culture turn the body into something it never was. A culture that protected its kind bodies would be a culture worth living inside.

Curiosity gets hidden too. The body that asks too many questions, that does not accept the official answer, that keeps wondering, has been called difficult, disruptive, immature, naive. The body learns to stop asking. To accept the room as it is. To not look too closely at what does not make sense.

Curiosity is not naivety. Curiosity is intelligence in motion. It is the form a body takes when it is still alive to the world. A culture that protected its curious bodies would be a culture that did not have to keep repeating its mistakes.

The bodies the culture has tried to hide are the bodies the culture most needs. The sensitive ones. The reflective ones. The kind ones. The questioning ones. The slow ones. The ones who feel too much, think too much, care too much, ask too much. The body that does not fit easily into the productivity machine is often the body whose presence the next iteration of culture will be built around.

If you have spent years being told that some part of you was too much, too sensitive, too slow, too kind, too questioning, too anything at all, hear this. That part of you is not the problem. That part of you is information. It is information about what the culture is missing and what the culture, if it ever becomes well, will need.

A Note on Hope

I want to say something about hope before this chapter closes.

The numbers in the first part of this chapter are real. They are heavy. They are evidence of social poisoning at a scale that is hard to hold without becoming numb to it. The temptation, when we look at numbers like that, is to despair. The conclusion that despair offers is that nothing will change.

Despair is itself a stress response. Despair is what the nervous system produces when it has been held in chronic activation without rest for so long that it has stopped believing rest is possible. Despair gives us information about the system we are inside of. Despair does not give us truth about the future.

Cultures have changed. They are changing now. The dismantling of regulated cultures into dysregulated ones happened over centuries and is still happening. The opposite movement is also happening. People are reclaiming ceremonies. Communities are rebuilding mutual aid. Workplaces are experimenting with four-day weeks. Schools are introducing somatic literacy. Healthcare is slowly acknowledging trauma. Therapies are integrating ancestral practices. The change is not fast enough. Change rarely is. The change is happening.

You are part of the change. The fact that you have read this far in a book like this one means you are part of a population of bodies in the world right now doing the work of returning. Your body is one of the regulated bodies entering the field. Your healing is one of the contributions that makes the field begin to shift.

The numbers are real. The hope is also real. Both can be held.

If you have read this chapter and recognized yourself in the numbers, if you have been one of the bodies inside the burnout statistics, the anxiety statistics, the suicidal-ideation statistics, the hypertension statistics, the violence statistics, the loneliness statistics, if you have lost someone to any of those numbers, hear this. You were not weak. You were not failing. You were one body inside a culture producing those numbers at scale. The fact that you are still here, reading this sentence, is itself a form of survival that deserves to be honoured.

If you have read this chapter from a place where you have access to some of the levers of design, as a policymaker, a workplace leader, a healthcare administrator, a school principal, a community organizer, a parent shaping the conditions of a household, hear this. The choices you make about structure shape the nervous systems of everyone inside those structures. Build rest in. Build connection in. Build permission in. Build ceremony in where you can. Build it slowly. Build it consistently. The bodies inside your structures will respond, often faster than you would expect, to a field that begins to hold them. Your role is not small. The structures you tend are where the field gets shifted.

For both, the same truth. The conditions can be different. The evidence is everywhere. We are not the first people to try.

The conditions producing the numbers in this chapter are not all recent. Some of them are. Industrial work design, social media, twenty-four-hour news cycles, the modern texture of chronic activation. Other conditions are much older. They reach back through generations and centuries to wounds that have not been named or healed at the cultural level. The next chapter looks at cultural trauma. The longer history of what has shaped the bodies that are now living inside these numbers. Some of the medicine for stress loops at the cultural level requires going back to wounds older than anyone now living. That is the work the next chapter takes up.

Chapter Seven
Cultural Trauma
The Erasure of Love, Connection, and the Holistic Body

A few chapters back I used a metaphor for what happens to a wound the body cannot metabolize. I said that shame, when it is not addressed, behaves the way a cancer cell behaves. It replicates. It travels. It does not stay in the cell where it began.

I want to bring that metaphor back here, because this chapter is about the same disease at the next scale up. The body of a single person. The body of a family. The body of a whole culture. The body of the human family on this earth. The disease moves through all of them by the same mechanism. A wound that was not held, in a generation that could not hold it, replicates forward into the bodies that come after.

Picture this at the scale of a forest. The cancer cell behaves at the scale of one body. The forest is what happens when many bodies are connected underground, through roots that touch each other, through soil they share. A toxin that enters one tree's roots reaches other trees through the mycorrhizal network the forest grows in. The trees on the surface can still look like trees. Underneath, in the network that ties the whole forest together, the sickness travels root to root. This is what cultural trauma is. A wound at the scale of one body, when it cannot be metabolized in that body, enters the network the human family lives inside. The descendants of those who first suffered carry it. The descendants of those who first caused the suffering carry a different shape of it. The bystanders, the people who lived nearby and looked away, carry their own version. Every body connected to the network is affected. None of us is outside it.

This chapter is not a hierarchy of suffering. There is no version of this conversation that is helped by ranking whose people had it worse. The pattern I am describing has touched every continent. Every lineage now living. The shapes of the wounds are different. The mechanism of the wounding is one mechanism. The bodies of the descendants are carrying it forward whether they know they are or not.

One body of the human family. One forest. One network of roots. One healing the entire body is being asked to do.

What Cultural Trauma Actually Is

The phrase cultural trauma is doing a lot of work in the last twenty years. Different scholars have given it slightly different names. The sociologist Jeffrey Alexander writes that cultural trauma occurs when members of a group feel they have been subjected to a horrendous event that leaves indelible marks on their consciousness, changing their identity in fundamental ways. Maria Yellow Horse Brave Heart, working from inside Lakota experience, calls it historical trauma. Eduardo and Bonnie Duran call it the soul wound. Joy DeGruy calls it Post Traumatic Slave Syndrome. Resmaa Menakem names it in the racialized body. Rachel Yehuda has shown it in gene expression itself.

Different vocabularies. One thing. A wound a whole people carries. A wound that moves through time the way fire moves through grass.

If you have ever sat across from a person whose face you cannot read, whose nervous system goes flat when certain topics come up, whose family seems to have decided something long ago that no one has ever spoken aloud, you have been in the presence of cultural trauma. It does not announce itself. It rarely uses its name. It shows up in the way someone cannot trust. In the way someone cannot rest. In the way a body braces in a room and cannot say why.

It is the inheritance you did not consent to. The activation you did not earn. The bracing your body did before you were old enough to know what it was bracing for. Most of us are carrying some of it. Some of us are carrying more than one kind. None of us is outside this.

The Pattern Beneath the Patterns

Underneath every form of cultural trauma I am about to name in this chapter is one pattern. The systematic erasure of what kept people whole.

What kept people whole, across cultures and continents, looked surprisingly similar. The body was understood as part of the land. The person was understood as part of a kinship system that included the dead and the unborn. Healing was understood as a relational practice, not a private transaction with a credentialed expert. Time was understood in cycles. Worth was understood as belonging to a person by virtue of being a person, not by virtue of producing. Ceremony was understood as the thing that knit everything together. Love and connection were understood as the medicine that made survival possible in a hard world.

These understandings were everywhere. They were the Indigenous knowledge systems of Turtle Island. They were the pre-Christian cosmologies of Europe. They were the African traditional religions. They were the women's healing traditions across every culture. They were the practices of the Sami, the Māori, the Aboriginal Australian, the Hawaiian, the Yoruba, the Celtic, the Slavic, the Andean, the Mayan. The vocabularies differed. The pattern was holistic.

The colonial-modern project, beginning in roughly the late 1400s and accelerating across the next five centuries, set itself the task of dismantling this. Not by accident. By design. By policy. By military force. By the church. By the school. By the courtroom. By the medical institution. The dismantling went by different names in different places. Christianization. Civilization. Modernization. Development. Whatever it was called, the work was the same. Tear the people away from the body. Tear the body away from the land. Tear the family away from each other. Tear the woman away from her healing traditions. Tear the child away from the elder. Tear the spirit away from the everyday. Tear the present away from the ancestors and the future.

In its place came something new. The body as a thing separate from the soul, treatable by a stranger with a credential. The person as a unit of productivity. The child as a project to be molded by an institution. Time as a clock to be obeyed. Worth as something earned. Land as property. Water as commodity. Animal as resource. Love as transaction.

This was the implementation. Not abstract. Concrete. The witch trials that killed tens of thousands of European women and destroyed centuries of vernacular medicine. The papal bulls that authorized Christian rulers to claim the lands of non-Christian peoples. The residential schools that took Indigenous children from their families and beat the language out of their mouths. The mother and baby homes that took Irish babies from unmarried girls and let them die. The plantations that severed African families and sold the children. The Highland Clearances that drove Gaelic families off ancestral land to make room for sheep. The country marriages of the fur trade era that produced thousands of Indigenous wives and Métis children left at the post when European men sailed home to wives back in Europe. The Stolen Generations. The Sami Norwegianization. The Cultural Revolution. The reservation system.

Every one of these institutions did the same thing at the level of mechanism. Tear the relationships apart. Replace the holistic framework with a transactional one. Make the body small and afraid and dependent on the institution for the love it had once received from kin.

Cultural trauma is not just what was done. Cultural trauma is what was taken. The right to belong. The right to be touched.

The right to know your own language. The right to grieve in ceremony. The right to be held by your people. The right to love and be loved inside a frame older than capitalism.

Every specific cultural trauma in this chapter is one implementation of that larger erasure. Keep that in mind as we walk through them. The implementations are different. The pattern underneath is one pattern.

The Child Who Was Sent

Between roughly 1869 and 1948, more than one hundred thousand children were sent from Britain across the ocean to Canada by organizations like Barnardo's, Macpherson's, and the Catholic Emigration Society. Some were as young as three. Most were under ten. They came from orphanages and from families judged too poor to keep them. They were placed with strangers on farms across the country to provide labour in exchange for board. Today, more than one in ten Canadians is estimated to descend from one of these children, according to Veterans Affairs Canada and the British Home Children Advocacy and Research Association. The Canadian government issued a formal apology to British Home Children in 2017.

The Orphan Trains in the United States moved approximately two hundred and fifty thousand children west between 1854 and 1929. Australia accepted child migrants from Britain until 1967. The Kindertransport carried ten thousand Jewish children out of Nazi Europe in 1938 and 1939. The Spanish Civil War evacuated children to Mexico, the Soviet Union, and Britain. The Second World War scattered children across continents.

Sending children away was something whole cultures did when the conditions had become unbearable enough that even the bond between parent and child began to feel expendable in the calculation of survival. The conditions were not gentle. The

Highland Clearances. The Irish Great Hunger. The wars of religion and empire. The recurring plagues. The enclosure economies. The famines and pogroms and conscriptions and cholera and homelessness. Inside those conditions, ancestors made the impossible decision of letting a small child go.

The science of what that does to a body is now well established. The attachment research of John Bowlby in the mid-twentieth century. The wartime nursery work of Anna Freud and Dorothy Burlingham. René Spitz's institutional infant studies. They converge on one finding. Early separation from a primary caregiver, especially between roughly six months and four years of age, can have lasting developmental effects, particularly in the context of inadequate substitute care or broader deprivation, though outcomes vary and later caregiving conditions still matter. The child learns, at the deepest somatic level, that connection cannot be trusted. That safety is a story other people tell, not a state the body knows.

That child grew up. That child had children. That child raised those children with the only template for love their body had been given. The wound did not stop when the ship docked. The wound became the family's template for what closeness looks like, generation after generation. The descendants can still carry measurable traces of what came before, through relationships, biology, culture, prenatal conditions, and the environments families continue to live inside. The imprint travels by more than one road.

If you have ever wondered why your grandfather could not show emotion. Why your great-grandmother held everyone at arm's length. Why one side of your family kept everything to themselves and called it strength. There is often a child on a ship somewhere back in the lineage. There is often a hand letting go of a smaller hand at a port. The grief was never spoken. The grief moved into the body. The body passed it forward as the only language it knew.

What is lost at three can echo for decades. Sometimes it reaches into the next generation before anyone understands where the echo began.

What the Body Carries Forward

The science of how a wound moves through generations has accelerated dramatically in the last fifteen years.

Rachel Yehuda's team at Mount Sinai has been studying Holocaust survivors and their descendants for decades. Her 2015 study compared survivors and their adult children to control families. The survivors and the children showed measurably different patterns of methylation at FKBP5, a gene that helps regulate the body's stress response. FKBP5 is involved in regulating aspects of the stress response. The study did not establish one single route through which these differences travelled. Biology, prenatal conditions, parental stress physiology, family relationships, and shared environments can all complicate the picture. What the findings did suggest was that intergenerational trauma may have biological dimensions alongside relational, social, and cultural ones. The wound may reach forward through more than words.

The evidence for that reaching is still being gathered, patiently, one study at a time, and it is worth seeing what it does and does not yet show. Michael Meaney's work at McGill showed that rat pups who received less licking and grooming from their mothers grew up with different stress-gene expression than pups who received more. In these animal studies, differences in maternal care were associated with changes in gene expression in the offspring's brain. Human research has since found associations between adversity and epigenetic differences in stress-related systems, although human lives are vastly more complex and these pathways cannot be isolated experimentally in the same way. Frances Champagne at Columbia. Research on the Dutch Hunger

Winter has shown long-term health and epigenetic differences in people who were directly exposed to famine in utero. Researchers have also asked whether effects reach a third generation. The human evidence there is mixed, and one adult-grandchild study found no clear adverse transgenerational health effect in the outcomes it examined.

Mi'kmaq researcher Amy Bombay and colleagues have documented associations between family residential-school attendance and poorer mental-health outcomes in later generations, including depression and suicidal thoughts or attempts in some samples. The work supports intergenerational effects while also showing that those effects move through complex social, familial, and structural pathways.

What this means is what your body may already have been telling you. The activation you carry exists inside a story larger than a single moment. The patterns you cannot explain are not automatically personal failure. The chemistry of your nervous system may carry influences from conditions that began long before you arrived. Some through biology. Some through pregnancy and early development. Some through family relationships, culture, stress, poverty, violence, and the worlds our ancestors handed forward.

The wound may be in the body. So is the medicine. The imprint travels by more than one road, and so can healing.

Wounds Across the Earth

I want to walk briefly through the broader field now. Not as inventory. As recognition. Every people group is somewhere in what follows. No one is outside this story.

The transatlantic slave trade forcibly carried approximately twelve and a half million Africans across the Atlantic between roughly 1525 and 1866. The cultural rupture this produced is what

Joy DeGruy has named Post Traumatic Slave Syndrome. The afterlife of slavery, as the scholar Christina Sharpe has named it, is still unfolding through every institution Black people meet in the Americas. The apartheid system in South Africa. The continuing mass incarceration in the United States. The poverty and the policing that grew on top of the original rupture.

The Holocaust murdered six million Jewish people between 1933 and 1945, along with hundreds of thousands of Roma and Sinti, disabled people, gay men, and political prisoners. It did not arrive without preparation. It was preceded by centuries of pogroms across Europe. The Spanish expulsion of 1492. The Inquisition. Blood libel accusations across medieval Europe. The Armenian Genocide of 1915 to 1923 killed approximately one and a half million Armenians at the hands of the Ottoman Empire. The Ukrainian Holodomor of 1932 to 1933, Stalin's engineered famine, killed somewhere between three and a half million and seven million Ukrainians. The Cambodian genocide under the Khmer Rouge from 1975 to 1979 killed approximately one point seven to two million people. The Rwandan Genocide of 1994 killed approximately eight hundred thousand Tutsi and moderate Hutu in one hundred days. The Bosnian genocide at Srebrenica in 1995. Darfur. The Rohingya. The list does not end.

Indigenous peoples of Turtle Island lived through the largest demographic collapse in recorded history. Some scholarship has estimated catastrophic population losses approaching ninety percent in parts of the Americas after 1492, driven by epidemics, warfare, forced labour, and colonial disruption. Exact continental totals and timelines remain debated but one of the most catastrophic demographic collapses in recorded history.

The American boarding school system from 1819 to 1969. The Stolen Generations in Australia from 1910 to 1970. The dispossession of Māori in Aotearoa. The suppression of the Sami in Scandinavia. The overthrow of the Hawaiian kingdom in 1893. The forced relocations of Indigenous Siberian peoples under

Soviet rule. For First Nations and Métis women in what is now Canada, an intimate pattern of betrayal ran underneath the land theft. Thousands of country marriages in the fur trade era ended in abandonment when European men returned to wives back in Europe. The Métis Nation, born of these unions, carried forward a three-part wound across generations. Separation. Betrayal. The hidden secret of an identity many families kept buried for generations. The Sixties Scoop took an estimated twenty thousand Indigenous children from their families between roughly 1960 and the early 1980s. The 2019 MMIWG National Inquiry concluded the continuing violence against Indigenous women, girls, and Two-Spirit people in Canada constitutes genocide without modifier. The 2020 BC report In Plain Sight documented widespread anti-Indigenous racism in BC healthcare.

European peasants and the wounded lineages of Europe itself. The witch trials of roughly 1450 to 1750 executed between forty and sixty thousand people, the great majority women, and destroyed centuries of women's vernacular medicine and lay healing. The forced Christianization of pagan Europe across the first millennium destroyed dozens of Indigenous European cosmologies and severed European bodies from their pre-Christian ceremonies. The Highland Clearances. The Great Hunger in Ireland. The Thirty Years' War. The Black Death. Russian serfdom. The two World Wars. The Iron Curtain. Resmaa Menakem has written that white bodies traumatized white bodies for centuries before they encountered Black bodies in the Americas. The unhealed wound those bodies were carrying did not heal when they crossed the ocean. It found a new shape on new land.

Asia and the Pacific carry their own. The Cultural Revolution in China, 1966 to 1976. The Partition of India in 1947, with up to one million dead and fifteen million displaced. Japanese internment in the Second World War. The comfort women, sexually enslaved by the Japanese imperial military across Asia.

The wars in Vietnam, Laos, and Cambodia, and their continuing afterlives in birth defects and unexploded ordnance. The Bengal Famine of 1943.

Latin America. The Guatemalan genocide of the Maya from 1981 to 1983. The Argentine Dirty War. The killings in Chile, Brazil, El Salvador, Colombia. The continuing dispossession of Indigenous land in the Amazon. The bodies of the disappeared whose families still do not know where they are buried.

This list is not complete. No list could be complete.

Every continent carries something. Every people group carries something. Look back far enough into any lineage and you will find a generation that lost something it was never given the conditions to grieve. That generation is somewhere in your body too.

Savage Primitive Gaslighting

Underneath every act of large-scale colonial violence was a piece of cultural work that had to be done first. The people doing the violence had to be conditioned to see the people receiving it as something less than fully human. So did the publics watching. Without that conditioning, the violence would not have been sustainable.

The conditioning had a vocabulary. Savage. Primitive. Barbarian. Heathen. Uncivilized. Pagan. Native, said in a certain tone. The words were carefully constructed to do specific work. They placed Indigenous peoples, African peoples, and Asian peoples on a developmental ladder beneath European peoples. They suggested the colonized were closer to animals than the colonizers were. They suggested the colonized were children in adult bodies, requiring civilizing the way children require discipline. They allowed violence to be framed as instruction. Theft as improvement. Murder as the unfortunate necessity of progress. I have come to call this whole apparatus savage primitive gaslighting, because what it was doing to entire populations was structurally identical to what an abuser does inside an intimate relationship. Make the victim doubt their own reality, their own worth, and their own perceptions, so that the violence becomes easier to enact and harder to name.

This vocabulary was theological, legal, and scientific. Every word of it was deliberate. In 1452, 1455, and 1493, three papal bulls (Dum Diversas, Romanus Pontifex, and Inter Caetera) authorized Christian rulers to capture, vanquish, and subdue non-Christian peoples and claim their lands. The bulls became known as the Doctrine of Discovery. They were the theological framework that gave Christian colonizers, in their own minds, the divine right to claim any land where the people had not yet been Christianized. The Doctrine was incorporated into United States law in the 1823 Supreme Court case Johnson versus M'Intosh and remains a precedent that has never been overturned. The Catholic Church formally repudiated the Doctrine of Discovery in March 2023, though it has not rescinded the original bulls.

In 1877 the American anthropologist Lewis Henry Morgan published Ancient Society. He proposed a three-stage scheme of human cultural evolution. Savagery. Barbarism. Civilization. European peoples, in his model, had reached civilization. Indigenous peoples were stuck at earlier stages. Morgan's scheme became the scaffolding of colonial anthropology for the next century. It shaped policy. It shaped curriculum. It shaped the everyday speech of ordinary settlers.

Anthropology as a discipline has been doing the long work of grappling with this. Decades of writing, much of it now by Indigenous anthropologists, has been dismantling the apparatus from within. The discipline that helped build the savage-primitive scaffolding is also part of how it now gets undone. Both are true.

What the vocabulary did is now measurable. In 2006 the social neuroscientists Lasana Harris and Susan Fiske published a study in Psychological Science in which they put subjects in functional MRI scanners and showed them images of various people, including members of groups commonly subjected to dehumanizing language. The medial prefrontal cortex, or mPFC, the region of the brain that activates when we recognize another person as a person with an inner life, did not activate for those images the way it activated for in-group members. The dehumanizing language had been working inside the brains of the viewers. Their nervous systems were responding to certain bodies as though those bodies were not fully other minds.

Frantz Fanon, a psychiatrist from Martinique who worked in colonial Algeria, wrote about this from the inside. Colonization, he said, reduces the colonized to the state of an animal in the colonizer's vocabulary, and the colonized then absorbs that designation into his own body. Aimé Césaire, also from Martinique, named in his 1950 Discourse on Colonialism that colonization does not only damage the colonized. It decivilizes the colonizer. The cruelty performed corrodes the moral architecture of the one performing it. Edward Said, working in literary studies in the 1970s, traced the same mechanism in how the Western imagination produced what he called Orientalism. A fictional East. Sensual, irrational, dangerous, requiring European management. The fiction served the policy. The policy served the fiction.

Here is what Harris and Fiske showed in a follow-up study that gives the body real hope. When subjects in their scanner were asked to imagine the inner life of the dehumanized person in front of them, even something as simple as guessing what food the person might prefer, the medial prefrontal cortex came back online. The brain that had stopped recognizing the other started recognizing them again. Within minutes. By a small individuating act of imagination.

Dehumanizing language builds nervous systems that can carry out and tolerate harm. The same nervous systems, when offered different conditions, remember how to see again. The remembering is fast at the level of the moment. The remembering of an entire culture is slower. Both are possible. Both are what the medicine is.

The Same Collective Cancer in Different Institutions

I want to do one piece of medicine on the page right now. I want to name a connection that the Catholic Church and its institutions have spent decades not wanting anyone to name.

In 2012 a local historian named Catherine Corless began to research the mother and baby home that had operated in the small town of Tuam, in the west of Ireland, from 1925 to 1961. The home was run by an order of Catholic nuns called the Sisters of Bon Secours. It housed unmarried Irish women who had become pregnant and the children they bore. The Irish Catholic state, working in close partnership with the Catholic Church, treated these women and their children as a moral problem to be hidden.

Corless tracked down death certificates for seven hundred and ninety-six children who had died at the Tuam home over thirty-six years of operation. She could find a burial record for only one of them. After years of further research, she concluded that the remains of the others had been placed in a decommissioned sewage tank on the grounds of the home. In 2017 forensic investigation confirmed the presence of significant quantities of children's remains. The full excavation began in July 2025. The Irish government's subsequent inquiry into eighteen mother and baby homes found that more than nine thousand children died across the Irish system between 1922 and 1998.

In May 2021, on the other side of the Atlantic, the Tk'emlúps te Secwépemc First Nation in British Columbia announced the discovery of approximately two hundred and fifteen suspected unmarked graves, identified by ground-penetrating radar at the site of the former Kamloops Indian Residential School. The school had operated from 1890 to 1969 under the Missionary Oblates of Mary Immaculate. Within weeks, the Cowessess First Nation in Saskatchewan announced seven hundred and fifty-one probable unmarked graves at the former Marieval Indian Residential School, also operated by the Missionary Oblates. Similar findings followed at other former residential school sites across Canada. Justice Murray Sinclair, who chaired the Truth and Reconciliation Commission, has estimated that more than six thousand Indigenous children died inside the system over its more than one hundred years of operation.

Now hold both facts together. The same crippling sickness that placed seven hundred and ninety-six Irish babies into a sewage tank in Tuam was the same crippling sickness that placed Indigenous children into unmarked graves at Kamloops and Marieval and so many other residential schools across this land. Not by coincidence. By the same institution. The same theological framework. Sometimes the same religious orders. Sometimes the same individual clergy moving between postings. The framework treated certain mothers as moral failures. Certain children as so contaminated by their origins that the institution's job was to break the connection between them and the people they came from. Certain bodies as bodies that did not fully count, because their souls were the wrong kind of soul, or their culture was the wrong kind of culture, or their birth was the wrong kind of birth. The same theology of disposable children. Continent after continent. Decade after decade.

The collective cancer does not pick countries. The collective cancer picks systems. Wherever the same theology of disposable bodies operates, the same outcome is produced. Mass child graves. Hidden for a generation. Found by the patient work of one or two people who refused to look away.

In July 2022 Pope Francis came to Canada and used the word genocide for what the residential schools had done. In March 2023 the Vatican issued a statement repudiating the Doctrine of Discovery. These are openings in a centuries-old wall. They matter. They are not enough. The bodies of the children are still in the ground. The descendants of those children are still alive, still carrying what was put into their lineage. The repair, if there is going to be repair, is going to take longer than the harm did. Len Pierre, the Coast Salish educator from Katzie First Nation who is writing the foreword to this book, calls this the tyranny of efficiency. The way institutions want to do reconciliation fast. Check the box. Move on. The body of the descendant does not heal on the timeline the institution would prefer. The body heals on the timeline of the body.

The Vectors of Violence

There are two mechanisms by which the collective cancer has spread so reliably through the underground network, across history and across continents, that this chapter would be incomplete without naming them directly.

Sexual violence. Physical violence.

Wherever unaccountable power has met vulnerable bodies, these two forms of violence have been the most efficient vectors by which the disease has traveled from one body to the next and from one generation to the next. The pattern is not specific to any one institution. It arises wherever the conditions are met, in any culture. Power that cannot be held to account. Bodies that cannot speak. Silence enforced by the same institution that committed or tolerated the violation.

Sexual violence first. In the mother and baby homes of mid-century Ireland, many of the women housed there were pregnant from sexual violence the institutions then concealed. Incest. Rape by employers. In some documented cases, sexual abuse by clergy. In the residential school system across Turtle Island, sexual abuse of children was systematic across many sites, documented in the testimonies of thousands of survivors, in court records, and in the findings of the Truth and Reconciliation Commission. In the plantation systems of the Americas, sexual violence against enslaved African women was routine and deliberately deployed as a tool of subjugation and forced reproduction. In wartime across the last century, rape has been used as a weapon across continents. The comfort women enslaved by the Japanese imperial military. The rape camps of the Bosnian war. The 1947 Partition of India. The Rwandan genocide. The ongoing weaponization of sexual violence in conflicts now.

Inside families across every culture, incest and the sexual abuse of children has been one of the most silenced and one of the most efficient transmitters of trauma through lineages. The body of a child who has been violated, when the violation cannot be metabolized and cannot be witnessed, often grows up either repeating the patterns of dissociation that made survival possible or, in some cases, repeating the violation itself in the next generation. The shame around it keeps it unspoken. The silence around it protects the conditions for the next round of violations to occur.

Physical violence carries the same way. The beatings administered in residential schools, in industrial schools, in workhouses, in orphanages. The corporal punishment that was the cultural norm inside many homes across many generations. The domestic violence that has shaped countless family lines. The violence of war reaching into the bodies of returning soldiers and from there into their children and grandchildren. The violence of policing inside communities that have been systematically overpoliced. The torture documented in conflicts on every continent. The lateral violence that arises inside oppressed communities when the wound of the original harm cannot find another outlet and turns sideways onto the people closest. Bodies that have been beaten, that have been threatened, that have been forced to live inside conditions of physical danger, carry the imprint into their nervous systems. The imprint shapes how those bodies parent. How they partner. How they move through rooms. The wound replicates through behaviour the body cannot quite explain to itself.

Both vectors cut across every category. Religious institutions have housed them. Secular institutions have housed them. Progressive families have housed them. Traditional families have housed them. The military has housed them. Universities have housed them. Hospitals have housed them. Sports organizations. The entertainment industry. The political system. The wellness industry itself. Anywhere in the human social fabric where unaccountable power has met vulnerable bodies in silence, the same patterns have shown up.

Naming these vectors is part of the medicine. The bodies of survivors have been carrying them alone for too long. The cultures around them have been agreeing to look the other way. The agreement is breaking now. The Me Too movement, which began in 2006 with Tarana Burke's grassroots work and accelerated publicly in 2017, has cracked open the cultural silence around sexual violence at a scale previous generations could not imagine. The reckonings inside religious bodies. The reckonings inside the residential school system. The reckonings inside the entertainment and political worlds. The growing public recognition that intimate partner violence and child abuse are public health emergencies, not private matters. The slow naming of state and military violence inside communities that have lived under it for generations. Each of these is one piece of the larger naming the human family is finally beginning to do.

The work is not finished. The disease has been replicating through these vectors for as long as human institutions have existed. The work now is to name the violence wherever it shows up, regardless of the institution housing it. Regardless of the power of the institution housing it. Regardless of who falls when the truth arrives. The disposability of certain bodies has been the collective cancer. The protection of those who harm them has been one of the most reliable ways the collective cancer has continued to replicate through the forest's underground. Both have to be addressed if the network is to clear.

Wherever unaccountable power meets vulnerable bodies in silence, the collective cancer spreads. The medicine is accountability without exception, even when accountability costs those in power their power.

What Repair Looks Like

This chapter cannot end with the wound. The medicine has to come into the room before we leave, or the chapter itself would be doing what unhealed cultural trauma does. Leaving the body inside the activation without showing where the discharge is.

The repair, when you look at what is happening across the human family right now, is fundamentally the same thing in every language. The reclamation of love and connection and the practices for holism that the larger erasure tried to dismantle. What was taken is being taken back, slowly, by hands all over the earth. Len Pierre calls this an Indigenous renaissance. He sees it in the matriarchs taking up land back. In Indigenous midwives reclaiming birth. In Indigenous politicians, entrepreneurs, nurses, physicians, teachers, and cultural leaders. In people who grew up without access to their language or ceremony, waking up to their own lineages later in life.

Truth and reconciliation processes have begun in many places. South Africa's Commission under Archbishop Desmond Tutu from 1996 to 2003. Canada's Commission from 2008 to 2015 with its ninety-four Calls to Action. The Norwegian Truth and Reconciliation Commission for the Sami, Kven, and Forest Finn peoples, which delivered its final report in 2023. Australia's Bringing Them Home report of 1997 and the National Apology of 2008. Rwanda's Gacaca courts. The processes are imperfect. They do not return the dead. They do create, where they have been allowed to function, a public record. A naming. A moment in which the cultural body acknowledges what was done and begins, slowly, to repair the relational fabric that the harm tore.

Land back is happening in pieces. The reclamation of Gwaii Haanas by the Haida Nation. The growing Land Back movement across Turtle Island. Māori land settlements in Aotearoa. The Sami pasture victories in Scandinavia. The body of an Indigenous person is regulated by being on the land their lineage knows. The return of land is the return of medicine.

Language revitalization is the work of bringing back what colonial education tried to extinguish. Hawaiian immersion schools. Māori language nests. Welsh, Irish, and Scottish Gaelic revival in the British Isles. The Indigenous Languages Act in Canada. The reclamation of Michif among Métis communities. The strengthening of Sami across Norway, Sweden, Finland, and Russia. The return of Mohawk, Cree, Anishinaabemowin, Halq'eméylem, Nuu-chahnulth, and dozens of other Indigenous languages on this continent. When a child can speak the language her ancestors spoke, something in her nervous system that had been waiting for the recognition begins to settle.

Ceremony and land-based healing. The reclamation of practices colonial governments criminalized for the better part of a century. Sweat lodges. Sun dances. Smudging. Fasting camps. The research on land-based healing for Indigenous youth is increasingly clear. The trauma symptoms decrease. The cultural pride increases. The nervous systems settle in ways no pharmaceutical has been able to produce. The medicine was always there. What was missing was permission and safety to practice it.

Reclamation in the bodies of European descendants matters here too. Sharon Blackie's work helping European descendants rediscover the older animist traditions of their own lineages. Martin Shaw's mythological work in England. The Slavic, Celtic, Norse, Germanic, Baltic, and Finno-Ugric reclamation movements across Europe. This work is the recovery of what was lost in their own continent, so the wound the colonizing peoples carried can stop replicating in the only language it knew.

Jewish trauma healing. Rabbi Tirzah Firestone in Wounds Into Wisdom has documented the work of Jewish descendants in metabolizing what was passed forward. The Hebrew concept of Tikkun Olam, repair of the world, frames this work in a tradition that is thousands of years old. African diasporic reclamation. The return of Ifa, Vodou, Santeria, and Candomblé to descendants who were severed from them. The work of bell hooks on love as the foundation of liberation. The slow return of ancestral foodways, music, dance, and spiritual practice in Black communities across the Americas, the Caribbean, and Europe.

Somatic abolitionism. Resmaa Menakem's framework of healing racialized trauma in the body. The slow practice of building what he calls a settled body. Decolonizing therapy itself. Jennifer Mullan's work. The recognition that western individualist therapy, on its own, is not adequate for cultural trauma. The integration of ancestral practices, somatic work, and political analysis into the clinical encounter.

Underneath all of it, the practice Len Pierre keeps returning his clients and colleagues to. Stillness. He writes that when we practice stillness we gain time, space, meaning, mindfulness, connection, and relaxation. When you are still, you can absorb more teachings. Go sit with the elders. Visit the youth. Be by the water. Touch the land. Be present with it. You might find connection, healing, happiness, and stillness.

We have everything we need for the journey ahead. The medicine is the reclamation of love and connection and the practices for holism. It is everywhere. It is winning in many more places than the news will tell you.

A Note on Responsibility

Before this chapter closes, one thing about responsibility, because I will be addressing it more fully in a later chapter and I do not want anyone to leave this one with a misunderstanding.

Naming cultural trauma is not the same as removing individual responsibility. Knowing you carry an inherited wound does not give you permission to enact that wound on the people around you. Knowing your ancestors were inside conditions that produced harm does not relieve you of the work of not passing that harm forward to the next generation. The conditions explain. The conditions do not excuse.

Every body alive today has both an inheritance and a choice. The inheritance is real. It shapes the field a body wakes up inside every morning. The inheritance is not destiny. What a body does with what it has inherited is the work of a single life. That work has been named, by every healing tradition in human history, as central to the meaning of being alive. The chapters to come will return to that work in detail. This chapter has been about the soil that the work is done inside of. The next chapters will be about the work itself.

If you have read this chapter and recognized your people in the bodies of the wounded, if your lineage was on the receiving end of any of the cultural traumas named here, hear this. You are not crazy. The activation you carry is not personal pathology. It is the accurate inheritance of what your people lived through. The work is to meet that activation with the medicine your lineage knew, and the medicine your lineage is now relearning, and the medicine the wider human family is finally beginning to gather. You are not alone in this field. You never were.

If you have read this chapter and recognized your lineage on the side of those whose ancestors caused harm, if you descend from settlers, from enslavers, from colonial officials, from perpetrators of any of these patterns, hear this also. You are not the villain alone. You did not personally do what your ancestors did. The wound you carry is also real, even if it has been less visible to you because the dominant culture has worked hard to keep it invisible. The work, for you, is to look at it. To grieve it. To recognize that the wound your ancestors inflicted is also a wound your ancestors carried, and that the wound your ancestors carried came from older wounds you have never been taught to see. The work is to break the inheritance pattern from inside the lineage. That is the work no one outside the lineage can do for you.

For both. The same truth. The collective cancer is one cancer. The forest is one forest. The body of the human family is one body. The medicine is one medicine, taken up in many languages, by many peoples, with different specific practices, in different specific places. We are inside one healing. The healing is asking each of us to do our specific piece of it where we are standing.

The collective cancer this chapter has named has been held in place, generation after generation, by something the next chapter is going to examine. The silence. The agreement, in nearly every wounded body and nearly every complicit body, not to talk about what happened. The silence is not the absence of speech. The silence is an active mechanism of the disease. It is what lets the toxin keep flowing through the underground network without anyone naming it. The next chapter looks at what the silence has been doing inside us, why it has been so hard to break, and what begins to shift when the speech finally arrives.

Chapter Eight
The Silence We Have All Been Keeping
Collective Fear, Collective Shame, and the Courage to Speak

The previous chapter ended with a bridge to a question this chapter has to take seriously. How has the collective cancer we have just spent so many pages naming been held in place for so long, across so many generations, in so many bodies, in so many places? The conditions were always there. The wounds were always there. The descendants were always there carrying them. Why did it take this long for any of it to be spoken?

The answer is one mechanism. Silence.

Silence is the active force that keeps unmetabolized wounds in place inside a body, a family, an institution, and a culture. The silence is not the absence of speech. The silence is the presence of a hush. An agreement, often wordless, that certain things will not be named. A certainty, in the bones of the people inside the agreement, that naming the thing will cost more than continuing to carry it.

This chapter is about that agreement. Where it comes from. What it has been doing inside us. Why it has been so hard to break. And what begins to shift when the speech finally arrives.

The wound that cannot be spoken cannot be healed. The wound that is spoken begins, slowly, to become something the body can put down.

The Fear That Has No Name

Underneath every silence in this chapter is one fear. The fear is old. The fear is collective. The fear lives in the body before it has any words for itself. I want to name it before we go any further, because the rest of the chapter is going to keep returning to it.

It is the primal, bone-deep terror of being called crazy.

Ask yourself honestly. When you have felt the most clearly that something was wrong with the world around you, what stopped you from saying so?

For most people, the answer is some version of the same fear. The fear of being dismissed. Of being labeled. Of being seen as unstable, unreliable, too much, unwell. The fear that if you name what you truly see and feel, the people around you will look at you in a particular way, and that look will cost you something you cannot afford to lose. Your job. Your relationships. Your standing. Your sense of belonging. Your credibility in rooms you depend on.

This fear is not irrational. It is not weakness. It is the accumulated inheritance of centuries of what has happened to people who speak uncomfortable truths, who feel too much, who refuse to perform wellness in the presence of genuine harm.

The fear is rational because the consequences have been real. Those consequences live in our nervous systems, passed forward through generations, as surely as eye colour or bone structure. The forest carries this fear in its underground. Every tree connected to the network has absorbed some version of it. Most of us inherited it before we were old enough to have any choice in the matter.

The fear of being called crazy is the deepest anchor of every silence this chapter is about. Naming it is the first move out from underneath it.

What Silence Actually Is

Silence in the body is something the body holds, the way a muscle holds tension. It costs energy. It uses resources. It shapes posture, breath, sleep, digestion, immune response, hormonal regulation, and the way a person walks into a room.

If you have ever sat with someone whose throat tightens when certain topics come up, whose voice drops to a whisper, whose eyes drift to the side when they begin a sentence they then do not finish, you have watched silence happen inside a body. The silence is doing work. The silence is protecting something. The silence is also exhausting the body that is keeping it.

Most of us are keeping more silences than we know.

There is the silence we keep about what happened to us. The silence we keep about what was done in our family. The silence we keep about what we did or did not do. The silence we keep about what we want, what we need, what we feel, what we know about ourselves that we are afraid would change everything if we said it out loud.

There is the silence we keep on behalf of someone else. The silence we agreed to before we were old enough to consent to agreeing. The silence about a parent's drinking. The silence about a sibling's mental illness. The silence about money. The silence about who slept where. The silence about why a certain photograph is no longer on the wall.

There is the silence we keep professionally. The thing we have noticed at work and have not raised. The colleague we know is struggling and we have not asked. The pattern we have seen repeating and have not named. The institutional thing that everyone in the building knows and no one says.

There is the silence whole cultures keep. The silence about the residential schools, until the unmarked graves arrived. The silence about the mother and baby homes, until Catherine Corless. The silence about the missing women, until the inquiry. The silence about what one's own ancestors did, until someone finally turns toward it.

All of these silences are doing the same kind of work. Holding something at bay. Protecting something. Performing membership in a group that has agreed not to speak. Buying safety, real or imagined, at the price of the body that is doing the holding.

Seven Moments That Taught the World to Stay Silent

To understand why the fear is so deep, we have to look at what created it. These are events and systems whose tremors still move through the bodies of their descendants today.

The witch trials of Europe and colonial America, from roughly the fourteenth to seventeenth centuries. Women who healed, who spoke, who saw clearly, who did not conform to the roles assigned to them, were labeled mad, demonic, or dangerous. Tens of thousands were executed. The message embedded into the collective nervous system of women across cultures was precise. To see too clearly, to speak too freely, to inhabit your power fully, is to risk your life. That imprint does not disappear in a few generations. It is still here.

The institutionalization era of the nineteenth and early twentieth centuries. Asylums across the Western world filled with people whose primary crime was nonconformity. Women who sought divorce. People who experienced grief or trauma. Those who refused to obey. Indigenous peoples who resisted assimilation. Queer people who existed visibly. The label of madness was used as a tool of social control with devastating efficiency. To be declared insane was to lose all legal rights, all bodily autonomy, all credibility. The fear of the asylum shaped entire generations.

The pathologization of political dissent in the Soviet Union across the twentieth century. The Soviet government formally used psychiatric diagnosis as a weapon against those who disagreed with the state. Citizens who protested, who wrote critically, who organized, were diagnosed with sluggish schizophrenia, a condition that conveniently only seemed to afflict people who threatened power. This was policy. It carried signatures. It demonstrated, with clinical precision, that mental health systems can be weaponized to silence truth-tellers, and that the label of mental illness can be deployed to destroy the credibility of anyone who speaks inconvenient things.

The residential school systems across Canada, Australia, and the United States. Indigenous children were removed from their families, forbidden their languages, their ceremonies, their ways of knowing. Those who resisted were punished. Those who grieved openly were disciplined. An entire relationship to land, to community, to the body, to healing, was systematically severed and replaced with shame. The nervous system responses of the survivors, and of their children, and of their children's children, carry the imprint of that forced silence. Speaking about it, for many families, still feels like stepping back into danger. The previous chapter walked through this wound in detail. The point here is the silencing.

The silencing of sexual violence survivors throughout recorded history. Women, children, and others who named sexual violence were historically, and often still are, disbelieved, blamed, and punished for speaking. The social consequence of being labeled hysterical, vindictive, or mentally unstable for naming abuse kept generations of survivors silent. The pain did not disappear because it was unspoken. It went inward. It became anxiety, depression, dissociation, and the particular exhaustion of a person who has been carrying something too heavy for too long, alone.

The stigmatization of mental health treatment itself, across the twentieth century to the present. In many families and communities, seeking help for emotional or psychological distress has been, and remains, a source of profound shame. The person who goes to therapy is weak. The person who takes medication is broken. The person who admits they are struggling is unreliable. This stigma is not accidental. It developed in cultures that equated emotional suppression with strength and vulnerability with failure. The result is that millions of people carry pain they cannot name, in a silence they have been taught to call dignity.

The everyday social punishment of emotional truth-telling. You do not need a historical event to learn that speaking your truth has consequences. Every person who was told they were too sensitive, too dramatic, too intense, too angry, too sad, who was met with eye rolls or dismissal or punishment for expressing what was real, learned the lesson. The accumulated weight of those small silencings across a lifetime produces a nervous system that has learned, at the deepest level, that the full truth is not safe to speak.

These seven forces did not stay in the past. They live in the body. In the hesitation before speaking. In the automatic self-censorship. In the quick scan of the room before saying something true. In the voice that drops to a whisper when naming what is real. In the shame that rises when you feel too much. *That is not your weakness. That is your inheritance.*

What the Silence Costs

There is now a substantial research literature on what unspoken wounds do inside a body. James Pennebaker, a social psychologist at the University of Texas, has been studying this for more than thirty years. His expressive writing protocols, in which people are asked to write about a traumatic event for fifteen to twenty minutes a day across several days, have produced measurable improvements in immune function, blood pressure, sleep quality, depression scores, and the number of doctor visits the participants make in the following year. The intervention is small. The shift in the body is real.

Bessel van der Kolk's work in The Body Keeps the Score documents what happens when traumatic experience cannot be put into language. The traumatic memory remains stored in non-verbal regions of the brain, in the body itself, in the muscles and the breath and the autonomic nervous system. It surfaces as flashback, as numbness, as somatic symptom, as relational pattern the person cannot account for. The body has been speaking the whole time. The mind has been unable to hear what the body has been saying because the language has been forbidden.

There is also a literature on alexithymia, the inability to name one's own emotions, coined as a term by psychiatrist Peter Sifneos in 1972. Research in this tradition, extended by writers like Gabor Maté in his book When the Body Says No, has connected the inability to name internal emotional states with higher rates of cardiovascular disease, autoimmune conditions, chronic pain, and addictive behaviour. The body that cannot find words for its experience finds other languages. Pain. Inflammation. Compulsion. Exhaustion. The silence in the language becomes a noise in the tissue.

This is the felt experience many of us know in ourselves. The tightness in the throat that never quite leaves. The headache that arrives on Sunday afternoon. The shoulder that holds the weight of every relationship we did not name. The stomach that knows what we will not let our mouth say. The body is keeping the silence with us, and the body is also paying the price for keeping it.

Silence is not free. The body always pays.

Why We Stay Silent

The silence is not a character flaw. It was learned. Often it was taught explicitly. Sometimes it was absorbed through the field of a family that had its own silences. Always there is a reason the silence felt safer than the speech.

The first reason is protection. A child who lives in a household with a volatile parent learns very early what topics produce more violence and what topics produce less. The child's nervous system makes a deal with the conditions it has. We will not talk about that. We will not name that. We will keep ourselves small around that subject so we do not draw the heat. This is not pathology. It is a survival strategy that worked at the time it was needed.

The second reason is loyalty. Families have systems. Families have rules about which stories belong to which person and which stories no one is allowed to tell. The unspoken agreement is the price of belonging. To break the silence is, in the family's logic, to break the family. Many people would rather carry the weight of an unspoken wound for the rest of their lives than risk the loss of belonging. The body knows this. The body chooses connection over truth, every time, when the two appear to be opposed.

The third reason is shame. The shame mechanism described in earlier chapters of this book is the engine of much of the silence we keep. We do not speak about what happened because we have absorbed the cultural message that what happened was somehow our fault. That speaking would expose us. That if people knew, they would withdraw the love we have been working so hard to earn. The shame replicates itself by keeping itself unspoken.

The fourth reason is the cost of not being believed. If you have ever told a true thing about your life to someone whose face went blank, whose response was a deflection or a defence, whose body language said this is too much for me to hold, you know the cost of speaking into a witness who cannot receive. Many of us tried once, were not received well, and put the words back inside where the body had been holding them. The body kept them safer than the room did.

The fifth reason is the institutional context. When the wound was caused by the institution, the institution often has more legal and reputational resources than the person who was wounded. Speaking up costs jobs. Speaking up costs custody. Speaking up costs reputation. Speaking up sometimes costs lives. The silence in these conditions is the rational response of a body inside a power structure built to make speech expensive.

Knowing why the silence exists is the beginning of being able to choose differently. The silence was a survival strategy. Survival strategies can be honoured for what they did. They can also, with the right conditions, be laid down.

Traum-our Speaks

Even when the mouth is closed, the armour is not. Traum-our, the protective shell I named in Chapter Four, the structure the body builds around what could not be metabolized, is always communicating. When the mouth has been forbidden, when the witness has not arrived, when the silence has been holding for so long that the speaker has forgotten the language, traum-our keeps speaking. It speaks through every channel it has. Pulse. Breath. Muscle tension. Sleep. Digestion. Dreams. The relational patterns we keep repeating without knowing why. The choices we make at three in the morning that we cannot explain to ourselves in the daylight.

This is the language I want to give back to you in this chapter. Traum-our-speech. The voice the armour uses when the voice of the person has been taken. Learning to listen to traum-our-speech is one of the most important reclamations available to anyone who has ever been silenced inside their own life.

Stephen Porges' polyvagal theory describes part of the mechanism. The autonomic nervous system continuously broadcasts the state of our internal world through subtle signals. The tone of voice. The micro-expressions of the face. The angle of the shoulders. The depth of the breath. Other nervous systems are reading these signals. Our own nervous system is reading itself. The information is moving whether we are aware of it or not. Traum-our is using every one of those channels to say what the mouth has been instructed not to say.

This is why family secrets do not really stay secret. The children growing up inside a family that does not speak about the alcoholic grandfather can feel the shape of his absence in the wallpaper. The children growing up inside the family that does not speak about the miscarriage can feel the grief their mother is holding in her body even when she smiles. The children growing up inside the family that does not speak about what happened on the reservation can feel the weight in the kitchen even before they know what a reservation is. Traum-our broadcasts. The children read the broadcast. They absorb the broadcast into the structure of their own developing nervous systems. The silence at the dinner table becomes the silence in their own throats one generation later.

Mark Wolynn's work in It Didn't Start With You documents how the unspoken griefs of one generation become the unaccountable symptoms of the next. People come into his office with phobias whose specifics match deaths in their grandparents' generation. With chronic illnesses whose patterns map onto traumas they never personally experienced. With anxieties that turn out, on careful inquiry, to be inherited from a family member who was never named. What he is documenting is traum-our-speech across generations. The armour of one body, unable to put down its load, transmitted the load forward through behaviour, attention, breath, and the small daily transactions of family life. The descendant's body is hearing traum-our-speech the ancestor never knew they were broadcasting.

Rachel Yehuda's epigenetic work, which we touched in the previous chapter, gives us part of the molecular mechanism. The methylation patterns at FKBP5 and other stress-related genes in the children of survivors are the literal molecular signature of traum-our that the previous generation could not put into language. The wound moves through chemistry because the wound was never given a voice. The body of the descendant is reading the chemical letter the ancestor was unable to write.

If you have ever wondered why your own body does things you cannot explain, why you flinch at things that did not happen to you, why you grieve at moments that have no occasion, why you brace for dangers that have never visited your particular life, the answer may be that you are reading the traum-our-speech of someone in your lineage who could not put down what they were carrying. Their armour spoke into yours before you had words for either.

Whatever is not spoken becomes traum-our-speech. The armour is the voice the wound finds when no other voice is available to it. Learning to read traum-our-speech is the beginning of letting the armour, at last, put its message down.

The Children Who Are Responding Most Clearly

There is a particular cruelty in what is happening to children and young people right now that we must name directly.

The children and youth who are being diagnosed in the highest numbers, who are being medicated at rates that would have been unthinkable a generation ago, are not the most disordered generation in human history. They are the most honest.

They are coming into bodies that carry generations of unprocessed ancestral trauma. They are being born into environments saturated with chemical, digital, social, and relational toxins that their nervous systems were not designed to metabolize. They are responding, clearly and loudly, to conditions that are genuinely harmful. The response of the systems around them is to treat the response as the problem.

Think of the plant. A plant growing in contaminated soil, deprived of adequate light, saturated with chemical runoff, begins to wilt. Its leaves yellow. Its growth becomes stunted and distorted. We do not look at that plant and say the plant is disordered. We look at the soil. We ask what has been done to the environment. We understand that the plant is doing exactly what a plant does when its conditions are wrong.

We do not extend this logic to children.

Instead, we look at the wilting and we give it a name from the DSM. We prescribe something to make the leaves look greener while the soil remains toxic. We send the child back into the same environment and wonder why the medication is not enough. We tell the child, in effect, that the problem is inside them. That their roots are defective. That their growth pattern is a disorder.

This is the gaslighting of entire generations. The children know it, even when they do not have words for it. The highly attuned child, the one who feels everything, who cannot perform wellness in an unwell environment, who cries or rages or shuts down in response to genuine harm, is often the most accurate diagnostician in the room. They are naming, with their bodies, what the adults around them have learned to normalize.

The forest, when it is sick, sends its earliest warnings up through the saplings. The young trees, whose roots are still tender, register the toxin in the soil before the older trees can. The wise forest watches the saplings closely. The wise forest understands that what the saplings are showing is information about the condition of the network, not pathology in the saplings.

The pathologization of these children is not a medical failure. It is a moral one.

The Moment Speech Arrives

Something extraordinary happens in a body the first time a long-held wound is finally spoken. The mouth opens around a word it has been avoiding for years. The breath catches. The tears arrive before the next sentence does. The body, which has been bracing for catastrophe, finds that the catastrophe is not happening. The room is still there. The witness is still there. The walls did not fall down.

Researchers who study the moment of disclosure have described it as a re-entry. The thing that was held outside the relational field becomes, in the speaking, part of the field. The wound that was carried alone becomes, in the moment of being heard, a wound that has a witness. The body that has been doing the work of holding the silence can begin, in tiny increments, to put the weight down.

The Truth and Reconciliation Commission of Canada built its entire architecture on this insight. The Commission gathered testimony from more than six thousand residential school survivors between 2009 and 2014. The testimonies were given in hearings across the country, often with elders and ceremony present. The Commission's 2015 final report makes clear that the public act of telling was, for many survivors, the first time in their lives they had spoken what happened to them in a context that received it as truth. The healing that began in those rooms did not erase what was done. It did begin the process of bringing the wound back into the relational field where repair becomes possible.

The South African Truth and Reconciliation Commission, the Norwegian Sami Truth Commission, the Guatemalan Commission for Historical Clarification, the Argentine Madres of the Plaza de Mayo. Every cultural body that has attempted to heal a collective wound has done so by creating conditions for the long-held silences to be brought into speech. Not all at once. Not without cost. The structure is always the same. Bring the wound back into relationship with witnesses who can receive it.

This is why the work of Catherine Corless in Tuam mattered so much. One historian. Death certificates retrieved one at a time. A name attached to a story that the institution had wanted to keep buried. The silence that the Bon Secours Sisters and the Irish state had maintained for sixty years began to break the moment one person started saying the names out loud. The bodies in the ground did not move. The bodies of the descendants did. The whole field around the wound shifted because someone finally spoke into it.

This same dynamic happens at the scale of one body in one room. The client who has been carrying a long-held secret about what happened in their childhood. The patient who has been carrying a diagnosis they have never told their family. The colleague who has been carrying an experience of harm at work and has never been believed. The first time the words come out, the room around them changes. The body around them changes. The trajectory of the next twenty years of their life changes.

It is the simple fact that wounds carried alone weigh more than wounds carried in relationship. No magic required. The wound being seen by another nervous system is the first condition of repair. Everything else follows from that.

The Witness as Medicine

If silence is the mechanism that holds the collective cancer in place, then the witness is the medicine that begins to dissolve it. A witness, in the sense I am using the word here, is a person whose nervous system can receive what another nervous system needs to put down. The witness does not have to fix it. The witness does not have to solve it. The witness does not have to make it stop hurting. The witness only has to be present, attentive, and unshaken enough that the speaker's body trusts that this room can hold what is being said.

The capacity to witness well is one of the most consequential capacities a human being can develop. It is the capacity at the centre of every healing profession. It is the capacity that good elders carry into every room they enter. It is the capacity that a beloved friend offers when the words finally come. It is also the capacity that almost none of us were trained in, because the culture that produced us was busy training us in productivity, problem-solving, advicegiving, and reassurance. Real witness is none of these things.

Real witness is the body of one human being saying to the body of another, with everything other than words, I am here. I see you. I am not going anywhere. Tell me what you need to tell me. The body of the speaker, registering the steadiness in the body of the listener, finds that it is safer to let the thing out than it is to keep it in. The speech follows. The disclosure follows. The healing follows.

This is the practice I have built so much of my work around. The sacred witness. The body that can hold the body of another while the other puts down what they have been carrying. It is ordinary and it is near: a friend, a therapist, a grandmother, a colleague who can stay in the room while we say the thing we have been afraid to say. The form is plain. The medicine is profound.

If you are wondering what you can give to the people you love, the people you work with, the people you encounter on a hard day, this is what you can give. The willingness to receive what they are carrying without flinching. The patience to let them find the words at their own pace. The trust that your nervous system, steady in the room, will allow theirs to begin to speak. You do not have to be perfect at this. You only have to be present and willing to learn.

The wound that finds a witness begins to become something other than the wound. The body that finds a witness begins to become something other than its silences.

How Speech Returns to a Body

People who have been silent for a long time do not, in most cases, suddenly start speaking. Speech returns to a body in stages. The body has been keeping the silence for reasons that were once real and that, for safety, the body still wants to honour even when the conditions have changed. The return of speech happens at the pace the body can tolerate. Pushed faster, the body braces and shuts down. Met at its own pace, the body opens by degrees.

The first stage is often non-verbal. The body begins to twitch around the unspoken thing. Tears arrive without context. The throat tightens or releases in patterns the person cannot account for. Dreams begin to show images that were not allowed during the daylight. This is the body announcing that it is approaching the territory of what has been held.

The second stage is often metaphor. The person finds themselves drawn to a film, a song, a poem, a story that, on close attention, is about something close to what they have been carrying. They cry at the story. They cannot say why. The metaphor is the body's way of approaching its own truth without yet using the literal language.

The third stage is fragmented speech. Half-sentences. Indirect references. Statements that begin and trail off. The person is testing whether the room can hold what is coming. The right response from a witness in this stage is patience and openness, not interpretation. The fragments are the body trying out the language. The fragments need to be received as they are.

The fourth stage is the disclosure itself. The thing said straight, in its own words, to a witness whose nervous system is ready to receive it. This is the stage in which the body actually puts down what it has been carrying. It is also the stage that, if the witness flinches or reaches too quickly for the rescue, can collapse back into silence and become harder to access in the future.

The fifth stage is integration. The speaking is done. The body begins to live with the new arrangement. The energy that had been used to hold the silence becomes available for other things. The person, often to their own surprise, finds themselves with more capacity. More patience. More joy. More breath. More groundedness in their own life. The healing is rarely dramatic. The healing shows up in the ordinary registers of a body that has more room inside it than it used to.

The work of helping speech return to a body is one of the most sacred forms of accompaniment available in human life. If you are a clinician, you do it. If you are a teacher, you do it. If you are a manager, a parent, a friend, an elder, a midwife, a nurse, a barista at the right moment, you do it. The skill of doing it well can be learned. The willingness to learn it is the only requirement.

The Collective Speech That Is Now Underway

Across the human family right now, a great unsilencing is happening. It is uneven. It is messy. It is already underway.

The Truth and Reconciliation processes I named in the previous chapter are part of this. So are the various national apologies that have been issued in the last twenty years. Australia's 2008 apology to the Stolen Generations. Canada's 2008 apology for residential schools. The United Kingdom's 2010 apology to child migrants. The 2017 Canadian apology to British Home Children. Pope Francis' 2022 statement of genocide in Canada. The Vatican's 2023 repudiation of the Doctrine of Discovery. None of these is sufficient. All of them are part of the cultural body beginning to speak about what was done.

The same dynamic is happening at the scale of intimate violence. The Me Too movement, beginning in 2006 with Tarana Burke's grassroots work and accelerating publicly in 2017, has brought the silence around sexual violence into the open at a scale that previous generations would not have thought possible. The Catholic Church's ongoing reckonings with priest abuse. The breaking of the silence around domestic violence. The breaking of the silence around men's mental health, which is finally beginning to crack in ways that may save many lives in the coming generation.

The same is happening with mental health more broadly. People are speaking publicly about depression, anxiety, suicidal ideation, addiction, eating disorders, and other conditions that previous generations were taught to hide. The speaking is itself part of the medicine. The next chapter of this book will look at what we should be saying about those conditions when we speak. For now, what matters is that the speaking is happening at all. The cultural body is putting down a layer of silence that has been weighing on it for centuries.

This unsilencing is uncomfortable for many. The dominant culture has built itself on the assumption that certain bodies and certain experiences and certain harms would remain unspoken. When the speech arrives, the structure that was built on the silence shakes. Some of that shaking shows up as backlash. Some shows up as defensiveness. Some shows up as the genuine work of institutions trying to learn how to listen to what they have never wanted to hear.

All of it is part of the same medicine. The unsilencing is the precondition for everything that follows. We cannot repair what we will not name. We cannot heal what we have agreed not to speak. The bodies of the wounded have been waiting, for generations, for the witnesses to arrive. The witnesses are arriving now. They are arriving slowly. They are arriving. The work of this generation is to be the ones who can finally listen.

The silence has been holding the disease in place. The speech is what begins to take it apart.

A Somatic Practice: Speaking from Your Roots

Before you read further, try this.

Sit with both feet flat on the floor. Feel the ground beneath you. Take three slow breaths, longer on the exhale than the inhale. Place one hand on your chest and one on your belly.

Now ask yourself, without judgment, what do I know to be true that I have not yet allowed myself to say out loud.

You do not have to say it yet. You do not have to say it to anyone. Simply notice that the knowing is there. Notice where in your body it lives. Notice what the body does when it is allowed to acknowledge what it already knows.

That noticing is the beginning of coming home to yourself. That noticing is the somatic truth of healing. The quiet, dignified, courageous act of being with what is.

You have always known more than you have been allowed to say. This page is the permission.

There is one more thing to say before this chapter closes.

Many readers of this book are people who hold silences they have never told anyone. Some of those silences are about things that happened to them. Some are about things they themselves did. Some are about what they have watched, what they have known, what they have absorbed from their lineage. Some are about the body itself. About sexuality, gender, addiction, mental health, illness, grief, longing, love. Some are about identity. About who they actually are underneath the version they have been showing the world.

I am not asking you to break every silence at once. I am not asking you to make a public declaration. I am not asking you to start with the hardest one. I am asking you to consider that the silences you have been keeping have been costing your body something, and that the speech, when it is safe enough to arrive, is one of the most reliable medicines this life makes available.

Start small. Start somewhere safe. Start with one trusted person, or one journal page, or one quiet hour with a body of water that has been hearing other people's confessions for a long time. The body knows what it has been holding. The body knows what it would like to put down. The body is also patient. It will wait for you to find the right conditions.

When you find them, when the first word arrives in the room, the collective cancer this book has been describing begins, in your particular body, to lose its grip. The collective cancer thrives on silence. The medicine begins in speech and movement=non-complacency. The next chapter looks at what we should be saying when we speak. What we should be calling the things we have always been told were wrong with us. Why so much of what gets called pathology is actually a body responding accurately to what was done to it, or to what was never given. The chapter ahead is the one this whole book has been building toward. You are not crazy. You are responding. That has always been the truth. We are about to look, together, at what it means to live in a society that finally accepts that truth as its starting place.

Chapter Nine
Anti-Pathologizing Society
From What Is Wrong With You to What Happened to You

This is the chapter the title of this book has been pointing at from the first page.

You are not crazy. You are responding. The activation in your body, the anxiety, the depression, the chronic pain, the dissociation, the rage, the freeze, the over-eating, the under-eating, the substances, the patterns you cannot break, the relationships you cannot leave, the sleep you cannot find. None of it can be understood honestly without asking what the body is responding to. Whether or not someone also meets criteria for illness, they are still responding. A response begins somewhere. A biology has a story. A nervous system has conditions. A human being has a culture. This chapter asks us to stop ending the investigation at the label.

This is not a new idea. People who have lived inside these responses have always known this in their bones. Indigenous healers have known it for as long as healers have existed. Somatic practitioners have known it for decades. Trauma specialists have been saying it for a generation. The biomedical model of mental illness, which has dominated Western medicine for the last seventy years, has had a very hard time hearing it.

This chapter is about the gap between what bodies actually need and what the dominant culture has been offering them. It is about the machinery that turns accurate responses into named pathologies. It is about the alternatives that have always existed, that are getting louder now, and that the next generation of medicine is going to have to take seriously if it wants to actually help anyone.

Your responses make sense. They always did. The question is not what is wrong with you. The question is what happened, and what your body has been doing about it ever since.

The Pathologizing Machinery

The Diagnostic and Statistical Manual of Mental Disorders, known as the DSM, is the book the American Psychiatric Association publishes to classify and name the conditions Western psychiatry treats. The first edition, published in 1952, was a hundred and thirty pages long and listed roughly a hundred conditions. The most recent edition, DSM-5-TR, published in 2022, runs more than a thousand pages and lists more than three hundred conditions. The manual expanded dramatically across the lifetime of one institution, depending on how categories, subtypes, and related conditions are counted. This expansion deserves examination not only as a medical history, but as an institutional and cultural one. Diagnostic systems do not develop outside economics, insurance structures, professional authority, research funding, or the values of the societies producing them.

This expansion did not happen because human beings suddenly became more disordered. It happened inside an ecosystem of changing science, professional authority, insurance requirements, pharmaceutical markets, research priorities, and shifting cultural definitions of normality. None of those forces operates in isolation. And that is precisely why diagnostic history deserves anthropological examination. A classification system is never produced outside the culture, institutions, and economies of the people producing it.

The trouble is that they are not. Diabetes can be measured with a blood test. Hypertension can be measured with a cuff. The conditions in the DSM cannot be measured with any biological test. They are descriptions of behaviour, gathered by committee, voted on by professional groups, and revised every decade or two as the social consensus changes. Homosexuality was a DSM diagnosis until 1973. Asperger's syndrome was a DSM diagnosis from 1994 until 2013. Premenstrual Dysphoric Disorder is a DSM diagnosis now and was not before 2013. The categories shift because they are social constructions about behaviour, not biological discoveries about disease.

This matters because the language of the DSM has migrated, over the last four decades, into the everyday vocabulary of how people talk about themselves and their loved ones. People do not say I have been struggling with grief I have not been able to put down. They say I have depression. People do not say my body is in constant alarm because of what I lived through. They say I have anxiety. People do not say my nervous system goes into states that look like another person taking the wheel. They say I have dissociative episodes. The translation from experience-language to diagnosticlanguage sounds more legitimate to the modern ear. It also quietly transfers ownership of the experience from the person who is living it to the institution that has named it.

Once an experience has been named as a disorder, several things happen inside the person who has been named. The person begins to relate to the experience as something foreign to themselves. Something that has happened to them rather than something their body is doing. The person begins to look for treatment from outside, primarily in the form of medication, because the institution has framed the experience as a chemical imbalance to be corrected. The person begins to expect the experience to be permanent, because that is how chronic diseases work, and the framing of the experience as a chronic disease implies that without continuous treatment it will return.

None of this is what the body actually needs. The body is not broken. The body is responding accurately to the conditions it was placed in. The medicine the body needs is rarely the medicine the institution has been selling.

There is one more pattern inside this machinery that has to be named, because it is the deepest layer of the harm.

The systems that create the trauma often pathologize the survivors of it.

The refugee parent whose child has been screened, in their new country, for behavioural disorders that turn out to be the somatic aftermath of war. The Indigenous student whose chronic stress response to a colonial classroom is diagnosed as ADHD instead of recognized as the body's accurate reading of a hostile environment. The Black child whose hypervigilance in a school that does not see them as fully human is treated as a disorder in the child rather than as information about the school. The woman whose response to ongoing intimate partner abuse is labelled as anxiety disorder rather than as the rational reporting of a body that has correctly assessed the room it is being asked to live in. The worker whose burnout under unsustainable conditions is diagnosed and medicated while the conditions go on. The patient whose response to repeated medical dismissal is recorded in the chart as somatization rather than as the predictable result of having been dismissed.

In every one of these cases, the body of the person who has been harmed is being given the diagnosis instead of the conditions that produced the response. The diagnostic vocabulary functions, in these cases, as a form of social control. It moves the problem from the system to the person. It protects the system from the demand that it change.

Pathology language, applied to bodies that are responding to harm, is one of the ways the harm continues.

What the Chemical Imbalance Story Got Wrong

For more than thirty years, the dominant public explanation for depression has been the chemical imbalance theory. The story, told in countless pharmaceutical advertisements and reinforced by many well-meaning clinicians, has been that depression is caused by low levels of serotonin in the brain, and that selective serotonin reuptake inhibitors correct this imbalance the way insulin corrects diabetes.

In 2022, the British psychiatrist Joanna Moncrieff and her colleagues at University College London published a systematic umbrella review in the journal Molecular Psychiatry that examined the entire body of research underlying the serotonin hypothesis. Their conclusion was unambiguous. There is no consistent evidence of a serotonin abnormality in people with depression. The chemical imbalance story, told to the public for decades, has not been supported by the research. The medications that target serotonin do help some people, by mechanisms that are not yet fully understood, while doing nothing or causing harm to many others. The certainty of the chemical imbalance story outran the science, while pharmaceutical marketing helped give it the language of an established biological finding.

Critics including investigative journalist Robert Whitaker, in Anatomy of an Epidemic, have argued that population-level disability trends and parts of the long-term outcomes literature challenge overly simple stories about psychiatric medication. These arguments remain debated. Long-term outcomes are difficult to study and vary considerably by diagnosis, medication class, severity, and the reasons a person remains on treatment. What the debate makes clear is that symptom reduction, long-term recovery, and population-level disability are not the same outcome. The rates of disability for diagnosed mental illness in the United States have risen continuously since the introduction of

SSRIs and atypical antipsychotics in the 1990s, in a country with more psychiatric prescribing per capita than anywhere else in the world. The fact that disability rates have continued to rise alongside expanding diagnosis and prescribing does not, by itself, prove that medication caused the increase or failed every person who received it. It does raise a larger question: if our dominant model were sufficient on its own, would we expect population-level suffering and disability to look the way they do now?

This is not an argument against medication in every case. Some medications help some people in some circumstances. The argument is against the story that human suffering, in its enormous variety, can be reduced to a chemical imbalance that medication corrects. The story has done damage in two directions. It has steered many people away from the slower, deeper work their bodies actually needed. It has also given a generation of people the impression that what was happening inside them was a disease they would never recover from, rather than a response their body could, with the right conditions, learn to settle. It also protected the violence culture and the behaviour that is condoned within a violence culture.

Sami Timimi, a child psychiatrist working in the United Kingdom, has been writing for over twenty years about how the diagnostic system specifically harms children. Behaviours that, in any other century, would have been understood as a child responding to its environment have been redefined as disorders in the child requiring medication of the child. Attention-Deficit Hyperactivity Disorder diagnoses in American children have risen substantially over recent decades, reaching more than eleven percent of children by recent reporting. The rise is real. Its meaning is more complicated. Increased recognition, changes in diagnostic practice, and access to assessment may all contribute. And still, wellness anthropology asks another question: while diagnosis has increased, how closely have we examined the environments children are being asked to function inside? The classroom. The family stress. Sleep. Movement. Technology. Food access. Poverty. Racism. The pace and sensory demands of modern childhood. Diagnosis may describe the child's experience. It should not end our investigation of the child's ecology.

Bonnie Burstow, a Canadian psychotherapist and scholar who worked at the Ontario Institute for Studies in Education until her death in 2020, named this whole apparatus psychiatric violence. Her language is sharper than mine. She made the case that the diagnostic-medication paradigm functions, at a structural level, to suppress accurate human response to oppressive conditions, to label the dissent as illness, and to keep the conditions intact. Her work is part of a critical psychiatry literature that has been growing for forty years and has not yet been allowed to reshape mainstream practice.

The Difference Between Symptom and Response

The most important shift this chapter is asking you to make is the shift from thinking of what your body does as symptoms to thinking of what your body does as responses.

A symptom is something a disease is doing to you. A response is something your body is doing in answer to what is happening or what has happened. The symptom framework looks at you and sees something foreign. The response framework looks at you and sees the intelligence of a living organism doing the best it can with the information and the conditions it has.

Anxiety is not meaningless. Call it a disorder if the label helps you get care. It is still information. Your nervous system may be scanning for a threat it learned, somewhere, to expect. The question is not only how we silence the alarm. The question is what the alarm might be reporting on, and what conditions might let it finally settle.

Depression is not contextless. Name it a disorder if the name opens a door to help. We should still ask what the body has been carrying. Low energy, withdrawal, the loss of capacity, these can live inside overwhelm, grief, chronic stress, illness, isolation. The question is not only how we reduce the symptoms. The question is what this person has been carrying, and what might help them set it down.

Your dissociation is not a disease. Your dissociation is your body's capacity to leave the room when the room becomes intolerable. It is one of the most sophisticated protections a nervous system has. It became your default because, at some point, you needed it. The question is not how do we stop you from leaving. The question is what is the room asking of you that your body cannot find another way to handle, and how do we make the room safer or build other capacities.

Addiction should never end the inquiry into function. Whatever we call it, the substance or behaviour is often doing a job. The body is trying to come down. To come up. To stop feeling what it is feeling. To feel anything at all. The question is not only how we end the behaviour. The question is what state the person is reaching for, what need is being met, and whether there is another way to reach it that does not cost so much over time.

Notice the structure of every question. The framework shifts from elimination to inquiry. From silencing the response to understanding what the response is doing. From treating the person as defective to receiving the person as informative. The body has been telling the truth all along. The medicine begins with believing the body.

The same shift applies one layer up. What the dominant model calls a disorder is, more accurately, an adaptation. The body learned to do this. The body, given the conditions and the resources it had at the time, found this particular shape because the particular shape was workable. Attention-Deficit Hyperactivity Disorder, in many of the children given the label, is an adaptation to conditions that asked the child to attend in ways the child's nervous system was never built to attend in. Obsessive-Compulsive Disorder, in many of the people given the label, is an adaptation to early conditions in which the body learned to manage unbearable internal states through small, controllable, repeatable actions. Borderline Personality Disorder, in many of the people given the label, is an adaptation to early relationships that taught the body that connection was both essential and unreliable. The adaptation is not the disease. The adaptation is the body's intelligent response to what was. Treating the adaptation as if it were the disease misses the point. The point is what produced the need for the adaptation, and what conditions would let the body's repertoire of responses expand beyond the one shape that survival required.

And one layer up again. The dominant model has been built around compliance. Does the patient take the medication. Does the student sit still. Does the worker meet the quota. Does the citizen follow the protocol. The body whose response does not fit the protocol is treated as a body that has failed to comply. Anti-pathologizing practice replaces compliance with mutual attunement. The practitioner reads the body in front of them and adjusts. The teacher reads the children in the room and adjusts. The leader reads the team and adjusts. The body, registering that it is being read, is able to come into deeper contact with the person reading it. Compliance produces an exhausted body performing wellness. Mutual attunement produces a settling body becoming well. The first is a transaction. The second is medicine.

Three shifts. One chapter's spine.

Symptoms become Responses

Disorders become Adaptations

Compliance becomes Mutual Attunement

Read the right side as the direction the next era of medicine is already moving in. The left side is what the dominant model has been doing for the last century. The right side is what the bodies inside the dominant model have always actually needed. The reframe is not abstract. The reframe is the practical, daily work of every clinician, teacher, manager, parent, and citizen who has begun to do this work where they stand.

The body is not the problem. The body is the messenger. The medicine listens before it intervenes.

Alternative Frameworks Have Always Existed

If the biomedical model has been failing so many people, what has been offered in its place? More than the dominant culture has been willing to acknowledge. The alternatives are old, ordinary, and already among us. They have been operating, mostly out of the mainstream press, for decades.

The Power Threat Meaning Framework, developed by Lucy Johnstone, Mary Boyle, and colleagues at the British Psychological Society, was published in 2018 as an alternative to psychiatric diagnosis. It asks four questions instead of one. What has happened to you? How did it affect you? What sense did you make of it? What did you have to do to survive? The framework reframes the experiences that get called mental illness as predictable human responses to power dynamics, threat conditions, and the meanings the person made of what they lived through. The framework does not require any biological evidence that does not exist. It does require listening to the person.

Open Dialogue, a network-based approach to acute psychiatric crisis developed in Western Lapland, Finland, by Jaakko Seikkula and colleagues beginning in the 1980s, has produced outcomes for first-episode psychosis that the biomedical model has not been able to replicate. People who go through Open Dialogue treatment have a roughly seventy-five percent recovery rate to full functioning. They have lower rates of medication use, lower rates of hospitalization, lower rates of long-term disability, and a fraction of the treatment cost of conventional psychiatric care. The method consists of bringing the person's entire support network into immediate, sustained, non-hierarchical conversation as the crisis is happening. The person is not pathologized. The person's experience is taken seriously as information. The network around them is mobilized as the treatment context. The recovery follows.

The Hearing Voices Movement, founded in 1987 in the Netherlands by Marius Romme and Sandra Escher, has built an international network of peer-support groups for people who hear voices that other people do not hear. The movement does not pathologize the experience. It does not insist on a single explanation. It welcomes spiritual, psychological, social, traumatic, neurological, and cultural explanations side by side. People who participate in Hearing Voices groups report dramatically improved functioning, reduced distress around their voices, and a sense of agency in their relationship to their own minds that the diagnostic-medication model rarely produces.

Trauma-informed care, in its strongest forms, is part of this same family of alternatives. Sandra Bloom's Sanctuary Model. SAMHSA's trauma-informed principles. Bruce Perry's Neurosequential Model. The work of clinicians like Janina Fisher, Pat Ogden, Peter Levine, Babette Rothschild. The common thread is the recognition that what people are experiencing is a response to something that happened, often very young, often unprocessed, often still alive in the body. The medicine works at the level of the body and the nervous system. The medicine does not begin by labelling the person as defective. It begins by asking what the body has been carrying and what it would take for the body to begin to put it down.

Peer-led recovery models. Survivor-led organizations. The neurodiversity movement, which has reframed autism, ADHD, and other conditions as natural variations in human cognition rather than disorders to be cured. Disability justice frameworks, led by people like Mia Mingus and Patty Berne, which have insisted that the answer to disability is the transformation of the world to accommodate the full range of human bodies. The answer is never the normalization of the disabled person. All of these alternatives have been operating, often quietly, often with less funding than the dominant model, often as the last resort of people who tried the dominant model and were harmed by it. The alternatives have been working. They have not been allowed to scale.

Indigenous and Holistic Frameworks Were Never Pathologizing

Underneath all of these alternatives is something older. The Indigenous healing traditions of every continent. The pre-colonial cosmologies of Europe and Africa and Asia. The medicine ways that the colonial-modern project tried so hard to erase. These traditions, in their authentic forms, were never pathologizing in the way the biomedical model became.

The Indigenous healing traditions of Turtle Island understood what happens in a body in distress as a response that called for restoration of relationship. Relationship with the land. Relationship with the ancestors. Relationship with the community. Relationship with ceremony. Relationship with the spirit. A person whose body was in distress was not a defective unit needing repair. They were a person whose relational field had become out of balance, requiring the community and the ceremony to come into right relation with them.

Curanderismo across Mesoamerica. Hmong healing traditions. Yoruba and Ifa traditions. Tibetan medicine. Ayurveda. Traditional Chinese Medicine. Aboriginal and Torres Strait Islander healing traditions. Sámi healing traditions. European folk practices that survived in fragments.

These are not one system. Their beliefs, ethics, medicines, and histories differ enormously. Many Indigenous, land-based, and traditional healing systems do not organize personhood through the same mind-body split that became dominant in Western biomedicine. Across diverse traditions, healing may include family, community, spirit, ceremony, land, and relationship alongside the individual. Colonial institutions often disrupted, criminalized, or displaced these systems of care. Western medicine, meanwhile, increasingly organized care through professional specialties and individual diagnosis. The biomedical model has extraordinary strengths. It is often insufficient on its own for cultural trauma, intergenerational harm, chronic relational injury, and the social conditions around distress. For many Indigenous communities, medicine has remained relational, embodied, cultural, and land connected. The exact forms differ by Nation and community. I believe decolonizing mental health may be one of the most important breakthroughs of our time.

The HEAL IT Framework

I want to share, briefly, the framework I have built my own work around. It is one example of what an anti-pathologizing practice can look like at the organizational level. I call it H.E.A.L. I.T. It stands for Humility, Equity, Antiracism, Lateral Kindness, Inclusivity, and Trauma-Informed. The six pillars are not arranged on a checklist. They function as a single living organism. When all six are present, an organization or a relationship or a practice becomes a place where bodies can begin to settle. When any one of them is missing, the others compensate for it imperfectly until the missing pillar is restored.

Humility is the recognition that no single person, profession, or framework holds the whole picture of what another body needs. The clinician learns from the patient. The teacher learns from the student. The leader learns from the team. The body of the practitioner is positioned as a body that is also learning, not as a body that has arrived. Humility is what makes the rest of the framework possible. Without it, the other five pillars become performances.

Equity is the structural distribution of access, voice, resources, and care across the people inside an organization or a system. Equity is not the same as equality. Equality gives every person the same thing regardless of what they need. Equity gives each person what they need so that all can flourish. Equity asks who is at the table, who is not at the table, whose body has had to work harder to be there, and what would need to change so that everyone could be present without paying disproportionate cost.

Anti-Racism is the active, ongoing dismantling of the structures and habits that produce racialized harm. It is more than the absence of racist behaviour. It is the deliberate work of identifying and changing the patterns that have been built up over centuries inside our institutions and inside our own nervous systems. Antiracism is a practice, not a credential. The work is never finished. The work is also not negotiable. Without it, the other pillars cannot function for the bodies who most need them.

Lateral Kindness is the practice of treating peers, colleagues, and people who share our experience with the care we extend to those above and below us in any hierarchy. Lateral violence, which I will say more about in a moment, is the corrosive pattern by which marginalized people turn the harm they have absorbed against each other rather than against the structures that produced it. Lateral kindness is the medicine for that pattern. It asks each of us to look at how we treat the people most like us, and to choose generosity even when the field around us has trained us in scarcity.

Inclusivity is the practice of building containers that can hold the full range of human bodies and human ways of being. Not as guests in someone else's house. As people whose presence belongs and whose ways of doing things are part of how the container will be shaped. Inclusivity is the active welcoming of difference, and the structural work of making the welcome real.

Trauma-Informed is the recognition that most of the bodies in any room are carrying something the room does not know about, and that the room's job is to be a place where activation does not produce more activation. Trauma-informed is not the same as trauma-treating. The room is not trying to do clinical work. The room is trying to be a place where bodies can be present without reentering the conditions that wounded them. Trauma-informed practice asks every leader, every facilitator, every clinician, every teacher to consider how their language, their pacing, their use of authority, and their attention to safety either supports or undermines the nervous systems present.

When the six pillars operate together, the conditions inside the container change. People bring more of themselves. People recover faster from setbacks. People can hold conflict without disintegrating. People can stay present with each other across difference. People can do hard work without burning out. The change is felt in the bodies of everyone inside the container, even when no one names what is producing it. The framework is one practical answer to the question this chapter is asking. What would a place look like that did not pathologize the people inside it. It would look something like this. We name psychological safety as crucial for all spaces, this is how we get there and maintain it.

Lateral Violence and the Wound Turned Inward, Why Lateral Kindness

One pattern that anti-pathologizing work has to take seriously is the pattern of lateral violence. This is the pattern in which wounded people, instead of directing their pain at the structures that produced the wounding, direct it at each other. Indigenous scholars including Paulette Regan, Phyllis Reid Jensen, and many community workers have written about how lateral violence operates inside colonized communities. The same dynamic operates inside any community that has been on the receiving end of sustained harm. Black communities, queer communities, immigrant communities, women's organizations, addiction recovery networks, every group that has carried disproportionate weight has lateral violence woven into its internal life. The definition of lateral violence is when the oppressed becomes the oppressor.

The pattern looks like this. The community has absorbed shame, harm, and powerlessness from the dominant culture. Those absorbed states have to go somewhere. They cannot, often, be safely expressed at the people in power because the people in power retain the capacity to retaliate. They get redirected, instead, at the people closest to the wounded person. Peers. Colleagues. Family members. Members of one's own community who are doing work similar to one's own. The harm is enacted laterally. The wound that came from above gets passed sideways.

Lateral violence inside healing professions is part of why so much of the work being done by people of colour, by Indigenous practitioners, by queer practitioners, by survivor-led organizations, is exhausting in ways that the work itself does not account for. The exhaustion is not the work. The exhaustion is the lateral wounding that comes from inside the field. People who have absorbed the shame of being marginalized often unleash that shame on each other in subtle and not so subtle ways. The judgment about who is doing it right. The competition over the small share of resources that has been allocated to the field. The withholding of credit. The whispering. The active sabotage.

Naming lateral violence is the beginning of being able to choose differently. Lateral kindness, the pillar in the framework I just described, is the practice that responds to it. The practice is simple in concept and demanding in execution. Treat your peers with the care you would offer a beloved elder. Resist the temptation to blame the person beside you for the conditions imposed from above. Use your voice to lift the people doing work similar to yours, especially in public, and especially when there is no obvious benefit to yourself. The dominant culture has been training us, for a long time, to compete with the people most like us. The medicine is to refuse the training. The lateral kindness training that I offer in HEAL IT is deep work, that is only for those who are ready to truly face the patterns and reclaim sovereignty into solutions.

Healership

I want to share one more word. It is a word I have been using in my own work for some years now. I have coined it because none of the existing words in English seemed to hold what I was trying to name.

The word is healership. It is the convergence of healing and leadership. It is what I believe the next generation of people who hold space for others, whether in clinical practice, in education, in management, in community work, in family, or in any other role of relational responsibility, will need to embody.

Healership is not the same as being a healer. A healer is a person who facilitates healing in others. Healership is broader. It is the practice of holding any container so that the bodies inside it can move toward healing whether or not the container was set up for that purpose explicitly. A manager who runs meetings with healership is simply running meetings, meetings that happen to leave the participants more regulated, more connected, and more capable than they were when they came in. A teacher with healership is simply teaching, in such a way that the students leave the classroom with their nervous systems a little more settled than they were when they walked in. A leader with healership is not running a healing organization. They are running an organization whose containers happen to support the recovery and the flourishing of the bodies inside it.

Healership is the answer to the question of what comes after the pathologizing model. The pathologizing model assumed that healing was the work of specialists in dedicated settings with diagnosed populations. Healership assumes that healing is the work of every body that holds another body, in every setting where bodies meet, regardless of credentials. The clinical work of trained specialists will always have its place. The everyday work of regulated, attentive, witnessing leadership is what holds the field around the clinical work. Without the field, the clinical work cannot stick. The medicine has to be in the water.

To practice healership is to recognize that every interaction you have with another human being is shaping their nervous system, whether you mean to or not. The pace at which you respond to their message. The tone in your voice when they walk into the room. The way you hold your own activation when they are activated. The willingness to apologize when you cause harm. The willingness to receive apology when harm is caused to you.

The capacity to be present without rushing to fix. The capacity to be honest without becoming brutal. The capacity to set limits with kindness. The capacity to receive feedback without collapsing. The capacity to laugh.

These are the skills the next era of leadership requires. They are the skills the bodies of the people you are responsible for need from you, whether they have named that need or not. The dominant culture has been training something else entirely. The body knows. The body always knows. The body, sitting in front of a person with healership, settles in ways it cannot settle in front of a person without it. The settling is the proof of the practice.

Healership is the convergence of healing and leadership. It is the practice the next generation of leaders is being called into. The bodies you hold are already telling you what it requires.

What This Chapter Has Been Asking

If you have made it this far in the book, something has been shifting in you. The shift is not a small one. The shift is the relocation of authority. From the institution that has been telling you what is wrong with you, to the body that has been responding all along, and to the lineage of healers and scholars and Indigenous knowledge keepers and ordinary witnesses who have been saying, for as long as there have been humans, that the body is not broken. The body is responding.

This relocation matters because everything you do next, in your own healing and in the way you accompany others, will be shaped by where you have placed the authority. If you place it in the institution, you will keep asking what the diagnosis is and waiting for the treatment to begin. If you place it in the body, you will begin to listen to what your body has been saying, and to give it the conditions it has been asking for, and to extend the same listening to the people around you.

The shift is not anti-medicine. It is anti-pathology. Medicines have their place. Diagnoses have their place. Specialists have their place. None of those places is the centre. The centre is the body in front of you, including your own. The centre has always been the body. The medicine works when it serves what the body actually needs. The medicine fails when it tries to override what the body is reporting. The next chapter of this book places this anti-pathologizing work back inside the particular body that is yours, and the particular lineage you are carrying. The chapter after that, the one that closes this book, walks us into what a society organized around what bodies actually need would look like at scale.

You are not crazy. You never were. You have been responding accurately to the conditions you were placed in. The work ahead is to change the conditions, hold the responses with kindness as they settle, and become someone whose presence makes the conditions kinder for the bodies around you. The well society is not somewhere in the future. The well society begins, every time, one person decides to do this work, and we join in to do it together.

Chapter Ten
Generational Reweaving
Untying What Was Tied Around You, Remembering Who You Were Before

The previous chapter described the framework that the next era of medicine is moving toward. The anti-pathologizing model. Symptoms examined as responses and context. Disorders examined for patterns, biology, and adaptation. Compliance replaced by mutual attunement. The body returning to its place at the centre of its own care. The institutions that have been silencing this knowledge learning, slowly, to listen.

The framework is not enough on its own. Frameworks are maps. Bodies do not heal inside maps. Bodies heal inside lineages, inside relationships, inside the small, ordinary, generational work this chapter is going to put in your hands. The framework is the map. The work is the territory.

The forest does not heal by command. The forest heals because enough trees have begun to circulate medicine instead of toxin through the underground network. Enough mother trees have begun to feed the saplings what they actually needed. Enough mycelium has begun to grow back in soil that had been compacted for centuries. The collective cancer loses its grip not because someone declared it so. The collective cancer loses its grip because enough bodies began to do the slow, ordinary, generational work of putting it down.

This is the work I want to place in your hands now. The work of generational reweaving. The work of untying what was tied around your body before you were old enough to consent to it, and reweaving the threads your lineage was meant to be carrying.

You are not separate from this work. You are not too small for it. You are not too late for it. You are not the wrong colour or the wrong class or the wrong gender or the wrong lineage for it. The work is built precisely for bodies like yours. It is the work the whole human family is being asked to participate in right now, each from where they stand, each from what they have inherited, each from the particular thread their particular lineage was carrying when the binding arrived.

The forest is being woven again. You are one of the trees the network is asking to feed it.

Individualism, the Architecture Underneath

Before the specific bindings can be named, the architecture that holds them all together has to be located. The architecture is so familiar that most readers will not have considered it as something a culture chose. They will have absorbed it as how things naturally are. It is the deepest binding the colonial-modern project ever tied around the bodies inside it.

The architecture is cultural individualism. You are a separate unit. You are responsible for your own wellbeing. Your healing is your work alone. Your suffering is yours to manage. You should not need others, and if you do, that need is itself a defect to be corrected. This is the water most readers have been swimming in for their entire lives. It has been doing daily damage to human bodies for centuries.

Your nervous system was not built for this architecture. Stephen Porges's polyvagal work, named in Chapter Eight, established that the ventral vagal state, the physiological state in which the body experiences safety, openness, and the capacity for genuine connection, can only be activated through actual social engagement. Eye contact. Soft prosody. The face of another regulated nervous system. The hand on the shoulder. The body co-regulating with another body in the same room. The human nervous system is wired for this. It is the social wiring our species came into the world with. Without the conditions co-regulation requires, the body cannot reach ventral.

A body that lives inside cultural individualism is rarely given those conditions. The body learns, very early, that connection is unreliable. That asking for help is shameful. That the proper response to overwhelm is isolation. That self-sufficiency is the marker of a competent adult. The body, denied the conditions ventral activation requires, retreats into the only physiological state it has available. Dorsal vagal shutdown. The numbness. The collapse. The depression. The dissociation. The exhaustion that does not lift after sleep.

The cultural architecture and the somatic state mirror each other. Individualism prescribes the disconnection. The body produces the shutdown the disconnection requires. The doctor diagnoses the shutdown. The patient is told the problem is inside them. The cycle continues, generation after generation, and the disconnection compounds.

Treating individualism is treating the core of many of the neurological shutdowns the dominant model has been wanting to medicate. It is hard to overstate how much of what gets called depression, anxiety disorder, burnout, and chronic disconnection is the predictable somatic consequence of a body that has been required, for years or decades, to function as an isolated unit when its physiology has been asking for the village.

The bindings that follow are the specific shapes individualism takes inside particular institutions and particular bodies. They cannot be undone without naming the architecture they sit inside.

The body knows what it was wired for. The culture has been lying to it for centuries. The reweaving begins when the body remembers the truth.

What Was Tied Around You

Before the reweaving can be named, the binding has to be located. You cannot untie what you cannot see.

Most of us are walking around carrying ties we have never identified, because the ties were tied early, the ties were tied steadily, and the ties were tied by everyone around us at the same time, so the ties came to feel like skin. They feel like us. They are not us. They are the things that were tied around us when we were small.

I want to name the most common ones. Read this as one reads a checklist. Notice whether any of them land in your own body.

The diagnostic tie. A label was placed on your nervous system. Anxiety disorder. Depression. ADHD. Bipolar. Borderline. PTSD. Some variant of one of these, or one of the dozens of newer labels the DSM keeps producing. For some readers, the label arrived as a relief, a permission, an entry point to services. For others, the label arrived as a verdict. Either way, the label has been doing work in your body since the day it arrived. The label located the wound inside you instead of inside the conditions that produced the wound. The label moved your nervous system response from a temporary adaptation to a permanent feature of who you are.

The chemical imbalance tie. For more than three decades the dominant cultural story for depression has been the chemical imbalance story. The serotonin theory. The pamphlet at the doctor's office. The advertisement on television. In 2022 a major review led by Joanna Moncrieff at University College London, after examining the totality of available research, found no convincing evidence that the serotonin theory accurately describes what happens in depressed people's brains. The certainty of the story outran the science, while marketing gave it the language of established fact. Many readers have been carrying that certainty in their bodies as if it were a finding. The certainty can be put down.

Many readers have been carrying that story in their bodies as if it were a finding. The story can be put down.

The individual pathology tie. Whatever is wrong with you is inside you alone. Separate from your family. Separate from your community. Separate from your land. Separate from your lineage. Separate from the conditions you have lived inside. The binding that severs the wound from the soil it grew inside is one of the most powerful bindings the colonial-modern project ever produced. It is also one of the easiest to identify once you start looking for it.

The expert-knows-better tie. Only credentialed strangers can name what is happening in your body. Your own felt sense does not count as information. The body's signals are unreliable until interpreted by someone whose authority comes from outside your lineage. This binding transfers authority over your body from your body to a system that does not know your body, did not raise your body, will not be in your kitchen when this conversation is over.

The productivity tie. You matter because you produce. Rest is a moral failure. Slowness is a personal flaw. The body that cannot maintain the pace of the dominant culture is a body that has failed. This binding is so familiar that most readers have stopped noticing it. Notice it now.

The body-as-machine tie. Your body is hardware to be repaired, not a living being that has been responding to conditions. Pain is malfunction. Fatigue is malfunction. Grief is malfunction. Joy is the output of a properly functioning machine. The binding strips the body of its intelligence and reduces it to a problem to be fixed.

The healing-as-transaction tie. Repair is something you purchase from a stranger in a sterile room. Healing has an hourly rate. Connection is what happens for fifty minutes on Wednesday afternoon. This binding works against everything the human nervous system actually knows about healing, which is that healing happens in relationship, in time, in place, in ceremony, in the long, ordinary, accumulated presence of bodies who care.

The forgetting tie. Whatever your lineage knew, before the binding came, is not worth knowing anymore. The traditional foods are quaint. The traditional languages are obsolete. The traditional ceremonies are inefficient. The traditional ways of raising children are unscientific. The traditional ways of dying are uncivilized. This binding asks you to forget, as the price of belonging to the dominant culture, what your people knew about being alive.

Each of these is a thread. Each one was tied around you before you were old enough to refuse. Each one has been doing work in your body for years, often decades. Each one is untieable.

You did not consent to the bindings. You are now, possibly for the first time, able to name them. The naming is the beginning of the untying.

How the Untying Begins

The ties do not come off all at once. They come off the way they were put on. Slowly. By the body. In the small daily transactions that, accumulated over time, change what the body knows to be true about itself.

Five practices, ordinary and free, are the heart of the untying.

Recognition. Notice the tie. See whether you feel it in your body. Locate it. Give it a name. Notice whether the tie has a felt location for you. A throat. Shoulders. Jaw. Chest. Behind the eyes. Or nowhere specific at all. Do not force the body to match my map.

Questioning. Ask, of every belief you hold about yourself, where it came from. Was this given by a doctor? By a parent? By a teacher? By a culture? By a diagnostic system? By an advertisement? By a story about who you were supposed to be? Ask the question without rushing to the answer. Many of the bindings begin to fall off in the asking.

Naming. Say out loud what was tied. To a witness who can receive it. The sacred witness work named in Chapter Eight is the same work here. The naming, in the presence of a nervous system that can hold the naming, begins the metabolizing. The body that says the thing in a room with someone who can hear it puts down some of the weight of having carried the thing in silence.

Embodying alternatives. Practice, in your body, the felt sense of being whole. Walk on land that has been allowed to be land. Cook foods your lineage knew. Move in ways the body wants to move. Sit with the elder. Listen to the child. Speak the language, even one word, even badly. Let the body remember what it knew before the binding was tied.

Receiving repair. Let other bodies meet yours in the places that were never witnessed. The therapist who can sit with you. The friend who can hear what no one else has heard. The community that can hold the speech the lineage never permitted. The grandmother who blesses you. The land that receives you. The water that holds you. Repair does not come from striving harder. Repair comes from being received.

These five practices are ordinary. That is their power. They are what bodies have always done to come back into themselves. The colonial-modern project made the ordinary practices feel inaccessible. The reweave is the return of the ordinary practices to the everyday lives of ordinary bodies.

The medicine has always been ordinary. The ordinary is what was taken from us.

The Remembering

In Chapter Seven I named the fourth pillar of a healing forest. Immune memory. Healing is not invention. Healing is remembering. I want to bring that frame back here, because the remembering is what the rest of this chapter rests on.

Every body alive right now is descended from people who knew how to weave. Even bodies whose recent lineages were placed inside conditions that broke the weaving carry, in their cellular substrate, the older memory of what weaving looked like. The wound did not erase all of it. Some of it survived underground, the way mycelium survives a forest fire.

The body remembers through several channels. I want to name them so you know what to look for in yourself.

The somatic. Your body feels at home in certain landscapes, certain weathers, certain foods, certain rhythms of breath, certain sounds. Those feelings are memory. The body that has never been to the mountains where your great-grandmother lived feels something when you finally stand there. The body that has never tasted the food your lineage ate feels something when it arrives on the tongue. Pay attention to those feelings. They are the lineage speaking through the substrate.

The symbolic. Your dreams. The objects that draw your eye. The artists, books, films, music that pierce your heart unaccountably. The metaphors that arrive on hard days. The animal that keeps showing up. The body is speaking through the symbol. The symbol is the lineage delivering messages the literal language cannot yet carry.

The relational. The person who feels like kin even though no blood connects you. The grandmother who passes you the recipe. The elder who tells you the story. The teacher whose presence steadies your nervous system in a way no diploma could explain. The body recognizes its people across thousands of miles and dozens of generations. Trust those recognitions.

The ancestral. The practices, languages, ceremonies, foods, songs that survive in pieces inside your lineage even after long erasure. Pieces are enough to begin from. Pieces lead to other pieces. The grandmother who taught you to fold dumplings was carrying the rest of the cuisine even when she did not know she was. The aunt who hummed the song was carrying the rest of the song even when she could not name it. The forest survives a fire underneath the forest floor, in mycelium that the fire never reached. Your lineage is doing the same thing inside you right now.

The land. The relationship a body forms when given time on land that has been allowed to be land. The body that has been bound to clocks and screens and concrete remembers itself, often quickly, when placed in the company of trees and water and weather and small animals. The land is doing some of the remembering for us. We have only to spend time inside it.

The remembering is not nostalgia. The remembering is the most accurate guide your body has to what wellness looked like before the disease arrived. Inside your lineage, somewhere, sometime, there was a generation that knew. The knowing did not disappear. It went underground. It is waiting for you to come find it.

Healing is not invention from an outside source or new idea. Healing is remembering. The body already knows. The lineage already knows. Everyone's ancestors have had healing practices. The work is letting yourself listen. Trusting the blood memory on how to connect beyond the last number of generations that have held carried stories and conditioning that have prevented healing.

Generational Reweaving Across the Human Family

This work is happening, right now, in every direction at once. I named some of it briefly in Chapter Seven. I want to walk through it more fully here, because seeing the breadth of the reweave is part of what makes it possible to believe in.

Indigenous renaissance across Turtle Island. Languages coming back. Ceremonies coming back. Land coming back. Birth coming back. Death practices coming back. Governance forms coming back. Foods coming back. Medicines coming back. Stories coming back. Len Pierre, the Coast Salish educator from Katzie First Nation, has named this an Indigenous renaissance. He sees it everywhere. In the matriarchs taking up land back. In Indigenous midwives reclaiming birth. In Indigenous politicians, entrepreneurs, nurses, physicians, teachers, and cultural leaders. In people who grew up without access to their language or ceremony, waking up to their own lineages later in life. The renaissance is underway. It never asked for permission.

African diasporic reclamation. The return of Ifa, Vodou, Santeria, and Candomblé to descendants who were severed from them. The return of foodways. The return of music, dance, and somatic practice. The work of bell hooks on love as the foundation of liberation. The slow rebuilding of kinship structures broken by the slave trade. The Black Lives Matter movement as one expression of bodies refusing to be disposable. The rise of Afrofuturism as a way of imagining wholeness that was always supposed to be there.

Jewish lineage repair. Rabbi Tirzah Firestone, in Wounds Into Wisdom, has documented the work of Jewish descendants in metabolizing what was passed forward from the Holocaust, the pogroms, the centuries of expulsion. The Hebrew concept of Tikkun Olam, repair of the world, frames this work inside a tradition that is thousands of years old. The Mussar tradition. The reclamation of Kabbalah. The return of the body to Jewish practice that had become heavily textual. The wave of Jewish therapists, rabbis, artists, and writers naming, in this generation, what their grandparents could not name in theirs.

European earth-tradition revival. Sharon Blackie's work helping European descendants rediscover the older animist traditions of their own lineages. Martin Shaw's mythological work in England. The Slavic, Celtic, Norse, Germanic, Baltic, and Finno-Ugric reclamation movements across Europe. The return of seasonal rites, plant medicine, ancestor work. This work matters because the descendants of colonizers untying their own bindings is part of how the collective cancer's transmission stops. The European reweave is the European lineage doing its own piece of the repair.

Somatic abolitionism. Resmaa Menakem's framework of healing racialized trauma in the body. The slow practice of building what he calls a settled body. The recognition that western individualist therapy, on its own, is not adequate for cultural trauma. The integration of ancestral practices, somatic work, and political analysis into the clinical encounter. Decolonizing therapy itself, as in Jennifer Mullan's work.

Asian reclamation. The return of traditional Chinese medicine as more than commercialized acupuncture. The integration of Ayurveda with embodied healing. The reclamation of mindfulness from its corporate captivity. The return of Confucian and Daoist understandings of human flourishing to bodies that had been told their healing had to be Western. The Asian American reckoning with intergenerational silence around the diaspora wounds.

Latin American and Caribbean reclamation. The integration of curanderismo, espiritismo, plant medicines, and ancestral practices. The recognition that the writers we now call magic realists were giving accurate description of cultures that had not lost what the dominant model had bound out of recognition. The reclamation of food sovereignty in Indigenous communities across

Mexico, Central America, the Andes, the Amazon, and the Caribbean.

Sami, Māori, Hawaiian, and Pacific Islander reclamation. Language nests. Land return. Ceremony return. The Sami Parliament. Māori sovereignty work. Hawaiian sovereignty work. The Pacific Islander reweave across the diaspora. Each is its own thread inside the same forest.

The everyday reweaving. Underneath every named movement above is the work that happens in millions of kitchens, on millions of patches of land, in millions of conversations between an elder and a child, in millions of small ordinary acts that the news does not report. The mother who teaches her daughter the song. The son who cooks the dish his grandfather cooked. The teacher who tells the children the true story of where they are. The midwife who holds the body of the new mother the way the old mothers held the bodies of new mothers. The neighbour who brings food when the death arrives. The friend who can stay in the room when the truth comes out. This is most of the reweave. This is the part the news will never tell you about. This is also the part you can join immediately. You may already be inside it.

Look around your own life. Notice the places where you have been doing this work without naming it as work. The grandmother whose recipes you remembered to write down. The friendship you built with someone whose lineage was on a different side of a historical wound. The thing you taught your child that your own parents could not teach you because their parents could not teach them. The body practice you have learned that your body knew before it learned it. Each of these is reweaving. Each of these is part of the world's medicine.

The reweave is not waiting for you to begin. The reweave is already underway. The invitation is to recognize yourself inside it.

The Reweave Does Not Wait for Permission

I want to name something direct, because some readers will still be waiting for permission that was never going to come. Like how grown children often wait for their parents to finally accept them, or say they can be who they are truly meant to be all along. The same is true for our other attachment. Our attachment to the wider caregiver-the system.

The systems that did the tying are not the systems that will untie. The systems that did the tying have, in many cases, an active interest in keeping the tying in place. The institutions of psychiatry, of education, of capital, of patriarchy, of empire, were built on assumptions that the reweave undoes. Some of those institutions are doing genuine repair work right now. Some are not. Either way, the reweave does not wait for them.

The reweave happens in the bodies. The reweave happens in the families. The reweave happens in the communities. The reweave happens in the lineages. The reweave happens in the rooms where two people who could not previously hear each other begin, slowly, to hear each other. The reweave happens in the kitchen at three in the afternoon when a grandmother teaches a four-year-old how to fold a dumpling, and the dumpling is the lineage, and the four-yearold is the future, and the kitchen is the medicine.

The reweave does not need a clinical trial. The reweave does not need a peer-reviewed publication. The reweave does not need a government grant. The reweave does not need a celebrity endorsement. The reweave is what the human family has always done in conditions of harm. It is what your great-grandmother did when she taught your grandmother how to be alive. It is what your grandmother did when she taught your parent. It is what you do, or do not do, in the next conversation you have with someone you love.

Every body in the reweave is doing it on its own terms, at its own pace, from its own lineage, in its own language, with its own particular contribution. There is no central authority of the reweave. There is no proper way to do it. There is no certification. There is no hierarchy. There is the work of each particular life, doing its particular piece, in the particular place where the body finds itself standing.

This is what makes the reweave unstoppable. It cannot be regulated. It cannot be defunded. It cannot be branded. It cannot be commodified, no matter how hard the dominant culture tries to do all four. The reweave is built into how human bodies actually heal. The reweave is the medicine the human family has always carried. The reweave is reasserting itself now because the conditions of the wounding have become so extreme that more and more bodies are remembering they have always had the medicine.

You are not waiting for the reweave to begin. The reweave is waiting for you to recognize you have already begun.

What Your Body Has Always Known

Here is the consciousness this chapter has been moving you toward.

You are not crazy. You have never been crazy. You have been responding, accurately and intelligently, to the conditions you were given. Your body has been doing exactly what bodies do when their conditions are wrong. The response was the report. The report was the truth. Your body has known the culture was sick, long before it had words for it. The body usually knows first.

You are also reweaving. Whether you have called it that or not. Every time you questioned what was tied around you. Every time you spoke a truth that had been kept silent. Every time you held a body in love when the dominant culture would have shamed it.

Every time you trusted what your body was telling you over what an expert told you about your body. Every time you cooked the food, walked the land, sat with the elder, listened to the child, lit the candle, said the name, sang the song, told the story, did the small thing that fed the network instead of feeding the disease. The reweaving has been happening in you already. You have only to recognize you are inside it.

The forest is being healed. The mycelium is growing back, slowly, in soil that had been compacted for centuries. The mother trees are speaking again. The saplings are absorbing medicine instead of toxin. The collective cancer is losing its grip. Not everywhere. Not yet completely. In enough places, in enough bodies, that the trajectory has begun to bend.

You are one of the bodies inside that trajectory. So is every body around you, even the ones who do not know it yet. So is the child you raise. So is the friend you call when the day is hard. So is the elder you visit. So is the stranger who turns to you on the bus and tells you something true.

The work of the rest of your life, if you choose to accept what this book has been placing in your hands, is the work of reweaving. The work of untying what was tied around your body. The work of remembering what your lineage knew. The work of feeding the network around you with whatever medicine your particular life is built to carry. The work of being, for the bodies that come after you, the kind of ancestor your body has needed someone to be for it.

This is the assignment, whole and entire.

You were never broken. You were responding. You are now also reweaving. The collective cancer that has been moving through the forest for centuries is losing its grip, one body, one lineage, one ordinary act of remembering at a time. Your body is one of the bodies the forest is using to heal itself.

You are not crazy. You are responding. You are also reweaving. The world that is being built around you right now, by ordinary people doing this work in ordinary places, is the world that has been waiting to be built. You are one of the ones building it. You always were.

The next chapter is the one that surfaces what will inevitably surface once we fully say yes to reweaving: the deep rooted reaction to suppress human emotion instead of allow it to flow and restore.

Chapter Eleven
Emotional Resistance
The Dam, the Wail, and the Return to Living Water

Every living body of water knows how to stay well. The creek moves. The river moves. Even the lake, which looks still from the shore, is turning over beneath its surface, circulating, exchanging what is below with what is above. Water that is allowed to move stays clear. Water that is dammed begins to change. The surface grows a film. The algae arrives and thickens until the light cannot get through. The oxygen thins. What was once living water becomes, slowly, a place where life struggles to survive. Nothing was ever wrong with the water. Something was wrong with the dam.

Emotion is the water of the human body. This chapter is about the dam.

I am calling the dam 'emotional resistance.' It is the learned refusal to let feeling move through the body and complete itself. It is taught to us early, enforced on us constantly, and rewarded so reliably that most of us mistake it for maturity. And it is, I believe, the root of much of the malignancy we now medicate at population scale. The anxiety that circles without landing. The depression that settles like sediment. The moral injury of people who have swallowed too many wrongs in silence. These are what a pond looks like after enough years behind a dam.

In Chapter Eight I named the silence: the wordless agreement not to speak certain things. Emotional resistance is the silence's twin, and it lives beneath language. It is the agreement not to feel them. The two hold each other in place. A person can find the courage to break the silence and still be dammed, telling the truth with a composed face while the body holds its breath. The hush governs what may be said. The dam governs what may move. This chapter goes beneath the words, to the water.

There is an irony at the centre of all of it, and I want to name it plainly before we go further. The way the dominant culture treats human emotion is built on fear of it. And the fear of the feeling is what creates the disease. Resisting the emotion creates the very pain point we are so desperately trying to escape. We create what we fear. And the reverse is also true, and it is the medicine of this entire chapter: when we turn toward what we fear with curiosity, it begins to dissolve. The wave crests, moves through, and completes. The body finds its way back to homeostasis, the way water finds its level, because that is what the body has been trying to do the whole time.

I write this from the discipline of medical anthropology, and from the diverse ways of knowing that have carried this understanding for far longer than any academic field, many of them rooted in worldviews that lessen hierarchy rather than enforce it. Across cultures and across centuries, human communities have known how to let the water move. That knowledge tells us something that the symptom checklists cannot: we are wise creatures, and the wisdom is within ourselves. This is true for all of us, in every ethnicity, every shape, every creation temple a spirit arrives in. The deciding factor was never our worth. The deciding factor is how aligned we are allowed to be with reality.

The Cultures That Kept the Water Moving

This is the anthropological record. I am only the one reporting it. Across the world, human communities built emotional expression into the very architecture of ordinary life, the way we build plumbing into houses, because they understood it as infrastructure for wellness rather than a threat to it.

In Aotearoa New Zealand, when a person dies, the Māori gather for tangihanga: days of communal mourning in which the body is almost never left alone and the bereaved family is held at the centre of an entire community's attention. No one, man or woman, is expected to conceal their grief. Open weeping is understood as therapeutic for everyone present. The whole event functions as emotional scaffolding, erected by many hands around the people who need it most, and taken down only when the grief has somewhere to live.

On the atoll of Ifaluk in Micronesia, the anthropologist Catherine Lutz found something that quietly dismantles one of our deepest Western assumptions. There, emotions are not understood as private weather inside an individual skull. They live between people. Feelings like fago, a braid of compassion, love, and sadness for another, are social acts, expected and honoured as the connective tissue of community life. The idea that a feeling belongs to you alone, to be managed alone behind a closed face, is a local custom that forgot it was one.

Among the Toraja people of Sulawesi, the dead are not surrendered on a deadline. A person who has died may remain in the family home for months, tended, spoken to, treated as one who is sleeping, while the family prepares the farewell. Years later, relatives return to clean and re-dress the ancestors, keeping the relationship alive across the threshold. Whatever we feel about that from inside our own frameworks, notice what it makes room for: a relationship with loss that moves at the speed of love rather than the speed of a work week.

Now watch how a whole civilization loses practices like these, because it does not happen in one dramatic decision. It happens the way a plane comes off its trajectory. One degree of drift at the runway is nothing; you would never feel it in your seat. Hold that same degree across an ocean and you land in a different country. The Western world drifted exactly like this, one degree at a time. A lament condemned here. A factory whistle installed there.

Composure rewarded, tears penalized, mourning shortened, the marketplace expanded. Each drift was small enough to absorb. Compounded across generations, we woke up somewhere our ancestors would not recognize: a culture that capitalized on productivity, with a fear of emotion running silently underneath the whole flight plan.

And what was lost in the drift was the compass. Because emotions were never the malfunction. They are nature's compass, baked into the body. Sacred, safe, wisdom teachers. They are the guide we were given to know ourselves more deeply: when something goes off inside us, that is the signal to tune in and ask why, the needle swinging to show us where reality and our lives have come apart. But a culture that profits from our productivity needs us to resign from that compass. It needs us to distrust the self, to treat our inner signals as noise, to outsource the reading of our own inner world to whoever holds the checklist. And when we legitimize ourselves anyway, when we say what we feel and what we see, we meet a culture that gaslights us at every turn, that makes us question our own reality the moment our truth counters the arrangements of patriarchy, capitalism, and individualism. In a productivity-producing culture, human beings are there to be extracted from, and disposable when the extraction slows. The instruction over the door is unmistakable: leave your humanness here.

I want to be gentle now, because none of this is an indictment of the people living inside it. It is no one's fault. It is cultural coping. Shutting this side of ourselves down is how we cope, endure, and survive the culture as it stands. It is how the bills get paid and the kids get fed, with a few feel-good moments scheduled in between to keep us going. Our grandparents did it. We do it. Most of us were never shown another way, because the people who raised us were never shown one either.

But here is the truth the drift hides, and it is the most hopeful sentence in this chapter. A culture is not weather. We shaped the

Western world this way based on a set of values, chosen, taught, and rewarded, which means we hold the power to reshape our cultural values for a new outcome. If you want new waters, you replenish what is upstream. And what sits upstream, at the very source of the water, is the set of social values we cocreate and choose together. Change what is chosen at the source, and it touches all the rest, every workplace, every classroom, every kitchen table downstream.

The Wail

Humans have always wailed.

In Ireland, they were the mná caointe, the keening women, called to the wake to raise the caoineadh over the body: an improvised, sustained lament, part poetry, part cry, in a form of grief older than the church that eventually set out to silence it. The keeners were skilled, often the finest oral poets of their communities, and their voices were so woven into the Irish imagination that the culture dreamed them into the banshee, the woman whose wail arrives ahead of a death. For centuries, church synods condemned the keen from the pulpit while colonial observers pointed to it as proof of barbarity, and still the women keened, because the community knew what the wail was for.

In the villages of Greece, women have sung the moirologia, ritual laments raised at the deathbed and then at the graveside, sometimes daily, sometimes for years, in antiphonal poetry passed between mourners like a shared load. Anthropologists who sat with these women documented grief that was neither hidden nor hurried: tended openly at the grave until, years later, the community completed the crossing with ceremony. Finnish and Karelian women carried their own lament tradition. Chinese funerals have long held space for loud, communal wailing. Across Egypt, West Africa, and the Middle East, communities honoured, and in places still honour, professional mourners, women whose work it was to give a family's grief a voice bigger than any one throat could produce. The wail was a technology. It told the community that a rupture had occurred. It gave the grieving body permission to move what was inside it all the way through and out. It was witnessed, held, and sanctioned. When the wailing was done, something in the body was done too. The water had moved.

I named wailing once before in this book, back in Chapter Six, in the list of communal discharges the dominant culture outlawed. It appeared there as one practice among many. I want to stay with it now, because the wail holds the whole teaching. Look at what happened here. North America built its institutions in an era that prized the absence of emotion. Composure was read as competence. Stillness of face was read as strength. The wail, the tremble, the open weeping, all of it got pained and pinned, reclassified from human expression into evidence of instability. And this is where so much diagnosis actually begins. A person is hurting. That is the whole of it. A person is hurting, and the culture around them has outlawed the expression that would let the hurt complete itself. So the hurt pools. The pooling deepens. And then the pooling is given a name, and the name is treated as the problem, and the person is treated for the name. The diagnosis arrives at exactly the place where the wail was refused.

And you have seen the modern version, because you live inside it. Picture the man at his father's funeral, jaw set, thanking everyone for coming, delivering the eulogy without a crack in his voice. Afterward, people tell him how well he held it together, and they mean it as the highest compliment. He goes home and cannot cry for a year, and the grief that was refused a voice goes looking for another exit through his sleep, his chest, his temper. Picture the woman who slips into the office washroom to cry, one eye on the door, fixing her face in the mirror before walking back to her desk, whispering to a colleague, I'm so sorry, I never do this. She is apologizing for the most honest thing that will happen in that building all day. Picture the wake where an elder begins to rock and moan the way her own grandmother once did, and feel the room stiffen, and watch how quickly someone rushes tissues to her, as if grief were a leak to be stopped rather than a river to be joined. Even the tissue, offered so kindly, so automatically, often carries a second message folded inside the first: here, contain that.

Expression is how the pond replenishes. The weeping, the shaking, the keening, the sound that comes from lower in the body than words do: these are the sluice gates. They were never the pathology. They were the prevention of it.

The Shudder

There is a truth beneath the wail that belongs to every mammal on this earth, and we are mammals, no matter how many floors of an office building we stack between ourselves and that fact.

In Chapter Six I showed you Sapolsky's zebra, chased by the lion and then returning, unburdened, to its grazing. Now I want you to watch what the body does in between, because the in-between is where our species keeps interrupting itself. Watch a deer after the coyote gives up the chase. Watch a dog after a fright. The animal trembles. It shudders, sometimes violently, sometimes for whole minutes, and then it shakes itself from nose to tail, and then it goes back to grazing as though nothing happened. Because in the deepest sense, nothing did remain. The nervous system mobilized an enormous charge to survive the moment, and then the body was allowed to discharge that charge, to let the cycle continue all the way through to its completion. The shudder is the sentence finishing itself. Regulation is a continuation. The wave has to be allowed to finish.

Human cultures have known this for as long as there have been human cultures, and many built the shudder into community life on purpose. In the Kalahari, the Ju/'hoansi hold healing dances that last the whole night: the women sing and clap the medicine songs while the dancers circle the fire for hours, until the energy they call n/um, boiling energy, rises hot up the spine and breaks into trembling and shaking. In that state the healers move through the gathering, laying hands, pulling sickness, and among them becoming a healer is not the calling of a rare few; most men and many women carry it at some point in their lives. The dance is held regularly, in crisis and in calm, because it does more than heal individuals. It releases the jealousies, tensions, and quiet conflicts of community life before they harden. It is maintenance of the pond.

The pattern repeats across the world, each tradition whole and distinct within its own cosmology, and I name them here with respect rather than flattening them into technique. Sufi orders whirl and chant the remembrance of the divine until the body itself becomes prayer. The Shakers earned their very name from trembling in worship. Pentecostal congregations are moved through the body, swaying, shaking, crying out. Across many Indigenous nations of Turtle Island, ceremony pairs drumming, heat, song, and prayer, sweat and rhythm carrying what words cannot. Yogic traditions have long recognized spontaneous shaking, the kriyas, as energy completing its path through the body. Different cosmologies, different meanings, and one shared understanding underneath: the body is where the water moves, and the community is where it is safe to let it.

We carry the same design as every one of those dancers, and then we interrupt it. We hold the shaking hands still under the table. We apologize for crying. We breathe the sob back down and call it pulling ourselves together. We are praised for the interruption. But the interrupted charge does not evaporate simply because we refused it an exit. It stores. It waits in the tissue, in the jaw, in the gut, in the startle that never quite settles. Years of held shudders is another name for the pond thickening. What we call symptoms are so often just the body's unfinished sentences, still asking, sometimes decades later, to be allowed to complete.

And here is what gives me hope: the shudder is coming back, wearing modern clothes. Peter Levine built an entire healing modality, somatic experiencing, from watching how animals complete what humans interrupt, gently guiding people to finish the responses their bodies were never allowed to finish. David Berceli developed simple exercises that invite the body's own tremor mechanism to switch on deliberately, and people lie on mats in community halls, shaking on purpose, releasing what decades of composure stored. Breathwork circles fill. Ecstatic dance floors open on Sunday mornings, sober and barefoot, no talking, just bodies moving what they carry. Therapies use rhythm and bilateral movement to help stuck experiences finally move through. Sound practitioners teach people to hum and tone, letting the vibration of their own voice loosen what gripping held. The wellness market calls all of this new. The anthropologist in me smiles, because none of it is new. It is a remembering.

You do not need a certification or a retreat to begin. You need permission, and I am formally handing it to you. Here are some ways to attune to your body and invite it to release, in the trust that it already knows how:

- Let the shaking happen. After a stressful call, a conflict, a scare, notice the tremble in your hands or legs and let it move instead of stilling it. Stand, soften your knees, and allow your body to shake and vibrate until it settles on its own. It will settle on its own.
- Give it sound. Sigh out loud. Hum. Groan. Let a long tone ride your exhale. The vibration of your own voice soothes the nervous system from the inside, which is part of why every wailing culture was onto something.
- Let tears finish. When crying arrives, let it complete instead of cutting it off at the first catch of breath. A cry that finishes ends differently in the body than a cry that is swallowed.

- Move it through. Put on one song and let your body move however it wants to, no mirror, no choreography. Shake out your wrists, bounce your heels, unclench your jaw, roll your shoulders like an animal shaking off water.
- Lengthen the exhale. Breathe in through the nose and out slowly through the mouth, letting the out-breath run longer than the in-breath, for a few quiet minutes. The long exhale is the body's own built-in downshift.
- Ask, then listen. Place a hand where the charge lives, the chest, the belly, the throat, and ask: what do you need to do right now? Then give permission to the smallest impulse that answers, the stretch, the sound, the reach, the push against a wall.
- Borrow a witness. Do any of this in the company of someone safe. The mammal body settles faster in safe company; we regulate together, which is exactly what the all-night dances always knew. None of it needs to be graceful. The mouse is not graceful when it trembles. Done is the goal of not pretty. The body is not asking you to perform its release. It is only asking you to stop preventing it.

Matriarch Wisdom and the Demonized Threshold

Nowhere is the punishment of emotional truth more visible than in what the dominant culture does to women at their thresholds. I want to stay here for a while, because there is a whole teaching in it.

Most cultures across the world and across time have understood a human life as a series of crossings. Birth. Coming of age. Union. Elderhood. Death. Anthropology has documented ceremony after ceremony marking these thresholds: rites of passage in which the community gathers to witness a person's transformation, to honour what is ending, and to welcome what is beginning. The crossing that is witnessed and honoured is lived differently than the crossing that is ignored or shamed. This is one of the quiet, profound findings of medical anthropology: how we interpret our inner world, and the meaning we apply to what is happening within us, shapes the experience itself. Meaning is not decoration laid over biology. Meaning reaches all the way down into how the biology is lived.

And we do not have to take that on faith, because the research exists, and it is some of the most beautiful work my discipline has produced. Margaret Lock spent years comparing the menopausal transition in Japan and North America and found that Japanese women reported dramatically fewer hot flashes and did not, on the whole, experience konenki, their word for this life chapter, as a crisis at all. It was understood as a natural turning in the long arc of aging, not a deficiency disease, and the bodies of the women lived it accordingly. Lock gave us the phrase local biologies for what she found: culture and biology in ongoing conversation, meaning reaching down into flesh. Yewoubdar Beyene sat with Mayan women in the Yucatán who welcomed the end of menstruation, and among the postmenopausal women she and her colleagues studied, not one reported hot flashes. The rural Greek women she compared them with told a similar story of an untroubled crossing. And Marcha Flint, working with Rajput women in India, found women who had lived veiled and secluded through their childbearing years, and who at menopause finally came downstairs, into public life, into laughter with the men, into visible standing in the household. Where the threshold was a promotion, the women reported few of the sufferings our culture treats as inevitable. Flint asked the question in the title of her research: is menopause a reward or a punishment? The honest answer is that it depends entirely on the culture the woman crosses it in.

Now place perimenopause inside the dominant Western framework, a framework that recognizes almost no rites of passage at all. There is no ceremony on offer. There is a symptom checklist. A woman entering her matriarch years finds her heat, her tears, her sleepless clarity, her suddenly lowered tolerance for what she once endured, all of it read as malfunction. She is handed language that frames her own becoming as a deficiency disorder. And she is demonized, over and over, in the oldest pattern this culture knows, for the sacred wisdom of expressing human emotion. The witch was this woman. The hysteric was this woman. The difficult woman in the meeting who has finally stopped absorbing what should never have been hers to absorb: this is that same woman, and the culture reaches for the same old pins.

Beneath it runs the glorification of youth and beauty, which carries its own quiet condemnation. To worship one stage of a woman's life is to sentence every other stage. The message lands subtly and constantly: your value was back there. But the truth held in cultures that honour their matriarchs is the opposite. The lowered tolerance is discernment arriving. The heat is truth burning off what was false. The tears are the dam finally, rightfully, giving way. This threshold, honoured, produces the wisdom keepers every community depends on.

So imagine the reinvention, because it is already beginning at the edges. Imagine the workplace where a woman's threshold is named without shame and met with flexibility instead of whispers. Imagine circles of women marking the crossing with ceremony, as many are now reclaiming, fire and story and witness where the culture offered only a prescription pad. Imagine the language shifting from symptoms to signals, and medicine that asks what is this transition asking of your life alongside what can we ease. Imagine daughters watching their mothers cross this threshold with pride instead of secrecy, so that their own future crossing is seeded with honour decades in advance. When a woman is offered the elder's seat instead of the exit, everything about the crossing reorganizes, in her mind and, as the research keeps showing us, in her body. She does not just think about it differently. She lives it differently.

And there is one more layer, the deepest one. The cultures that hold the earth as sacred tend to be the cultures that hold women as sacred, and this is no coincidence, because many traditions never separated the two. The same worldview that reduces the earth to a resource, valuable only for what can be extracted from it, reduces a woman to her productive and reproductive years and calls everything after them decline. And the same worldview that meets the earth as kin, as a living relation to be in reciprocity with, meets a woman's every season as sacred. When the earth is treated as sacred instead of merely extracted from, we will see women that way again too. And when we honour the matriarch, we will remember how to honour the land. They are not separate. They never were. Heal one lens and the other begins to clear.

Symptoms Without Stories

The intake form asks you to describe your symptoms. It almost never asks you why you have them.

Rate your sleep. Rate your appetite. Rate your mood on a scale of one to ten. The form is fluent in smoke and has no vocabulary for fire. A person can complete the entire assessment, receive the diagnosis, begin the treatment, and never once be asked the only question that would have explained everything: what are you living inside of? What has been done to you, asked of you, taken from you? What are you responding to?

Nowhere does this play out more plainly than at work, so let me make it concrete, because you will recognize someone in these stories, and it may be you. The nurse in her fourth understaffed year, running a ward short six bodies every shift, is invited to a lunchtime resilience webinar while nothing about the staffing changes. The warehouse worker's targets are set by a system that never tires, never grieves, and never needs the washroom, and when his body starts to fail the pace, the conversation is about his performance. The young manager raises a workload concern in a meeting, factually, calmly, once, and discovers afterward that the word attached to her now is negative, and everyone who watched it happen learns the lesson without a word being spoken to them. The employee gathers the courage to report a bullying supervisor, into a process that, one way or another, reports back to the supervisor. None of these responses can be understood honestly without the conditions around them. Whether or not someone also meets criteria for illness, all of them are responding.

The modern workplace was characterized from its beginning as a goal-oriented production factory, and the emotional self was never in the blueprint. But the emotional self shows up every single day, because a human being cannot leave it in the car. So the worker is trained to stuff it down and stay quiet. Be grateful. Be lucky you are here at all. And when the conditions themselves are the harm, when the psychological safety risks have never been assessed, when the exposures go unacknowledged and the accountability never comes, and the worker's health finally begins to answer for all of it, look closely at the only door the system leaves open.

To be granted leave, even for right reasons, even under entirely normal human circumstances, a person must declare themselves ill. They must go to a doctor and be pathologized, must symptomize themselves in writing, must carry a diagnosis back to the very workplace that produced the injury. There is no form that says the conditions were unsafe and my body responded accurately. There is only the form that says something is wrong with me. It is a degrading passage. The person who could not get respect, safety, or accountability discovers that the one thing the system will readily hand them is a label. And the label completes the shutdown, because it turns the story inward. It teaches the worker to conclude that the problem lived in them all along. This is how the silencing sustains itself: it leaves self-blame as the only exit that pays the bills.

If this sounds dramatic, the numbers are worse. More than seven in ten Canadian workers report having experienced harassment or violence on the job, and the impacts extended into workers' health and ability to work, with particularly substantial disruption reported among those experiencing sexual harassment and violence. In Sun Life's 2024 Canadian long-term disability claims data, mental health was the most common diagnostic category, representing almost four in ten claims. In the United Kingdom, work-related stress, depression, and anxiety now make up nearly half of all work-related ill health, hundreds of thousands of workers and more than sixteen million working days lost in a single year. And at the global scale, the World Health Organization and the International Labour Organization did the accounting no one wanted to see: long working hours were linked to roughly three quarters of a million deaths from stroke and heart disease in a single year, making overwork the single largest occupational disease burden ever identified. Chronic work stress writes itself into blood pressure, into hearts, into immune systems, into depression. The disease is thoroughly documented. It is only the story that keeps getting left off the chart.

Now hold that against the anthropological record, because human beings have organized work very differently, and for most of our existence, we did. Marcel Mauss studied the gift economies of the Pacific and beyond and found whole societies bound together by giving, receiving, and reciprocating, where what moved between people carried relationship with it, and contribution wove the giver deeper into belonging. Robin Wall Kimmerer writes of the gift economy still alive in Indigenous lifeways, where the harvest is honourable because it takes only what is needed and gives back in return. Southern Africa gave the world the philosophy of ubuntu: I am because we are, a person is a person through other persons. And across many Indigenous nations of Turtle Island runs the teaching that every person arrives carrying gifts, and that the community's sacred task is to see those gifts and receive them. Inside frames like these, every role has a purpose and every role is significant. The fisher, the firekeeper, the one who watches the children, the one who remembers the songs. Work is contribution woven into belonging, reciprocity flowing in both directions, and the humanness of the worker is the entire point rather than the problem to be managed. There is a wisdom in that approach that we did not outgrow. We only drifted from it.

And the return is not a fantasy; the tools are already on the table. Researchers have given us the concept of psychological safety, the shared belief that it is safe to take interpersonal risks, to speak up, to say I am at capacity, without punishment. Canada created the world's first national standard for psychological health and safety in the workplace, and an international standard now exists alongside it. But a standard is only a document until it becomes a norm, so let me tell you what the norm looks like, because it looks like the old cultures. It looks like leaders who ask what do you need and then act on the answer. Workloads designed to actual human capacity instead of extraction curves. A debrief after the hard event instead of straight back to it. Accountability that flows up as readily as it flows down. The ability to name a harm without the process quietly punishing the namer. Every one of those practices is reciprocity. Every one of them is the village remembering what it always knew: that the wellbeing of the worker and the wealth of the community are the same water.

And nowhere does the employer's clock reach deeper into sacred territory than when someone we love dies. That is where I want to take you next, because it is the same machinery, and it is holding a stopwatch over the most human thing we do.

Grief on a Timer

Three to five days. In most of the Western world, that is the standard bereavement leave: three to five days to bury the person, notify the bank, empty the closet, and grieve, before the production line expects your face composed and your output restored. Some of those days are often unpaid.

And the diagnostic manuals have been keeping pace with the payroll calendar. In 2013, the exclusion that once protected the bereaved was removed, so that grief could be assessed as a depressive disorder within weeks of a loss. In 2022, a new diagnosis arrived that draws an official line for adults at one year, after which enduring grief becomes eligible for reclassification as disorder. Clinicians themselves are divided over that timer, and no wonder. The message underneath it is unmistakable: grieve faster, or your sanity comes into question. Wail at the funeral if you must, quietly, and then return to the line.

Now set that against how humans have actually mourned. Jewish tradition holds the bereaved in widening rings: seven days of shiva when the community comes to you, thirty days of shloshim, and a full year of mourning for a parent, each ring with its own permissions and practices, grief given a landscape instead of a cliff edge. In the Greek villages, the women lamented at the graveside across years rather than days, until the community completed the crossing with ceremony. A Māori tangi stops ordinary life for days, because a person has died, and that matters more than anything else on the calendar. These cultures did not fear that honouring grief would trap people in it. They understood the opposite: that grief which is witnessed and given its season is grief that can eventually transform, while grief that is timed and hidden is grief that goes to ground in the body.

You can see now that this section is the same section as the last one. It is the same employer clock, the same symptomizing of the self to justify an absence, the same form that asks what is wrong with you because there is no box for something sacred is moving through me. And it is the wail again, refused again. Grief on a timer is nothing more and nothing less than the dam applied to love. Grief is love with nowhere left to land, and it moves on the timeline of the relationship, of the body, of a season, never on the timeline of a pay period. Keep the flow flowing, and grief does what water does: it moves, it carves, it eventually finds the sea. Dam it, and it does what dammed water does.

Hold all of this together and the cruelty comes into focus, and so does the sanity of the grieving. A person can be wailing and be sane. A person can be undone by loss and be responding with perfect accuracy to the size of what they loved. Both can be true at the same time. The both-and is the ground the dominant framework keeps refusing to stand on, and it is precisely the ground the grieving need us to hold.

From the First Bell

I want you to see how early this begins and how long it runs, because it is one system wearing different uniforms, from birth to the end of our cycles.

It begins at the first school bell. And there is a reason the day begins with a bell. More than a century ago, Ivan Pavlov rang a bell before feeding his dogs, again and again, until the bell alone made them salivate. The food no longer needed to be present; the signal had been written into the body. He called it a conditioned reflex, and we have been organizing childhood around bells ever since. Human beings are the most conditionable creatures on this earth, and there is a humbling reason for it: we are wired to absorb the norms of the group that keeps us alive. Belonging is survival to a human nervous system, so we ascribe to our society's norms as automatically as we breathe. There is no fighting this in ourselves, and no shame in it. Social conditioning is not a personal weakness. It is part of our makeup.

But that truth carries a hard edge, and I will not soften it: if the norms we are absorbing are unwell, then the conditioning faithfully installs the unwellness in all of us. If our society is unwell, we are all unwell, no matter how privately and cleverly we cope. There is no individual wellness plan that exits a collective condition. There is only the honesty of admitting we are in one.

Our school systems were never designed around the neurodevelopmental needs of the children who enter them. Small bodies built for movement, play, attachment, and rhythm are seated in rows and measured against standardized competencies. Adolescents whose circadian rhythms are biologically shifted toward later sleep are summoned to first period in the dark. If schools were built for the students, they would look vastly different. They were built for the factory the students were being prepared for, bell to bell, from the first one to the last.

And then watch what happens to the ones who cannot endure the model. They are othered. They are assessed, labelled, and streamed, when in fact they are built exactly how they need to be. Chapter Nine showed you the machinery that turns a child's accurate response to a hostile classroom into a diagnosis in the child. This is that same machinery, seen from the level of design: the environment is never asked to account for itself, so the body that could not endure it must. Their thresholds of capacity are real and legitimate; the model simply refuses to recognize any threshold it did not standardize. Falling outside of Western systemization was never grounds for pathology. It is grounds for redesign.

From the school bell to the workplace to the grief timeline to the demonized matriarch, the pattern holds, and here is the hardest part to say: the system maintains itself through us. We operate inside it, and to meet our need for survival, literally our ability to pay our bills, we replicate it. We arrive on time, we stuff it down, we symptomize ourselves for the leave form, we teach our children to sit still. Nobody offers us a more natural way, a way built on the configuration of our actual human development, so we pass the dam forward, generation to generation, and call it life.

Naming this is the beginning of refusing it, and I want to be honest about what the naming feels like, because it is not a single clean realization. Accepting that the water we swim in is unwell is itself a grieving process, and it is natural for it to move through everything grief moves through: the denial, the anger, the bargaining, the sadness, and, in its own time, the acceptance. Those stages were first written about the dying, and they were never meant to be a straight line; they spiral, they repeat, they arrive out of order. Let them. This is part of the soul's journey: coming far enough out of the fishbowl to finally see the water, while still having to live in the water. That is exactly what we are called to and asked to do. And it is powerful work, and it goes better together. We are here for it in a far better way when we witness one another becoming through it, because on the other side of the acceptance waits the only question that matters: so now what? What do I actually have power over? We do have power. We only need to see the situation for what it is first, and be willing to.

And I understand completely why so many of us check out instead, because the checking out is also the body's wisdom. Screening research suggests that roughly one in ten of us lives with significant dissociation, and far more of us live in its milder weather, scrolling, numbing, floating somewhere just behind our own eyes, in a world engineered to catch every spare glance. Dissociation is built as a means to cope, to endure, to survive an environment the body does not want to be fully present in. Hold that sentence, because it is not an indictment of the dissociated. It is a review of the environment. Here is the reframe I want to leave you with: if we build a culture that is genuinely desirable to be in, we will live in it fully, in our bodies, in our minds, in our hearts and souls. The spirit wants to ground itself into a body when the life is livable, and it pops out, quietly, partially, when it is not. That is how we know. That innate, powerful compass is the answer one more time: whatever brings us back in means we are figuring it out. Presence is the pulse-check of a culture. And a culture that people no longer need to escape is precisely what the final chapter of this book is for.

The Pond Between Us

Before I close my own cycle, I want to name where the dam does its most intimate damage: between us.

Emotional resistance sits upstream of so much of what we now call, as a society, toxicity in relationships. When we name the patterns of abuse and dysfunction, what we are usually describing is coping strategy stacked upon coping strategy, built by people who refuse to look at the underlying emotion that made the strategies necessary in the first place. And the refusal does not keep the feeling small. It builds pressure. The intensity increases until it can only exit sideways, in unhealthy explosions, in ruptures that seem to arrive out of nowhere, in the fight that was never actually about the thing it was about.

The unlooked-at parts do not stay quietly where we left them. The parts of ourselves we reject inevitably become our biggest wounds, because rejection at that depth leads to heartache, and heartache unfelt becomes the pain we hand to each other, cycle after cycle, generation after generation of hurt passing between people who never meant to pass it. We stop listening to our own truth, and then we build an entire world out of that not-listening. Rarely one great betrayal. More often a million micro moments of avoidance, of denial, of safeguarding the heart from the emotions and from the freedom to truly express them.

When there is no safety to feel hurt, abandonment, the fear of rejection, shame, or any of the other deep waters, the internal world does exactly what the pond does. It builds up. It thickens. And a pond in that condition becomes a place where healthy relationships cannot form, because there is no clear water left to meet another person in. Two dammed ponds cannot make a river.

And I want to let the naming breathe here, because where dammed ponds can go is far more common than most people believe, and the silence around it is part of what keeps it going. In Canada, forty-four percent of women who have ever been in an intimate partner relationship, nearly half, report experiencing intimate partner violence in their lifetime, along with roughly a third of men. In the United States, the figures tell the same story: about four in ten women and one in four men. And violence wears many uniforms beyond the fist. There is the emotional and psychological abuse that erodes a person's sense of reality. There is financial abuse that quietly removes the means of leaving. There is coercive control that shrinks a life decision by decision until the world fits inside someone else's permission. And there is the cycle so many survivors know by heart, first mapped by Lenore Walker decades ago: the tension building, the explosion, and then the honeymoon of apologies and promises, the sweetness that keeps hope alive and the pond dammed, before the tension begins to build again. If you have lived inside any of this, you are not rare, and you are not crazy. You are surrounded by neighbours who have lived it too, most of them in the same silence Chapter Eight named.

The research on emotional suppression closes the loop with almost painful precision. People who habitually suppress their emotions report less closeness, less support, and less satisfaction in their relationships. Read that again: the composed face, held to protect the relationship, costs the very intimacy it was trying to protect. Suppression never makes a feeling smaller. It only makes it less visible, less shared, and more likely to surface as something worse.

And once again, the anthropological record holds alternatives worth naming, because human beings have known how to keep the water clear between them. The Semai of Malaysia, long documented as among the most nonviolent peoples on earth, meet conflict with the bcaraa': a community assembly, unhurried, sometimes running deep into the night, where everyone touched by a dispute speaks until the matter is genuinely finished, so that nothing is left to ferment in silence. Hawaiian families have practiced ho'oponopono, to set right: a structured gathering of prayer, truth-telling, confession, forgiveness, and release, untangling a relationship the way patient hands untangle a cord. Across many Indigenous legal traditions, peacemaking and restorative circles treat a harm as a rupture in relationship to be repaired with the community's help, rather than a private failing to be hidden or a crime to be punished in isolation. And modern relationship research lands, almost sheepishly, in the same place the old cultures started: what predicts whether love lasts is the presence of repair: the small reach across the gap in the middle of the argument, and whether it is received.

So here are some windows into practice, some ways to create clear water between you and the people you love:

- Name the feeling early and small. Say I felt hurt when, while it is still a trickle. Feelings named at the size of a seed never have to become the size of a tree.
- Build a repair ritual together. Agree in a calm moment on a word, a gesture, a cup of tea that either of you can offer midconflict that means I am still on your side. And decide together that receiving the repair matters as much as offering it.
- Let each other finish. Try a household bcaraa': each person speaks until they are truly done, uninterrupted, before the other responds. Most of what we call communication problems are completion problems.
- Make the implicit explicit. Hold a regular checkin where small resentments and unspoken needs get aired on

purpose, so nothing has to grow in the dark to get attention.
• Separate the feeling from the verdict. I feel abandoned is water moving; you are selfish is a dam thrown at someone else's pond. Speak the water, not the verdict.
• Know when the pond needs more than the two of you. Reaching for a counsellor, an elder, or a circle is not failure; it is repair in its communal form. And where there is abuse, safety comes before repair, always, and leaving can be the most honest act of self-love there is. And here is the sorrow underneath all of it. This is the biggest self-abandonment of all: the abandonment of the soul's truest desires. Every micro-moment of avoidance is a small no to the life the soul actually came here to live. The medicine has not changed since the first page of this chapter. Turn toward it with curiosity. Make it safe to feel, first within yourself, then between you and the people you love. The safety to feel is where every relationship worth having begins, including the one you are in with yourself.

Closing My Own Cycle

Earlier in this book, I opened my story to you. I told you what I lived through and what my body did to carry me through it, and I did that because I will not ask a reader to walk anywhere I have not walked myself. Before this book closes, I want to close the circle I opened. This is the end of that cycle, offered in the same openness.

Here is where I have arrived. I have a heart of compassion now, and it began with accepting that there is nothing I can do perfectly, because humans were never built for perfect. We were built for learning. And the image that has become my daily practice, the one I offer you now to keep, is the baby deer.

When a fawn is learning to walk, its legs are too long for its body. It stumbles. It splays. It sorts out its feet, its muscles, its trust in the ground, one wobbling attempt at a time. And no one laughs at a fawn. No one shames it. No one blames it for not already knowing. We watch it with our breath held and our hearts open, because we understand, without needing to be told, that it is learning something new, and that the stumbling is the learning. I have come to treat myself like a baby deer learning to walk. Every human being who is learning or unlearning anything is a fawn on new legs, and deserves to be met the way we would meet one.

My own neurodevelopmental wiring and my own experiences have shaped how I walk through this world and how I see it. That shaping is real, and it does not close the story. I can keep growing. I can let myself feel vulnerable and step into new meadows instead of staying only where my footing is sure. The world is not fully safe yet. People are not yet fully accepting of one another. And still, I can model what safety looks like, through my own self-advocacy, and by reminding others that they are allowed to advocate for themselves too. I can offer myself the same grace, compassion, and encouragement I would offer a fawn finding its legs, and I can offer it to you, and to everyone still sorting out their feet.

I do not have power over what has already happened in my experience. That water has moved through the valley it moved through. But I do have power over how I internalize the narrative, over what I allow the story to tell me about who I am and what I am worthy of experiencing. That power is real, and it is mine, and yours is yours. From that ground, I can hold a profound yes to compassion in the circles I keep, and a profound no to those who do not embody it yet. The no carries no hatred. It simply keeps the pond clear, and it leaves the door unlocked for the day they are ready. And for the ones who are still learning, I can guide with the same compassion, grace, humility, and acceptance that was extended to me when I was the one stumbling.

We are all incredible in our journeys, no matter what our stories are. Every one of us is shaping the social ecosystem we share, each nervous system feeding the field around it. The cocreation of a humanity that lets the water move is not a dream held somewhere above us. It starts with the lens we turn on ourselves. That lens becomes the lens we turn on each other. It is beautiful. It is sacred. And it is the reclaiming of wholeness.

Chapter Twelve
Moving Toward a Well Society
The Reclamation of Love, Connection, and the Practices for Holism

This chapter and the one that follows are the last of this book. They are also, in many ways, the chapters the rest of the book has been preparing you for.

Every page so far has been describing what happens when a body, a family, a culture is not given the conditions it needs to be well. The myth of brokenness. The soul echoes. The survival responses. The trauma armour. The social conditioning. The stress loops at population scale. The cultural trauma carried across generations. The silence that has kept it all in place. The pathologizing machinery that has translated accurate response into named disease. The generational reweaving that begins in one body at a time and feeds the network around it. The dam of emotional resistance that has kept the water from moving through any of it.

Every page has also been gesturing, sometimes quietly, sometimes directly, at what wellness actually requires. Safety. Witness. Belonging. Ceremony. Land. Language. Kin. Time. Rest. Permission. Love that is not transactional. Connection that is not conditional. The practices for holism that the larger erasure tried to dismantle, returning now in many languages, by many hands, in many places.

This chapter is about what a society would look like if it organized itself around what bodies actually need. I want to say at the beginning that I am not promising you a utopia. I am not asking you to wait for some future arrangement that does not yet exist. The well society is being built right now, in fragments, by ordinary people doing ordinary things in the rooms they are responsible for. The vision I am about to describe is an emergence.

Pieces of it are already alive. You are inside it. The question this chapter is asking is what your particular piece of it is.

The previous chapter placed the work of the reweaving in your own body and lineage. This chapter places the field of that work in front of all of us. The well society is what becomes possible when enough bodies inside it are doing what the previous chapter asked of you. The field and the body grow each other.

The well society is not a place we arrive at. The well society is a practice we take up. Every body that takes it up moves the whole field a little closer to it.

What a Well Society Would Feel Like

Before I describe what a well society would do, I want to describe what it would feel like, because the felt sense is the test of whether the structure is working.

In a well society, a body could walk into a public space and find its nervous system settling, rather than activating. The volume of the environment would not assault. The pace of the environment would not demand more than the body could sustain. The faces in the environment would meet the body's face with recognition rather than indifference or threat. The body would not have to spend energy bracing. The energy that bracing currently consumes would be available for other things.

In a well society, a body could feel hunger and know that food would be available. Could feel cold and know that shelter would be available. Could feel tired and know that rest was permitted. Could feel grief and know that the grief would be witnessed. Could feel joy and know that the joy would be welcomed without anyone needing to puncture it. The basic conditions of a body in time would be met as a baseline rather than as a prize earned through correct behaviour.

In a well society, the people who are responsible for children would have the time, the resources, the support, the rest, and the regulation to attune to those children. The children would grow up inside nervous systems that knew how to receive them. They would learn, at the somatic level the previous chapters have described, that connection can be trusted. That safety is real. That their own perceptions are accurate. That they belong here. The next generation would carry forward the inheritance of having been held.

In a well society, sickness would not be a personal failing. It would not be a financial catastrophe. It would not require navigation of a labyrinth designed to wear the sick body down further. The body that became unwell, for whatever reason, would be received by a network of care that included relational support, somatic attention, ceremonial space if the body wanted it, biomedical intervention where it was actually needed, and the time and resources for recovery. The body would not have to argue for its right to be cared for. The care would be the default.

In a well society, age would not be hidden. The elders would be present. The dying would be tended. The grieving would be held. The babies would be welcomed by communities ready to receive them. The transitions of a body across its life would be marked, witnessed, supported, and made meaningful. The body would not move through its years inside a privatized loneliness. The body would move through its years inside a field of relation that knew how to recognize each season as it arrived.

In a well society, the wounds of history would be visible, named, attended, and being repaired. The cultural traumas the previous chapters have walked through would not be treated as embarrassing details that the dominant culture should be allowed to forget. They would be treated as ongoing work the entire society is engaged in. The descendants of the wounded would receive the medicine the wider field could offer. The descendants of the wounding would do their own work without being asked to disappear or be ashamed. The whole field would be tilted, slowly, toward repair.

This is not abstract. Each of these felt qualities is something some bodies, in some places, are already experiencing. The well society is uneven. It is partial. It is interrupted. It is also real. It is the texture you have probably felt in a particular room with a particular elder, or at a particular ceremony, or in a particular kitchen with a particular friend, or in a particular forest at a particular hour. The texture is what tells you that the well society is recognition of what we have all, at moments, already touched.

The Soil a Well Society Grows In

Every garden is a function of its soil. A well society grows in particular soil. The soil has features. Some of these features have been steadily eroded for centuries by the colonial-modern project. Some have survived underground. Some are being deliberately rebuilt by the work being done right now in many places. The soil consists, at minimum, of the following.

Safety as a baseline rather than a prize. Bodies that are chronically braced cannot do the work of being well. Safety, in the somatic and material sense, is the precondition for everything else. This means food, shelter, freedom from violence, freedom from racialized harm, freedom from gendered harm, freedom from the kind of work that destroys the body that does it. The well society treats these conditions as floor, not ceiling.

Witness as default rather than as luxury. Every body, in every community, should have access to at least one other body that knows how to listen. The capacity to witness should be cultivated in schools, in workplaces, in families, in clinical settings, in religious communities, in any container where bodies meet. The capacity is teachable. The capacity is also undertaught. A well society would build the capacity deliberately.

Belonging that is not earned through performance. The body of a child belongs to its people without having to be impressive. The body of an elder belongs to its people without having to be productive. The body of any person belongs to the field without having to justify its presence through what it produces, what it earns, what it achieves, or how attractive it is. Belonging is the precondition of personhood. A well society treats it as such.

Time that is paced to bodies rather than to clocks. Bodies have their own rhythms. They need rest. They need slow meals. They need long conversations. They need seasons. They need to be allowed to be still. The colonial-modern project pulled bodies away from their own rhythms and demanded that they synchronize to industrial time. A well society would return time to the body. Not entirely. Enough.

Land relationship as constitutive rather than as decorative. The bodies that are well are the bodies that are in active relationship with the land they live on. They know the seasons. They know the names of the local plants. They know the watersheds. They know the local sacred sites. They know the Indigenous nations whose territory they are on and they are in some kind of right relationship with that fact. Land relationship is not a hobby for retired people. It is a foundational condition of nervous system regulation. The well society treats it as such.

Ceremony as ordinary rather than as exotic. Ceremony is the deliberate creation of conditions inside which bodies can do things they cannot do without ceremony. Mark transitions. Grieve. Celebrate. Reconnect. Forgive. Receive. The colonial-modern project privatized and commercialized ceremony. A well society would return ceremony to the ordinary fabric of communal life. Births. Deaths. Marriages. New jobs. Returns. Departures. The body knows it has lived through something when ceremony has marked it. A society without ceremony is a society that asks its bodies to absorb every transition without the witness the body requires.

Honest reckoning with what has been done. A society that refuses to look at its own history cannot heal. The well society looks. The well society listens to the descendants of those who were harmed. The well society makes the reparations it can make, even when they are partial, even when they are imperfect. The well society allows the descendants of those who caused harm to do their own work of grief and accountability without being shamed or being let off. The reckoning is the soil out of which any future arrangement can actually grow.

These are the features of the soil. None of them is impossible. None of them is utopian. All of them are being practiced, in various places, by various communities, right now. The well society is not waiting to be invented. The well society is waiting to be generalized.

Building Containers

A society is made of containers. Families. Friendships. Neighbourhoods. Workplaces. Schools. Clinics. Faith communities. Recovery groups. Online communities. The political institutions that hold the larger frame. Each container has its own quality of soil. Each container either supports the wellness of the bodies inside it or undermines it. A well society is one in which the containers have, on average, become places where bodies can settle and grow.

Container design is a skill. It can be taught. It can be learned. It has features. Pace. Tone. Use of authority. Treatment of conflict. Treatment of difference. Treatment of mistakes. Treatment of grief. Treatment of joy. Distribution of voice. Distribution of resource. Each of these is a design choice. Each choice either invites bodies to settle or signals to bodies that they had better brace.

The work of building better containers is work everyone is qualified to do, in the containers they have access to. If you are a parent, you are designing the container that your children's nervous systems are growing inside. If you are a manager, you are designing the container that your team is working inside. If you are a teacher, you are designing the container that your students are learning inside. If you are a clinician, you are designing the container that your patients are recovering inside. If you are a friend, you are designing the container that the people who love you live inside in their moments with you. The design is happening whether you are paying attention or not. Paying attention is the choice.

There are some general principles for building containers that support wellness. Slow the pace where you can. Reduce the volume where you can. Make the rules clear and apply them consistently. Apologize when you cause harm. Receive apology gracefully when it is offered to you. Allow people the time and the conditions to settle before you ask them to perform. Give people more voice in shaping the container than the dominant culture has trained you to give them. Notice who is not at the table and inquire about why. Notice your own activation and regulate it before you ask others to regulate around you. Take your own rest seriously so that the container you hold can be steady. Laugh more than the dominant culture suggests is appropriate. Cry without apology when grief is in the room.

None of this is mysterious. All of it is countercultural. The dominant culture, having been built on the suppression of bodies and on the demand that bodies produce regardless of cost, has trained most of us in patterns that work against wellness in the containers we hold. Choosing differently requires noticing the training and refusing it. The refusal is not dramatic. The refusal happens in small choices, made consistently, in the rooms you are responsible for.

Every container you hold is either a place where bodies can grow or a place where bodies have to brace. You get to choose. The bodies you hold will tell you what you have chosen, even when they do not say it in words.

The Individual Work

Every reader of this book has individual work to do. The work is not the same for every reader. The work depends on which lineage you carry, what was done to you, what you have absorbed, what you have already addressed, and what is still operating inside you that you have not yet looked at. I will not prescribe the work. I will name the kinds of work the path requires.

Listening to your body. Your body has been speaking to you for as long as you have been alive. The dominant culture trained most of us to override it. The work, slowly, is to begin listening again. The hunger you have ignored. The tiredness you have powered through. The grief you have not let yourself feel. The desire you have suppressed. The boundary you have not enforced. The body knows. Begin asking it. Begin acting on what it tells you.

Finding the witnesses. The previous chapter described the centrality of witness to the healing process. The individual work includes finding at least one body that can receive what you have been carrying. A therapist if you have access to one and one is the right fit. A friend if you have a friend who can hold what you need to put down. A community if the community is real and not a substitute for the work. An elder if you are lucky enough to have access to one. A ceremony if the ceremony is alive in your lineage or you have been invited into one that is alive in someone else's. Whatever the form, do not try to do this work alone. The work was never meant to be done alone.

Breaking specific silences. There are silences inside you. Some of them have been there for a long time. The work is to identify the next one that is ready to come out and find the conditions in which it can be spoken safely. Not all of them at once. The next one. Then the one after that. The pace is the pace of your body. The destination is a body that holds fewer silences than it used to.

Reclaiming what was taken from your lineage. Whatever your lineage is, something was taken from it. The language. The cosmology. The practices. The land. The names. The recipes. The songs. The forms of grief. The forms of joy. The relationship to the seasons. The relationship to the ancestors. The work is to begin recovering what is recoverable. Read about it. Ask the elders who are still alive. Travel to the land if you can. Learn the language even if you stumble. Wear the inherited symbol if it is yours to wear. Speak the names. The lineage is waiting for someone in this generation to call it back. You might be that someone.

Working with your own activation. Your nervous system was shaped by what your people lived through. It will keep doing what it was shaped to do until you give it different conditions and the practice to settle. There are many practices that work. Somatic experiencing. Yoga. Breathwork. Walking. Cold water. Singing. Drumming. Dancing. Time in the trees. Time near water. Sleep. Touch. Laughter. The specific practice is less important than the consistency. The practice is teaching the nervous system that the conditions are different now. The teaching takes time. The teaching works.

Holding yourself with kindness when the work is hard. The work will be hard. You will fail at it. You will revert. You will catch yourself doing the very thing you have been working to stop doing. This is what progress looks like inside a nervous system that has been shaped by hard conditions for a long time. The capacity to come back to the practice after you have fallen off it is the practice. The kindness toward yourself in the moments of falling is part of what makes the coming back possible. Self-cruelty does not produce healing. It produces more of what produced the wound in the first place. Be patient. Be kind. Keep going.

The Collective Work

The individual work is necessary. The individual work is also not sufficient. A society in which only a few people have done their inner work but the structures around them remain unchanged is a society of regulated individuals trying to function inside dysregulated systems. The bodies of those individuals will keep paying the cost of the systems. The well society requires that the work scale.

The collective work is the work of changing the conditions inside which bodies live. This includes the work of policy. Housing policy that ensures every body has shelter. Food policy that ensures every body has nourishment. Labour policy that ensures rest, fair wage, dignity at work, freedom from the most extractive forms of labour. Health policy that decouples access to care from employment and wealth. Education policy that supports children to grow into themselves rather than to be processed into productive units. Climate policy that takes the long view of a living planet rather than the short view of quarterly profit.

The collective work also includes the work of organization. Building the institutions, networks, and movements that hold the policy work and the cultural work over time. Mutual aid networks. Community land trusts. Cooperative housing. Worker-owned enterprises. Indigenous-led organizations. Disability justice collectives. Grief tending circles. Peer-led mental health support. Birth circles. Death doulas. The infrastructure of a well society is being built right now, in fragments, in many places. Joining one of those fragments, supporting one of those fragments, learning from one of those fragments, is collective work.

The collective work also includes the work of reparation. The descendants of those who were harmed have ongoing claims that have not been met. Land back. Restitution. Treaty implementation. The honouring of the ninety-four Calls to Action of the Canadian Truth and Reconciliation Commission. The honouring of the Calls for Justice from the MMIWG inquiry. The implementation of UNDRIP. The slow, contested, necessary work of unmaking what was made over centuries and remaking it more justly. None of this is finished. All of it is underway. The work is ours to advance, not to complete.

The collective work also includes the work of ceremony at scale. Public mourning for public losses. Public celebration of public joy. The work of reweaving a cultural fabric that has been deliberately torn. National Indigenous Peoples Day. Orange Shirt Day. Truth and Reconciliation Day. Holocaust Remembrance Day. The growing recognition of cultural holidays that the dominant culture had previously excluded. They are training in collective attention, disguised as small gestures. A society that learns to attend to its losses begins to be a society that can prevent the next round of them.

The collective work includes the building of bridges across lineages. The work of getting the bodies of people whose ancestors were on different sides of the same wound into rooms together, with skilled facilitators, with adequate time, with willingness to be uncomfortable, and with the long-term commitment to keep showing up. This is some of the hardest work of all. It is also some of the most important. The collective cancer the previous chapters described will not be healed by the wounded lineages alone or by the complicit lineages alone. The medicine requires the rooms where both can be present. The rooms are being built. Some of them are being built well. We are still learning.

What This Asks of Those Who Hold Bodies

If you are a clinician, a therapist, a counsellor, a coach, a nurse, a physician, a midwife, a chaplain, a teacher, a manager, a leader, a parent, a grandparent, an elder, an organizer, a facilitator, or any other role in which bodies look to you for steadiness, this section is for you. The work I have been describing throughout this book happens through you whether you have framed it that way or not. The quality of your own regulation is part of the medicine you offer the bodies you hold. The quality of your own ongoing healing is the limiting factor on what the bodies you serve can do in your presence. The work begins inside the practitioner.

This is what I mean when I use the word healership. The convergence of healing and leadership. The recognition that you cannot take a body further than your own body has gone. You cannot regulate a room more deeply than your own nervous system is regulated. You cannot offer presence to another body that your own body has not yet practiced offering to itself. Your inner work is not separate from your outer work. Your inner work is the foundation of your outer work. Without it, every container you hold will quietly carry whatever you have not yet metabolized.

The bodies in front of you are reading your body all the time. They are reading your breath. They are reading your eye contact. They are reading the speed at which you respond. They are reading the words you use and the words you avoid. They are reading whether you are present or whether you are mentally elsewhere. They are reading whether you can hold what they have to say or whether they will need to manage your reaction. Most of this reading is happening below the threshold of either party's awareness. All of it is shaping what the encounter produces.

This means that the inner work I have been describing is the prerequisite for those of you in positions of relational responsibility. The continuing education most healers and leaders take is mostly about technique and content. The continuing education most healers and leaders need is the slow, demanding, lifelong work of becoming a more regulated, more attentive, more honest, more humble, more available body. There are no shortcuts to this. There are also no end points. The work continues for as long as you are in the field. It is the work itself.

Make your own healing a non-negotiable part of your practice. Find your own witness. Tell your own truths. Cry your own tears. Grieve your own losses. Speak your own silences. Receive your own care from the people who can give it to you. Be in supervision, in your own therapy, in your own ceremony, in your own community of practice. The bodies you serve will benefit from every increment of your own work, even when you cannot trace exactly how the benefit travelled.

Give yourself permission to set the work down sometimes. Rest is medicine. Joy is medicine. Time away from the work is part of the work. The dominant culture has trained many of us in heroic patterns of overwork in helping professions. The training is wrong. The bodies we serve are best served by practitioners whose own bodies are well. The well practitioner takes care of themselves first. This is the precondition of being able to take care of anyone else.

The capacity to be present with another body cannot be borrowed from a credential. It can only be built inside the practitioner's own ongoing healing. Healership is built one breath at a time, in the body of the one who would hold others. The work begins again every morning.

What This Asks of Institutions

Institutions, in their dominant current forms, are not yet places that hold bodies well. They were designed, mostly, for other purposes. Efficiency. Productivity. Profit. Control. The bodies that work inside them and the bodies they serve have, for a long time, been required to set aside their own needs in order to fit. The cost of this arrangement is visible everywhere now. Burnout. Turnover. Disengagement. The quiet quitting that is really the body protecting itself. The sick leave numbers. The mental health claims. The recruitment crises. The bodies are reporting on the conditions. The institutions, if they are paying attention, are starting to hear it.

Institutions that want to move toward being well will have to take on serious work. Some of this work is structural. Reasonable workloads. Adequate staffing. Living wages. Stable schedules.

Meaningful benefits. The basic material conditions inside which a body can function without being depleted. Many institutions have known this for decades and have not done it because the cost would reduce short-term profit. The cost of not doing it is now becoming visible in ways the financial reports can no longer hide.

Some of the work is cultural. The pace of communication. The treatment of mistakes. The relationship between authority and care. The way feedback is given. The way feedback is received. The treatment of difference. The way conflict is handled. The honouring of grief when a colleague is going through it. The honouring of joy when a colleague is having it. The treatment of bodies that need accommodation. The treatment of bodies that look or move differently from the institutional norm. These questions are the daily fabric of whether the institution is a place where the people inside it can be well.

Some of the work is reparative. Institutions, especially institutions that have operated inside Canada or any other settler colonial state, have inherited specific obligations that have not yet been met. The implementation of the TRC Calls to Action. The implementation of UNDRIP. The integration of Indigenous knowledge systems into the institution's operating logic. The active recruitment, retention, and meaningful authority of Indigenous and racialized employees as people whose perspectives are meant to change how the institution does its work, never as token presences arranged for institutional optics. The acknowledgement of harm the institution has caused and the actual work of repairing it. This work is hard. It is also overdue. The institutions that take it on will be the ones that survive the transitions that are already underway.

Some of the work is spiritual, in the broad sense of that word. The recognition that institutions are containers that bodies live inside. The bodies have souls. The bodies have lineages. The bodies have grief and joy and longing and hope. The institutions that recognize this and build accordingly become places where the people inside them want to stay. The institutions that refuse to recognize it become places that people leave as soon as they can find somewhere else.

If you are inside an institution, in whatever role, you are part of how it changes. Not all of the change. A part of it. The change happens through every voice that asks the harder question, every leader who refuses to perpetuate the dysfunction they inherited, every employee who insists on being treated as a body with a soul, every committee that takes the recommendations of the people most affected seriously. Institutional change is slow. Institutional change is real. Your part in it matters more than the institution will admit.

What This Asks of Anyone Holding a Body in Pain

There is one more category of reader I want to address before this chapter closes. The reader who is, right now, accompanying another body that is in pain. A child. A partner. A parent. A sibling. A friend. A patient. A client. A student. A colleague. A neighbour. Whoever that body is for you. You are doing the most important work this book has been pointing at, in the most ordinary form available. Here is what I want you to know.

You do not have to fix it. Most of the bodies in pain around you cannot be fixed. They can be accompanied. They can be witnessed. They can be heard. They can be allowed to be in pain while you are present. The body in pain that finds another body present with it is not a body in pain alone. That is the gift you can give. The gift is enormous. It will sometimes feel like it is not enough. It is enough. It is more than enough. It is the medicine the body in front of you actually needs.

You do not have to know what to say. The dominant culture has trained you to respond with words. Often the most healing thing you can offer is the quietness of your own steady body in the room with the body that is hurting. Sit. Breathe. Stay. The body in front of you knows you are there. The body in front of you is regulating off your nervous system whether you can see the regulation happening or not.

You do not have to carry it. The body of the accompanying person is not designed to absorb the pain of the body in pain. Boundaries are part of how the accompaniment works. You can be deeply present with someone in pain and also go home, rest, eat well, sleep, attend to your own life. Carrying their pain inside your body, in the long run, will deplete you to the point that you cannot accompany them anymore. The practice of not carrying it, while remaining present with it, is the skill. It is teachable. It is hard. It is essential.

You will not always do this well. You will say the wrong thing. You will be too tired to be present when the moment requires it. You will fail to show up. You will reach for the rescue when the witness was what was needed. This is part of being human and part of doing this work. The practice is to keep coming back. The practice is to apologize when you can apologize. The practice is to learn from each encounter and bring more of yourself to the next one. The bodies you accompany do not need perfection. They need a witness who is committed to keep returning.

Know that what you are doing matters more than the dominant culture will tell you. The dominant culture rewards production. The dominant culture barely sees accompaniment. The bodies that have been accompanied through their hardest moments know what was done for them. The lineages of the bodies you accompany will remember. The work you are doing, often invisible, often unpaid, often misunderstood, is the work the human family has always run on. Without it, the species would not have survived this long. With more of it, the species can begin to do more than survive.

The Multigenerational Frame

I want to say one thing about timing before I close this book. The work I have been describing is not work this generation will finish.

The wounds we have been looking at took centuries to accumulate. The medicine will take generations to fully take. We are the advancers of this work. The finishing belongs to hands that come after ours. The generation before us did its piece. The generation after us will do theirs. Our job is to do what we can do in the body we have for the time we have it, and to pass forward to the next generation a slightly less wounded field than the one we received.

This frame matters because the dominant culture has trained us to expect short-term results. Quarterly outcomes. Five-year plans. The pace of a news cycle. None of that is the pace of healing. The pace of healing is the pace of a season, a generation, a century. The bodies that took five generations to be wounded will not be unwounded in one. The cultural fabrics that took five hundred years to be torn will not be rewoven in twenty. Knowing this is part of the medicine. The knowing protects us from the despair that would arrive if we measured the work by the timelines of the wounding.

Robin Wall Kimmerer, in her writing on Indigenous knowledge and gift economies, has named the importance of what she calls the long view. Joy Harjo, in her poetry, has named it through the figure of the ancestors who are watching and the descendants who are coming. The Haudenosaunee Great Law of Peace asks that decisions be made with the seventh generation in mind. The well society is built on these timelines. It is not built on the timelines of the institutions that have to report next quarter.

If you give your one life to this work, you will not see the well society fully arrive. You will see fragments of it. You will see it in particular rooms. You will see it in particular bodies you accompanied. You will see it in the children who grew up in containers you helped build. You will not see the whole. You are not supposed to see the whole. The whole is the work of generations. Your piece is to advance the work in the years you have, and to trust that the descendants will continue what you began.

We do not have to finish the work. We have to advance it. The well society is the inheritance of a long line of ordinary people, in every generation, who refused to pass forward, untouched, what they had been handed.

The last chapter takes you inside it. Not the argument for a well society. The feeling of one, from the first cry of a life to the rooms you will walk into tomorrow.

Chapter Thirteen
The Feeling of a Well Society
Sensing the Echo in Our Blood Memory

The last chapter made the argument. This one sets the argument down. Because there is a kind of knowing that arguments cannot reach, and it is the kind this book has been walking toward the whole time. You can be persuaded of a well society and still not believe in it, the way you can memorize a map of a country you have never stood in. Belief lives lower than persuasion. It lives in the body. So before I let you go, I want to do something different. I want you to feel it.

I believe you already can. Not because you have lived in a well society. Almost no one reading this has. But your body carries reference points for wellness that your biography never gave it. Many traditions call this blood memory: the knowing that travels in the body, passed down the line the way the wounds were passed, older than your story, patient as ground water. Chapter Ten showed you that the wounds travel through the generations. It would be strange if the wounds travelled and the wisdom did not. We may only sense the echo of it now. The echo is enough to navigate by.

Have you ever felt homesick for a place you have never been? That ache may not be confusion at all. It may be the compass again, the same one from the dam chapter, pointing at the design. The body recognizes what it was built for even when it has never once received it. That recognition is what this chapter is for.

The Sacred and the Social Ecosystem

Before I take you inside the feeling, I want to lay one more piece of ground, because it is the ground everything else stands on. The world is a sacred place. It did not become sacred when a doctrine declared it so, and it will not stop being sacred when a market says otherwise. But there have always been those who wanted to take the sacred out of it, because a world stripped of the sacred is a world that can be extracted from without ceremony or apology. And people across lifetimes have fought, bled, and burned over whose version of the sacred is the right one. So I will not name it fully here. I cannot, and I should not. The sacred does not need our agreement in order to be real. It only needs our reverence, in whatever language reverence arrives in you.

Nor will I pretend the world holds still. Life is a mixed relational dance, always moving, and consistency was never the promise. What a society can offer is a way of moving together. Stillness was never the promise.

That way of moving together is what I mean by a social ecosystem. Every society, everywhere, in every era, is a living network of understandings: how we govern ourselves, how we feed ourselves, how we heal, how we teach, how we trade, and how we touch the sacred. Each of those domains takes its shape from the values chosen at the source, and there is deep wisdom in how the old shapes were made. They were formed around the land and its seasons, around what the place itself could teach, and they were repeated and refined by so many wise ones before us that the foundation became a kind of inheritance. Which is why the resourceful move, when a society begins to fail its people, was never to invent a new way and then a newer way and then a newer way still. It was to return to the root and restore it there. You have heard this before in this book, because it is the book: tend the fire, and stop chasing the smoke.

And here is the measure of whether an ecosystem is well, the single diagnostic I would hand you if I could hand you only one. In a well society, no one profits from the vulnerabilities of the exploited. Vulnerability is not the weakness the extractive world taught us it was. It is the most useful signal a community has. Our vulnerabilities show us our set point within the ecosystem, the places where we need each other, the exact coordinates where kinship becomes possible. They are how we find each other and how we stay akin to those around us. A society that mines them for profit has read the map upside down. A society that meets them with relationship is reading it the way it was drawn.

The First Cry

So let us begin where every nervous system begins. A baby is born, and the first thing she does in this world is cry. That cry is the first communication any human being ever makes. It is not a demand and it is not a manipulation. It is a signal, pure and accurate: something is needed. It is the first vulnerability any of us ever offers the world, and it is offered in total trust. And what happens next, in the first weeks and months of answering or not answering that signal, is the first lesson any of us is ever taught about the world.

In Chapter Six I showed you how infant care drifted, over generations, from constant carrying and co-regulation to swings, cribs, and schedules. I want to stay now with the method that sits at the centre of that drift, because it is the crib-sized version of everything this book has named. And I need to pause here and distinguish established science from my own grounded opinion.

We do not currently have evidence establishing that the cry-itout method causes anxiety or depression in adulthood. Some behavioural sleep studies, including follow-up into childhood, have not found measurable long-term harm in the outcomes they assessed. I want to say that honestly.

I also remain deeply unconvinced by the practice.

My concern comes from the wider developmental rationale I have spent this entire book tracing. An infant's cry is a biological signal. The youngest nervous systems develop in relationship. Responsive caregiving can buffer stress, and our earliest repeated experiences help shape our expectations about whether distress brings connection, comfort, or response.

So this is my grounded opinion and my hypothesis. I believe that intentionally and repeatedly leaving an infant's distress unanswered may be one upstream contributor to anxiety, emotional suppression, or disconnection for some people later in life. I believe it deserves far more longitudinal research into adult mental health than currently exists. I cannot tell you science has proven that connection. It has not. I can tell you the rationale is strong enough that I am unwilling to dismiss the question.

The cry-it-out method instructs parents to leave a baby crying for periods of time as part of teaching independent sleep. The crying often does stop. Where I depart from the dominant interpretation is in what I believe we should remain curious about. Did the nervous system learn to self-soothe? Did sleep pressure simply win? Did the child adapt to the pattern? Did nothing harmful happen at all? Does the meaning change depending on the infant, the age, the wider caregiving relationship, the frequency, or whether repair and responsiveness are abundant everywhere else?

I do not think we know enough to shut those questions down.

And my body, my work, and everything I understand about relational development make me ask a deeper one. What do we teach a human nervous system when its earliest signal of distress is intentionally left unanswered?

That question is the first dam I am asking us to examine. Chapter Eleven traced emotional resistance through the funeral, the workplace, the classroom, and the family table. This is where I am asking us to stay curious about where the training may begin: in a dark room, in a crib, in the moment a small body calls out and the world, on advice, does not come. The society that will later hand her a tissue to stop her crying, a form to symptomize her exhaustion, and a timeline for her grief begins its instruction in the first months of her life. She will be praised, at every later stage, for the same skill she learned in that room: needing without showing it.

And now the paragraph I will not write this chapter without. If you sleep-trained your children, put the guilt down. You were an exhausted parent inside an economy that took your village away, handed you a baby and a job and no help, and then sold you a method with the word expert on the cover. You did what loving parents do: you reached for what you were told was best, with the resources you had. That is cultural coping, the same coping this book has refused to blame anyone for from its first page. And here is what your nervous system and your child's nervous system both deserve to know: the wiring is not a sentence. Rupture followed by repair is one of the most healing sequences a relationship can hold, at any age. You met the Still Face experiment in Chapter Six; what that same body of research went on to show is that babies never needed perfect attunement. They needed enough of it, and they needed the repair after the misses. It is never too late to become a person who comes when called. Children feel that change. So do grown ones.

So here is the first feeling of a well society, and see if you can let yourself feel it, in your own body. Imagine being small, and calling out into the dark, and hearing footsteps. Imagine the world's first lesson being: when you signal, someone comes. Feel what that would have built. A well society is that lesson, kept, at every scale, for a whole lifetime. The rest of this chapter is that lesson growing up.

A Day Inside It

Come inside it with me, then. Not the argument. The day.

You wake when your body finishes sleeping, because the rhythms of the day were built around bodies rather than bells. You lie there for a moment and notice something it can take a lifetime to name: you are not braced. The floor of your stomach is not preparing for anything. The day ahead of you wants you in it.

You go to your work, and your work receives your particular gifts, because in this place every role has a purpose and everyone knows it. Someone asks what you need to do this well, and then waits for the answer, and then acts on it. In the late morning, word moves through the community that someone has died. Things pause. Not everything, and not forever. Visibly, though, because a person has died and that matters here. You hear the grief being given its voice from across the way, and nobody moves to quiet it. Your own chest aches in the old way, and you let it, and the ache moves through and completes, the way you were taught it would.

In the afternoon you say a no in a meeting. The no is received as information rather than as insubordination. Nobody writes a word on you for it. The children are outside longer than they are inside, and the teenagers are still asleep when the morning starts, because the schedule was built for them. An elder sits at the centre of a room, and the room came to her.

In the evening there is food and there are people and there is no performance. Nobody at the table is managing their face. Someone cries at a story, and the story simply waits for them. Notice your own body as you read this. Your shoulders. Your jaw. Your breath. If something in you loosened, even slightly, that is worth trusting. It may be recognition.

And at night, the dark is not a thing to brace against. In a well society, the children grow up able to sleep with the light off.

Nourishment, Kin, and the Doorway

There are textures inside that day I want to slow down for, because they are the load-bearing walls of the feeling.

The first is nourishment, and I mean it in the fullest sense. The gut and the brain are in constant conversation along the body's great wandering pathways; the belly is wired into the very systems that decide whether the world feels safe. Nourishment is central to the nervous system, which means that how a society feeds itself is never just logistics. It is regulation. Food grown with care, prepared with presence, and eaten in company lands in the body as a message: you are provided for, and you belong here. The same meal eaten alone, standing, scrolling, delivers a different message entirely, and the body files both.

The second is kin beyond the human. There is a relationship between how we care for the plants and the animals and how we care for ourselves, and it has never been a coincidence. The hands that learn gentleness with a seedling or an old dog are practicing the same gentleness they will offer a child, an elder, their own tired body. A society's treatment of its gardens and its creatures is a preview of its treatment of its people. Everything in the way we do life is connected to everything else in the way we do life. That is what ecosystem means.

The third is creativity. Where relationships are safe, expression follows, because a nervous system that no longer spends itself on bracing has energy left over for making. In a well society, creativity is the ordinary overflow of people who are allowed to be true: the song while cooking, the carving, the garden laid out for beauty as much as for food, the story told properly with all its pauses. Expressing what is true for ourselves is evidence of a life being lived.

And beyond expression there is purpose, the question of who you truly want to be, which stops being a crisis and becomes a becoming when the ecosystem around you is designed to receive your answer. Purpose carries a meaning that always ends up making sense, later, when you have grown into it and can look back at the path that only your particular gifts could have walked.

But the best of it, the texture I would choose if I could only keep one, is the doorway. Watch what happens when love is doing the greeting. Someone rises when you enter. The kettle goes on. Your name is said like it matters. Across so many cultures, arrival was ritualized on purpose: greetings that mean I see you, blessings spoken at the threshold, the guest seated first and fed first. The doorway was understood as a small ceremony, repeated daily, telling every nervous system that crossed it the same thing the answered cry told the baby: you are expected here, and someone comes. Ritualizing connection and love is maintenance, the daily kind that keeps a home standing. It is the daily tending of the pond between us.

Already Arriving

Now let me say plainly what the wellness of a society is not, so that nothing in this chapter gets romanticized on its way into you. It is not utopia. Utopia is an idea, and ideas do not have bodies. What I am describing is homeostasis: a natural way of being together that self-corrects the way any living system self-corrects, with rupture and repair, with seasons, with loss that is honoured and conflict that is finished properly. There will still be death in a well society. There will still be heartbreak, hard winters, poor harvests, and people who take longer to learn. The difference is not the absence of pain. The difference is that nothing has to pool behind a dam.

And you do not have to wait for it, because it is already arriving, in fragments, wearing modern clothes. Look:

- A workplace runs a real debrief after a hard event, asks its people what they need, and adjusts the workload instead of the worker. Psychological safety moves from the poster to the practice.
- A school district moves its start time later so its teenagers can sleep the way their biology asks to, and mood, attendance, and learning all rise to meet the decision.
- A circle of women gathers with fire and story to mark a friend's crossing into her matriarch years, and a daughter watches a threshold being honoured instead of hidden.

• A death is met with a grief circle, a home vigil, or simply a workplace that says take the time you need, and the mourner discovers their tears have somewhere sanctioned to go.
• A neighbourhood grows food together in a shared garden, and the harvest moves between houses the way gifts do, binding the block into something older than an address.
• A school replaces suspensions with restorative circles, and a harm becomes a rupture the community repairs together instead of a child sent away with a label.
• A father wears his baby through the market, answering the small sounds before they become cries, and nobody calls it spoiling anymore.
• A men's circle sits weekly in a garage or a hall, and men who were trained for silence practice finishing their sentences in front of witnesses.
• A community answers a crisis with mutual aid: meal trains, tool libraries, time banks, neighbours trading skills without an invoice in sight, and commerce remembers that it began as reciprocity.
• A household keeps its small rituals of the doorway: the greeting, the shoes, the kettle, the goodnight said properly. The sacred returns to a society the same way it left, one ordinary act at a time. None of these are utopia. Every one of them is happening somewhere in the modern world right now. They are the ecosystem restoring itself at the root, value by value, room by room. When you find one, join it. When you cannot find one, be the first fragment. Chapter Five handed you the image this whole vision rests on: the petri dish. A dysregulated organism, placed in a field that holds regulation, comes back into regulation on its own, without anyone forcing it. The nervous system reads the field. Now widen the dish. The well social ecosystem is the petri dish grown to the size of a life, and the culture inside it

is something we name and choose to value. That is the whole turn of this book, arriving at its plainest form: the field is a choice. Nobody gets to choose the field they were born into. Every one of us gets a say in the field we are building around the people we love, in the rooms we are responsible for, at the values we water at the source. A well society is worked toward the way a garden is worked toward: chosen, tended, and returned to daily. And every fragment on the list above is someone, somewhere, already choosing it.

Blood Memory

Why did your body respond to all of that? You have never lived that day, and the fragments may not have reached your street yet. And yet perhaps something in you moved toward it anyway, like a plant toward a window. If it did, that movement is worth trusting. It is memory. Your line lived versions of that day. Some of them recently, in a grandmother's kitchen, at a fire, in a language you may no longer speak. Some of them so long ago that no story survives of them, perhaps a settling in your chest when the shape comes near. The wounds travelled down the line; this book has spent many chapters on that. The wisdom travelled too, in songs, in hands, in the body's stubborn recognition of what it was designed for. We may only sense the echo of it in our blood memory now. Sensing the echo is not a small thing. Migrating birds have never seen the place they are flying to, the first time they go. They go anyway. Something in them knows.

But I want to press on the question underneath all of this, because it is the question this section exists to answer. When people do not know what has been lost to them, how do they know what is worth reclaiming? The wisdom knowledges of connection, to our whole selves, to each other, to the land, to the sacred, were suppressed through many generations, deliberately in some places, carelessly in others, until whole lineages arrived in the present with no picture of what was taken. You cannot grieve a treasure you never saw. You cannot fight for an inheritance you were never told existed. This is the cruelest efficiency of the erasure: it removes the loss and then removes the memory of the loss, so that the descendants come to defend the emptiness itself as normal. And this is exactly why blood memory matters. It is the part of the inheritance that could not be confiscated. When the stories were interrupted and the practices were outlawed and the languages went quiet, the body kept a copy. Not a detailed one. An echo. And an echo is enough, because an echo tells you two things the erasure tried to hide: that there was a sound, and the direction it came from. To feel that knowing rise through our dominant values and societies again is crucial, because it is the only compass a dispossessed people carries that cannot be marketed to them. We reclaim by resonance. If it rings in the blood, it was ours.

I know this because it happened in my own body, and I want to tell you when. The birth of my daughter was the reigniting of my soul echoes, the very ones I named for you back in Chapter Two. When I became pregnant, I had no one. I mean that literally: there was not one woman in my life I could turn to for guidance. I was in the fog with no lighthouse. And something in me already knew that most of what the world was offering me was marketing, that so much of the guidance on the shelves was really a list of what a mother needed to buy. So I started researching, young and alone, and somewhere in that searching, something older than my biography switched on. Out of sheer need, I turned toward some kind of matriarchal wisdom, and an activation occurred. Because of everything I had been through, I could see the why of what I was doing with total clarity: keeping my daughter safe in a world I did not yet fully understand, a world that hurt its own without knowing why. The feeling of knowings deep within, that was the blood memory. What felt innate and raw and true and real. I began asking my questions through it. Did having her sleep on the other side of the house feel right? Would our ancestors have done that? I was the young girl who grew up on the outside of town asking questions, and I had become the woman growing a being into the world, still asking them. Modernity was never my fishbowl. I was always on the outside looking in, and for once that vantage was a gift. I learned to trust the echo far more than the social messaging, and the echo did not fail me. It has not failed me since.

That is when the burning questions of this chapter first lit in me, and they have not gone out. What does it mean to have a well society for our young ones? For ourselves? To create together? And why have we not created one? What stopped us in the first place? What are we saying yes to? What are we saying no to? And who decides?

This is why glimpses matter so much more than they appear to. Every time you have been heard all the way to the end of a sentence, you were inside a fragment of the well society. Every time someone's hand landed on your shoulder at the exact right moment. Every meal where you did not manage your face. Every room where your no was safe. Those moments are not consolation prizes on the way to the real thing. They are the real thing, arriving early, in pieces, the way dawn arrives in pieces before the sun clears the hill.

So practice the feeling on purpose. Here are some ways to taste the well society today, with the life and the people you already have:

- Answer a cry within your reach. The friend's message you have been meaning to return, the child calling from the other room, your own body's signal to rest or eat or move. Let your response time be the culture you keep.
- Give one person your unhurried witness. Let them speak until they are truly finished, without rehearsing your reply. The well society is built one completed sentence at a time.

• Mark a threshold out loud. Someone near you is crossing something: a birthday into elderhood, a retirement, a first year of grief, a becoming. Name it and honour it, even in a single sentence. Rites of passage begin returning the moment one person witnesses another on purpose.

• Thank a role. Tell one person today that their contribution was seen, especially a contribution the culture has been trained to look past.

• Keep one table free of performance. One meal, however simple, where every nervous system present is allowed to arrive exactly as it is. None of this waits for policy. All of it is upstream work, because every one of those acts is a value being chosen, and Chapter Eleven already told you what sits at the source of the water. When enough of us choose the same values in enough small rooms, the culture is no longer being resisted. It is being replaced. You are still in the fishbowl. So am I. We do not get to live outside the water we were born into. But we have come far enough out of it to see it now, and we know the direction the compass points, and we have felt, even for a few minutes, what the destination feels like from the inside. Whatever brings you back into your body is the way. Follow the settling. Follow the loosening jaw. Follow whatever makes your spirit want to ground itself deeper into your one life. That is the echo, getting louder.

If Not Now, Then When

So here is where I hand it all back to you, because it was always yours. You are the master of your own life. You light the fire of your own desire, your own motivation, your own purpose. Only you. Do not take my processes and my writing and wear them as your own. Do not think I am trying to convince you of anything, or asking you to adopt a doctrine, because it is not that, and this book will have failed if that is what it becomes. What I am asking is smaller and harder: feel into your own core beliefs and see if they align with wellness. If they do not, then why not? What is the root of that? Track those answers, honestly, all the way down, and they will reveal one of two paths. Do you want a well world, or not?

If you do, then allow it to be known in your own spaces. Or reach out. Join the wider community of people doing this work and let us cocreate together. Because we truly can create whatever we decide in a social ecosystem, and here is the fact that changes everything once it lands: we are creating every single day, in every single way, regardless. Period. We are creating. There is no neutral. Every doorway greeted or ignored, every cry answered or trained away, every table with or without performance is a brick laid in one world or another. So why not create the world that is worth staying fully in our bodies for? A world we can be home in ourselves in, a world that is actually enjoyable to experience? Why not create a world built for wellness, for self-actualization, for loving ourselves? Why not celebrate each other for being resilient and creative, and put down the comparing, the contrasting, and the ridiculing for good? Normalize human love and connection. That is the whole revolution, and it fits inside an ordinary day.

If not now, then when?

And now, before I let you go, there is one more thing I want to say to you, directly, reader to reader of the same water.

A Final Word

If you have read this book all the way through, something in you has been doing significant work. The reading itself is part of the work. The reader's nervous system has been processing, integrating, recognizing itself, sometimes being activated, sometimes being soothed, sometimes being asked to look at things it had carefully placed out of view. That work is real. It has changed something in you. It will continue to change things in you for some time after you set the book down.

I want to thank you for that. The fact that you stayed with this material, when so much of the dominant culture trains us to look away from it, is itself an act of healership. You held yourself through it. You let it land. You may have cried at some sections. You may have set the book aside for days. You may have written in the margins or shared passages with the people in your life. All of this is the work the book was written to invite. The book was always going to be the smaller part. You are the larger part. The book hands the work to you. What happens next is yours.

Here is what I want you to take with you.

Your responses make sense. Every one of them. The exhaustion, the activation, the grief, the rage, the longing, the freeze, the substances, the patterns, the relationships, the choices that have looked, on the outside, like failure. They are not failure. They are a body responding accurately to what it has been placed in. The body has been telling the truth. The medicine begins by believing the body.

You are inside a lineage. The lineage carried wounds. The lineage also carried medicine. Both are available to you. You did not choose what you inherited. You can choose what you do with it. What you do with it shapes what gets passed forward. Every act of healing in your one body is, simultaneously, an act of healing in the line behind you and the line ahead of you. You are doing the work on behalf of more than yourself, whether you have framed it that way or not.

You are inside a wider field. The field includes every person reading this book, every person who could not read it because they did not have access, every body across the planet that is engaged in the same work in its own language. The field is bigger than you can see. The field is also smaller and more intimate than you can see. It includes the elder you saw at the grocery store, the child in your neighbourhood, the colleague who has been struggling, the friend who texted you yesterday. The field is the medium the well society grows in. You are part of how it gets tended.

You are not alone. You never were. The loneliness many of us have felt is a symptom of the field having been torn. The remedy is the active rebuilding of relation. With your body. With your people. With your lineage. With the land you live on. With the ancestors who are waiting to be remembered. With the descendants who are coming. The well society grows in these relations. Tend them. They will tend you back.

Remember the practice. Stillness. The teaching the Coast Salish educator Len Pierre has shared so many times. When you are still, you can absorb more teachings. When you are still, the body can put down what it has been carrying. When you are still, you can hear what your life is asking of you. When you are still, you remember what was forgotten.

The work ahead is long. The work is also good. The work is the meaning of being alive in a body in a time on this earth. The bodies who came before you did their piece. The bodies who come after you will do theirs. The piece in front of you is yours. It is enough. It is what you came here for. Take it up with the others who are taking it up. Take it up with kindness, including for yourself. Take it up knowing that what you offer matters, even when it is invisible, even when no one names it, even when the dominant culture refuses to count it.

May the wounds you carry begin, in this body, to soften.

May the silences you have kept find, in their own time, the witnesses they need.

May the lineage behind you feel itself remembered.

May the lineage ahead of you receive an inheritance kinder than the one you received.

May the people you hold feel held, even on the hard days.

May you remember to be still.

May you remember that you were never broken.

May you remember that you have been responding all along.

May you remember that you are not alone.

May the well society we are building together rise around you, in your time, by your hands, and by the hands of all the others who are building it with you.

With every blessing of the long lineage of healers who came before me, and with every hope for the bodies that come after, I thank you for reading. The work continues.

Take good care of yourself. Take good care of each other.

References

This is a working bibliography for readers who want to follow any of the threads this book has touched into the literature. It is organized by category rather than strict alphabetical order, because most readers will be looking for a way into a particular conversation rather than for a specific citation. Within each category, sources are listed alphabetically by author or organization.

Foundations

Blackie, Sharon. If Women Rose Rooted: A Life-Changing Journey to Authenticity and Belonging. September Publishing, 2016.

Bloom, Sandra L. Creating Sanctuary: Toward the Evolution of Sane Societies. Routledge, 1997.

Burstow, Bonnie. Psychiatry and the Business of Madness: An Ethical and Epistemological Accountability. Palgrave Macmillan, 2015.

DeGruy, Joy. Post Traumatic Slave Syndrome: America's Legacy of Enduring Injury and Healing. Joy DeGruy Publications, 2005.

Firestone, Tirzah. Wounds Into Wisdom: Healing Intergenerational Jewish Trauma. Adam Kadmon Books, 2019.

Fisher, Janina. Healing the Fragmented Selves of Trauma Survivors: Overcoming Internal Self-Alienation. Routledge, 2017.

Hari, Johann. Lost Connections: Why You're Depressed and How to Find Hope. Bloomsbury, 2018.

Herman, Judith. Trauma and Recovery: The Aftermath of Violence from Domestic Abuse to Political Terror. Basic Books, 1992.

hooks, bell. All About Love: New Visions. William Morrow, 2000.

Johnstone, Lucy, and Mary Boyle. The Power Threat Meaning Framework. British Psychological Society, 2018.

Kimmerer, Robin Wall. Braiding Sweetgrass: Indigenous Wisdom, Scientific Knowledge, and the Teachings of Plants. Milkweed Editions, 2013.

Levine, Peter A. Waking the Tiger: Healing Trauma. North Atlantic Books, 1997.

Maté, Gabor. The Myth of Normal: Trauma, Illness, and Healing in a Toxic Culture. Avery, 2022.

Maté, Gabor. When the Body Says No: Exploring the Stress-Disease Connection. Wiley, 2003.

Menakem, Resmaa. My Grandmother's Hands: Racialized Trauma and the Pathway to Mending Our Hearts and Bodies. Central Recovery Press, 2017.

Moncrieff, Joanna. The Myth of the Chemical Cure: A Critique of Psychiatric Drug Treatment. Palgrave Macmillan, 2008.

Mullan, Jennifer. Decolonizing Therapy: Oppression, Historical Trauma, and Politicizing Your Practice. W. W. Norton, 2023.

Ogden, Pat, Kekuni Minton, and Clare Pain. Trauma and the Body: A Sensorimotor Approach to Psychotherapy. W. W. Norton, 2006.

Perry, Bruce D., and Maia Szalavitz. The Boy Who Was Raised as a Dog: And Other Stories from a Child Psychiatrist's Notebook. Basic Books, 2006.

Porges, Stephen W. The Polyvagal Theory: Neurophysiological Foundations of Emotions, Attachment, Communication, and Self-Regulation. W. W. Norton, 2011.

Putnam, Robert D. Bowling Alone: The Collapse and Revival of American Community. Simon & Schuster, 2000.

Rothschild, Babette. The Body Remembers: The Psychophysiology of Trauma and Trauma Treatment. W. W. Norton, 2000.

Sapolsky, Robert M. Why Zebras Don't Get Ulcers. Third edition. Holt Paperbacks, 2004.

Shaw, Martin. Smoke Hole: Looking to the Wild in the Time of the Spyglass. Chelsea Green Publishing, 2021.

Simard, Suzanne. Finding the Mother Tree: Discovering the Wisdom of the Forest. Knopf, 2021.

van der Kolk, Bessel. The Body Keeps the Score: Brain, Mind, and Body in the Healing of Trauma. Viking, 2014.

Whitaker, Robert. Anatomy of an Epidemic: Magic Bullets, Psychiatric Drugs, and the Astonishing Rise of Mental Illness in America. Broadway Books, 2010.

Wilkinson, Richard, and Kate Pickett. The Spirit Level: Why Greater Equality Makes Societies Stronger. Bloomsbury Press, 2009.

Wolynn, Mark. It Didn't Start with You: How Inherited Family Trauma Shapes Who We Are and How to End the Cycle. Viking, 2016.

Key Research Papers and Scientific Studies

Felitti, Vincent J., Robert F. Anda, *et al.* Relationship of Childhood Abuse and Household Dysfunction to Many of the Leading Causes of Death in Adults: The Adverse Childhood Experiences (ACE) Study. American Journal of Preventive Medicine, 14(4), 1998, pages 245 to 258.

Harris, Lasana T., and Susan T. Fiske. Dehumanizing the Lowest of the Low: Neuroimaging Responses to Extreme Out-Groups. Psychological Science, 17(10), 2006, pages 847 to 853.

Holt-Lunstad, Julianne, Timothy B. Smith, and J. Bradley Layton. Social Relationships and Mortality Risk: A Meta-analytic

Review. PLOS Medicine, 7(7), 2010.

McEwen, Bruce S. Stress, Adaptation, and Disease: Allostasis and Allostatic Load. Annals of the New York Academy of Sciences, 840, 1998, pages 33 to 44.

Moncrieff, Joanna, Ruth E. Cooper, *et al.* The Serotonin Theory of Depression: A Systematic Umbrella Review of the Evidence. Molecular Psychiatry, 28, 2022, pages 3243 to 3256.

Pennebaker, James W. Writing About Emotional Experiences as a Therapeutic Process. Psychological Science, 8(3), 1997, pages 162 to 166.

Sifneos, Peter E. Short-Term Psychotherapy and Emotional Crisis. Harvard University Press, 1972. (First academic use of the term alexithymia.)

Weaver, Ian C. G., *et al.* Epigenetic Programming by Maternal Behavior. Nature Neuroscience, 7(8), 2004, pages 847 to 854. (Meaney lab.)

Yehuda, Rachel, *et al.* Holocaust Exposure Induced Intergenerational Effects on FKBP5 Methylation. Biological Psychiatry, 80(5), 2016, pages 372 to 380.

Emotion, Expression, and Lament Across Cultures

Alexiou, Margaret. The Ritual Lament in Greek Tradition. Cambridge University Press, 1974.

Danforth, Loring M. The Death Rituals of Rural Greece. Princeton University Press, 1982.

Feld, Steven. Sound and Sentiment: Birds, Weeping, Poetics, and Song in Kaluli Expression. University of Pennsylvania Press, 1982.

Lutz, Catherine A. Unnatural Emotions: Everyday Sentiments on a Micronesian Atoll and Their Challenge to Western Theory. University of Chicago Press, 1988.

Lysaght, Patricia. The Banshee: The Irish Supernatural DeathMessenger. Glendale Press, 1986.

Nikora, Linda Waimarie, Ngahuia Te Awekotuku, Mohi Rua, and colleagues. "Tangihanga: The Ultimate Form of Māori Cultural Expression." University of Waikato Tangihanga Research Programme, 2010.

Salmond, Anne. Hui: A Study of Maori Ceremonial Gatherings. Reed, 1975.

Volkman, Toby Alice. Feasts of Honor: Ritual and Change in the Toraja Highlands. University of Illinois Press, 1985.

The Body, Discharge, and Somatic Healing

Berceli, David. The Revolutionary Trauma Release Process: Transcend Your Toughest Times. Namaste Publishing, 2008.

Katz, Richard. Boiling Energy: Community Healing Among the Kalahari !Kung. Harvard University Press, 1982.

Levine, Peter A. In an Unspoken Voice: How the Body Releases Trauma and Restores Goodness. North Atlantic Books, 2010.

Women, Menopause, and Rites of Passage

Beyene, Yewoubdar. From Menarche to Menopause: Reproductive Lives of Peasant Women in Two Cultures. State University of New York Press, 1989.

Flint, Marcha. "The Menopause: Reward or Punishment?" Psychosomatics 16, no. 4, 1975.

Lock, Margaret. Encounters with Aging: Mythologies of Menopause in Japan and North America. University of California Press, 1993.

Martin, Mary C., Jon E. Block, Sarah D. Sanchez, Claude D. Arnaud, and Yewoubdar Beyene. "Menopause Without Symptoms: The Endocrinology of Menopause Among Rural Mayan Indians." American Journal of Obstetrics and Gynecology 168, no. 6, 1993.

Turner, Victor. The Ritual Process: Structure and Anti-Structure. Aldine, 1969.

van Gennep, Arnold. The Rites of Passage. University of Chicago Press, 1960. First published 1909.

Work, Reciprocity, and Psychological Safety

Canadian Labour Congress, Western University, and University of Toronto. Harassment and Violence in Canadian Workplaces: It's [Not] Part of the Job. Canadian Labour Congress, 2022.

CSA Group and Bureau de normalisation du Québec. Psychological Health and Safety in the Workplace (CAN/CSA-Z1003-13). CSA Group, 2013.

Edmondson, Amy C. "Psychological Safety and Learning Behavior in Work Teams." Administrative Science Quarterly 44, no. 2, 1999.

Health and Safety Executive. Work-Related Stress, Depression or Anxiety Statistics in Great Britain. HSE, 2024.

Hyde, Lewis. The Gift: Imagination and the Erotic Life of Property. Vintage, 1983.

International Organization for Standardization. ISO 45003: Occupational Health and Safety Management — Psychological Health and Safety at Work. ISO, 2021.

Karasek, Robert A. "Job Demands, Job Decision Latitude, and Mental Strain: Implications for Job Redesign." Administrative Science Quarterly 24, no. 2, 1979.

Mauss, Marcel. The Gift: The Form and Reason for Exchange in Archaic Societies. Routledge, 1990. First published 1925.

Pega, Frank, and colleagues. "Global, Regional, and National Burdens of Ischemic Heart Disease and Stroke Attributable to Exposure to Long Working Hours: A Systematic Analysis from the WHO/ILO Joint Estimates." Environment International 154, 2021.

Siegrist, Johannes. "Adverse Health Effects of High-Effort/LowReward Conditions." Journal of Occupational Health Psychology 1, no. 1, 1996.

Sun Life Financial. Designed for Health: Mental Health and Long-Term Disability Claims in Canada. Sun Life, 2024.

Grief, Conditioning, and Dissociation

American Psychiatric Association. Diagnostic and Statistical Manual of Mental Disorders, 5th ed., 2013; and 5th ed., text revision, 2022. American Psychiatric Association.

Eisma, Maarten C. "Prolonged Grief Disorder in ICD-11 and DSM-5-TR: Challenges and Controversies." Australian & New Zealand Journal of Psychiatry 57, no. 7, 2023.

Kübler-Ross, Elisabeth. On Death and Dying. Macmillan, 1969.

Pavlov, Ivan P. Conditioned Reflexes: An Investigation of the Physiological Activity of the Cerebral Cortex. Oxford University Press, 1927.

Şar, Vedat. "Epidemiology of Dissociative Disorders: An Overview." Epidemiology Research International, 2011.

Wallace, David Foster. This Is Water: Some Thoughts, Delivered on a Significant Occasion, About Living a Compassionate Life. Little, Brown, 2009.

Relationships, Violence, and Repair

Cotter, Adam. "Intimate Partner Violence in Canada, 2018: An Overview." Juristat, Statistics Canada, 2021.

Dentan, Robert Knox. The Semai: A Nonviolent People of Malaya. Holt, Rinehart and Winston, 1968.

Fry, Douglas P. The Human Potential for Peace: An Anthropological Challenge to Assumptions About War and Violence. Oxford University Press, 2006.

Gottman, John M., and Nan Silver. The Seven Principles for Making Marriage Work. Crown, 1999.

Johnson, Susan M. The Practice of Emotionally Focused Couple Therapy: Creating Connection, 2nd ed. Routledge, 2004.

Leemis, R. W., N. Friar, S. Khatiwada, and colleagues. The National Intimate Partner and Sexual Violence Survey: 2016/2017 Report on Intimate Partner Violence. Centers for Disease Control and Prevention, 2022.

Shook, E. Victoria. Hoʻoponopono: Contemporary Uses of a Hawaiian Problem-Solving Process. University of Hawaii Press, 1985.

Srivastava, Sanjay, Maya Tamir, Kelly M. McGonigal, Oliver P. John, and James J. Gross. “The Social Costs of Emotional Suppression: A Prospective Study of the Transition to College.” Journal of Personality and Social Psychology 96, no. 4, 2009.

Walker, Lenore E. The Battered Woman. Harper & Row, 197

Reports and Public Inquiries

Government of British Columbia. In Plain Sight: Addressing Indigenous-specific Racism and Discrimination in B.C. Health Care. Independent investigation by M. E. Turpel-Lafond, 2020.

National Inquiry into Missing and Murdered Indigenous Women and Girls. Reclaiming Power and Place: The Final Report. Government of Canada, 2019.

Norwegian Truth and Reconciliation Commission. Final Report on Sami, Kven, and Forest Finn Peoples. Norwegian Parliament, 2023.

Promise of the Republic of South Africa. Truth and Reconciliation Commission of South Africa Report. Volumes 1 to 7. 1998 to 2003.

SAMHSA. Trauma-Informed Care in Behavioral Health Services. Treatment Improvement Protocol (TIP) Series 57. Substance Abuse and Mental Health Services Administration, 2014.

Truth and Reconciliation Commission of Canada. Honouring the Truth, Reconciling for the Future: Summary of the Final Report. Government of Canada, 2015.

World Health Organization. Global Hypertension Report. WHO, 2025.

World Health Organization. World Mental Health Today. WHO, 2025.

World Health Organization. Violence Against Women: Global Estimates. WHO, November 2025.

Apologies

Australia. National Apology to the Stolen Generations. Delivered by Prime Minister Kevin Rudd, House of Representatives, 13 February 2008.

Canada. Statement of Apology to Former Students of Indian Residential Schools. Delivered by Prime Minister Stephen Harper, House of Commons, 11 June 2008.

Canada. Apology to Former British Home Children and Their Descendants. House of Commons, 16 February 2017.

Holy See. Statement Regarding the Doctrine of Discovery. Vatican Dicasteries for Culture and Education and for Promoting Integral Human Development, 30 March 2023.

Pope Francis. Statement on Residential Schools, Canada. Iqaluit, Nunavut, 29 July 2022. Use of the word genocide.

United Kingdom. Apology to British Child Migrants. Delivered by Prime Minister Gordon Brown, House of Commons, 24 February 2010.

Mother and Baby Homes Ireland

Commission of Investigation into Mother and Baby Homes. Final Report. Government of Ireland, January 2021.

Corless, Catherine. Research papers and public reporting on the Tuam Mother and Baby Home, 2012 onward.

Government of Ireland. Tuam Excavation Programme. Office of the Director of Authorised Intervention, 2025.

Healing Movements, Frameworks, and Networks

Berne, Patty, and Sins Invalid. Skin, Tooth, and Bone: The Basis of Movement Is Our People. Sins Invalid, 2019. (Disability justice framework, Berne, Mingus, and collaborators, 2005 onward.)

Bloom, Sandra L. The Sanctuary Model: Trauma-Informed Care in Therapeutic Communities. Ongoing program since 1985.

Burke, Tarana. Unbound: My Story of Liberation and the Birth of the Me Too Movement. Flatiron Books, 2021. (Movement founded 2006.)

Hearing Voices Movement, International Network. Founded by Marius Romme and Sandra Escher, Netherlands, 1987.

Seikkula, Jaakko, and Mary E. Olson. The Open Dialogue Approach to Acute Psychosis: Its Poetics and Micropolitics. Family Process, 42(3), 2003, pages 403 to 418. (Western Lapland, Finland, since 1980s.)

Critical Psychiatry and Anti-Pathologizing Voices

Boyle, Mary, and Lucy Johnstone. A Straight Talking Introduction to the Power Threat Meaning Framework. PCCS Books, 2020.

Critical Psychiatry Network. Ongoing publications and position statements. UK-based, founded 1999.

Timimi, Sami. Pathological Child Psychiatry and the Medicalization of Childhood. Routledge, 2002.

Timimi, Sami. Insane Medicine: How the Mental Health Industry Creates Damaging Treatment Traps. Independently published, 2020.

Indigenous and British Columbia Sources

Government of British Columbia. Health Professions and Occupations Act (Bill 36), enacted 2022, in force April 2026.

Pierre, Len. Cultural Safety and Humility teaching materials. Simon Fraser University, 2024.

Pierre, Len. On Stillness. Drishti Magazine, 2022.

Somé, Sobonfu E. The Spirit of Intimacy: Ancient African Teachings in the Ways of Relationships. William Morrow, 2000.

Somé, Malidoma Patrice. Ritual: Power, Healing, and Community. Penguin, 1997.

This bibliography is not exhaustive. Many of the sources cited in

passing across the chapters, particularly the works of Frantz Fanon,

Aimé Césaire, Edward Said, Byung-Chul Han, Mark Fisher, Jeffrey

Alexander, Maria Yellow Horse Brave Heart, Eduardo and Bonnie

Duran, Christina Sharpe, Anne Case and Angus Deaton, Eric

Klinenberg, Vivette Glover, Frances Champagne, Stephen Porges,

Bruce Perry, John Bowlby, Anna Freud, Ed Tronick, Alicia Lieberman, Mary Dozier, Jack Shonkoff, Nadine Burke Harris, Urie Bronfenbrenner, Joy Harjo, the Haudenosaunee Great Law of Peace, and

others, are widely available through any university library or open —

access archive. Readers are invited to follow whichever thread calls

them most. The literature is large. The work is shared.

Every author named here, and many more not named, is part of the

long lineage of bodies who chose to put their work in writing so that

the bodies coming after would have a place to begin.

About the Author

Auroara Leigh is a Canadian wellness anthropologist, educator, and the founder of Simply Sacred Solutions. She holds an undergraduate degree in anthropology and a Master of Education from the University of British Columbia, and she has spent years studying the places where culture, trauma, neuroscience, and healing meet. Her work walks in two worlds, the academic and the embodied, and it refuses to sever the mind from the body when both are carrying the story.

She writes from the other side of her own healing, albeit a continual spiral, within and without. What she offers her readers and her clients did not arrive through theory alone. It came through her own body, through the slow work of metabolizing what she had survived, through the years it took to understand that her responses had always made sense. That understanding became her life's work: to return people to themselves, and to return our systems to the human-centered values they were never meant to abandon.

Her teaching reframes how we treat mental health, addiction, and the pathologizing of pain. She tends the fire instead of chasing the smoke. She believes a well society is possible, and that we build it the way our ancestors always have, by reweaving care, reciprocity, and belonging back into the places that forgot them. She lives in British Columbia, where she raises her daughter and continues the work of helping bodies, families, and institutions remember their own wholeness.

Continue the Work

If something in these pages returned you to yourself, there is more for you here, and there is a way to carry this work further into your own life and into the lives of the people you serve so we can tend one another like we would plants, and watch one another bloom:

Sacred Witness™ My book for those who long to hold trauma-informed space for others. Where this book was about coming home to yourself, Sacred Witness™ teaches you how to become the steady, grounded presence that helps another person find their own way home. It is written for the helpers, the healers, the parents, the practitioners, and everyone who has ever wanted to witness another's pain with dignity instead of rushing to fix it or flee from it.

The Healership Academy™ My online learning community on Skool, built around the practice of healership, the convergence of healing and leadership. This is where healed humans learn to lead from that place, and where your inner work becomes the steady ground you stand on as you guide others. I also support deeper mentorship for leaders who are ready to accept the challenge of anchoring new values in society that shape a healing culture together.

Somatic Regeneration™ Practitioner Certification A pathway for holistic wellness and the slow, embodied work of somatic regeneration. Here we tend the nervous system the way you would tend a garden, returning the body to its own rhythm, its own homeostasis, its own quiet capacity to heal once it finally feels safe enough to. Offered in The Healership Academy.

Presentations and Speaking. I bring this work to stages, teams, and gatherings, reframing how we treat mental health, addiction, and the pathologizing of pain. These conversations call us back to our human-centered values and ask a braver question together: what would it take to become a well society?

Trauma-Informed Consulting. I partner with organizations across disciplines and sectors to weave trauma-informed, equitable practice into the bones of how they work and programming. I also guide in social determinants of health and restorative justice frameworks. This is systems-level care, the kind that treats the fire instead of the smoke, so that the people inside an institution, and the people it serves, are met with safety, dignity, and belonging. Wherever you begin, begin gently. The wholeness was never lost. It was only waiting for you to feel safe enough to return to it.

HEAL IT Certification™. I offer full certification for social competencies on the HEAL IT framework. These support leaders to develop their ability to discern, and create psychological safety in workplaces. As people come into healing, it will be even more important that they have environments that can be trauma informed and supportive. The quality of life that is connected to work is incredibly important for a thriving culture to be possible.

Together, we can cocreate a well society!

With love and with truth,

Auroara Leigh
www.simplysacred.ca ·

www.ingramcontent.com/pod-product-compliance
Lightning Source LLC
LaVergne TN
LVHW050804061126
851857LV00012B/672

* 9 7 8 1 7 7 8 1 0 8 2 2 8 *